Grade Aid Workbook with Practice Tests

for

Berk

Infants, Children, and Adolescents

Fifth Edition

Prepared by

JoDe Paladino
Illinois State University

Laura E. Berk
Illinois State University

Gabrielle Principe
Ursinus College

Boston   New York   San Francisco
Mexico City   Montreal   Toronto   London   Madrid   Munich   Paris
Hong Kong   Singapore   Tokyo   Cape Town   Sydney

To obtain permission(s) to use material from this work, please submit a written request to Allyn and Bacon, Permissions Department, 75 Arlington Street, Boston, MA 02116 or fax your request to 617-848-7320.

ISBN: 0-205-43998-5

Printed in the United States of America

10 9 8 7 6 5 4   08 07 06 05

CONTENTS

PREFACE

As you embark on the fascinating journey of studying child development, it is our hope that this workbook will help you master the material in your text, *Infants, Children, and Adolescents,* by Laura E. Berk. Our intention in preparing the workbook is to provide you with active practice in learning the content in your textbook and thought-provoking questions that help you clarify your own thinking. Each chapter in the workbook is organized into the following six sections.

BRIEF CHAPTER SUMMARY

We begin with a brief chapter summary of the material, mentioning major topics covered and general principles emphasized in text discussion. Each chapter of your textbook includes two additional summaries: an informal one at the beginning of the chapter, and a structured summary at the end of the chapter. Thus, the brief chapter summary in the workbook will be your third review of the information covered in each chapter. It is intended to remind you of major points in the text before you embark on the remaining activities in the workbook.

LEARNING OBJECTIVES

We have organized the main points in each chapter into a series of objectives that indicate what you should be able to do once you have mastered the material. We suggest that you look over these objectives before you read each chapter. You may find it useful to take notes on information pertaining to objectives as you read. When you finish a chapter, try to answer the objectives in a few sentences or a short paragraph. Then check your answers against the text and revise your responses accordingly. Once you have completed this exercise, you will have generated your own review of chapter content. Because it is written in your own words, it should serve as an especially useful chapter overview that can be referred to when you prepare for examinations.

STUDY QUESTIONS

The main body of each chapter consists of study questions, organized according to major headings in the textbook, that assist you in identifying main points and grasping concepts and principles. Text pages on which answers can be found are indicated next to each entry. The study question section can be used in a number of different ways. You may find it helpful to answer each question as you read the chapter. Alternatively, try reading one or more sections and then testing yourself by answering the relevant study questions. Finally, use the study question section as a device to review for examinations. If you work through it methodically, your retention of chapter material will be greatly enhanced.

ASK YOURSELF . . .

In each chapter of your textbook, critical thinking questions that appear at the end of each major section. Answering these questions will help you analyze important theoretical concepts and research findings. Three types of questions are included: *Review* questions, which assist with recall and comprehension of information in the text; *Apply* questions, which encourage application of your knowledge to controversial issues and problems; and *Connect* questions, which help you to integrate what you have learned across age periods and aspects of development, thereby building an image of the whole person. Each question is answered on the text's Companion Website, where you may compare your reasoning to a model response.

PUZZLES

To help you master the central vocabulary of the field, we have provided crossword puzzles that test your knowledge of important terms and concepts. Answers can be found at the back of the workbook. If you cannot think of the term that matches a clue in the puzzles, your knowledge of information related to the term may be insecure. Reread the material in the text chapter related to each item that you miss. Also, try a more demanding approach to term mastery: After you have completed each puzzle, cover the clues and write your own definitions of each term.

PRACTICE TESTS

Once you have thoroughly studied a chapter, find out how well you know the material by taking the two multiple choice practice tests. Then check your answers using the key at the back of the workbook. If you answered more than a few items incorrectly, spend extra time rereading the chapter, writing responses to chapter objectives, and reviewing the study questions of this guide.

Now that you understand how the workbook is organized, you are ready to begin using it to master *Infants, Children, and Adolescents.* We wish you a rewarding and enjoyable course of study.

JoDe Paladino
Laura E. Berk
Gabrielle Principe

CHAPTER 1
HISTORY, THEORY, AND RESEARCH STRATEGIES

BRIEF CHAPTER SUMMARY

Child development is the study of all aspects of human growth and change from conception through adolescence. Researchers often segment the first two decades of life into five age periods. In addition, development is often divided into three broad domains—physical development, cognitive development, and emotional and social development. These divisions make the vast, interdisciplinary study of human constancy more orderly and convenient.

Theories lend structure and meaning to the scientific study of children. This chapter provides an overview of philosophical and theoretical approaches to child study from medieval to modern times. It also reviews major research strategies used to study child behavior and development. When compared and contrasted, historical philosophies and contemporary theories raise three basic issues about what children are like and how they develop: (1) Is development continuous or discontinuous? (2) Is there one course of development or many? (3) Is nature or nurture more important in development? Theories also differ in the degree to which they emphasize stability versus potential for change. Many theories, especially modern ones, take a balanced point of view and recognize the merits of both sides of these issues.

Research methods commonly used to study children include systematic observation, self-reports, psychophysiological methods, the clinical, or case study, method, and ethnography. Investigators of child development generally choose either a correlational or an experimental research design. To study how their participants change over time, they use special developmental research strategies—longitudinal, cross-sectional, longitudinal-sequential, and microgenetic designs. Each method and design has both strengths and limitations.

Conducting research with children also poses special ethical dilemmas. Ethical guidelines for research and special committees determine if the benefits of research outweigh the risks and ensure that children's rights are protected.

LEARNING OBJECTIVES

After reading this chapter, you should be able to:

1.1 Explain the importance of the terms *interdisciplinary* and *applied* as they help to define the field of child development. (p. 4)

1.2 Explain the role of theories in understanding child development, and describe the three basic issues on which major theories take a stand. (pp. 6–10)

1.3 Trace historical influences on modern theories of child development, from medieval times through the early twentieth century. (pp. 12–14)

1.4 Describe the theoretical perspectives that influenced child development research in the mid-twentieth century, and cite the contributions and limitations of each. (pp. 15–22)

1.5 Describe six recent theoretical perspectives of child development, noting the contributions of major theorists. (pp. 23–29)

1.6 Identify the stand that each modern theory takes on the three basic issues of child development presented earlier in this chapter. (pp. 31, 32)

1.7 Describe the methods commonly used to study children, and cite the strengths and limitations of each. (pp. 31, 33–38)

1.8 Contrast correlational and experimental research designs, and cite the strengths and limitations of each. (pp. 39–42)

1.9   Describe four research designs used to study development, noting the strengths and limitations of each. (pp. 42, 43, 45, 46)

1.10   Describe children's research rights, and explain why research involving children raises special ethical concerns. (pp. 46–48)

STUDY QUESTIONS

The Field of Child Development

1. Child development is an *interdisciplinary* field. Explain what this means. (p. 4)

_____

_____

_____

Periods of Development

1. List the six age periods used to segment the first two-and-a-half decades of life. (p. 5)

    A. _____ Age span: _____

    B. _____ Age span: _____

    C. _____ Age span: _____

    D. _____ Age span: _____

    E. _____ Age span: _____

    F. _____ Age span: _____

Domains of Development

1. List and describe the three domains of development. (p. 5)

    A. _____

    _____

    B. _____

    _____

    C. _____

    _____

Basic Issues

1. What are the three elements of a good theory? (pp. 6–7)

    A. _____   B. _____

    C. _____

2. Cite two reasons that theories are important to the study of child development. (p. 7)

A. _____

B. _____

3. Explain how theories differ from opinions. (p. 7)

_____

_____

_____

4. Match each theoretical approach with the appropriate description. (pp. 7–9)

_____ Considers development to be universal across children and across cultures

_____ Views development as a process of gradually building on preexisting skills

_____ Regards the environment as the most important influence on development

_____ Considers child development in light of distinct contexts

_____ Views development as a progression through a series of qualitatively distinct stages

_____ Views heredity as the most important influence on development

1. Multiple courses of development
2. Single course of development
3. Continuous development
4. Discontinuous development
5. Nature
6. Nurture

5. True or False: Most modern theories of development take a strong position on controversial issues such as the nature-nurture debate. (p. 10)

Biology and Environment: Resilient Children

1. What is *resiliency*? (p. 10)

_____

_____

_____

2. List and briefly describe the four broad factors that appear to offer protection from the damaging effects of stressful life events. (pp. 10–11)

A. _____

_____

B. _____

_____

C. _____

_____

D. _____

_____

Medieval Times

1. In medieval times, childhood (was / was not) regarded as a distinct developmental period. Cite evidence to support your response. (p. 12)

   _____

   _____

The Reformation

1. True or False: Puritan doctrine stressed the innate goodness of all children. Briefly explain your response. (p. 12)

   _____

   _____

2. True or False: The Puritans placed a high value on the development of reasoning in children. (p. 12)

Philosophies of the Enlightenment

1. During the Enlightenment, the British philosopher John Locke regarded the child as a *tabula rasa,* which means_____. Explain his view. (p. 13)

   _____

   _____

2. Summarize Locke's stance on each of the three basic issues of human development. (p. 13)

   Continuous or discontinuous development?:

   _____

   _____

   One course of development or many?:

   _____

   _____

   Nature or nurture as more important?:

   _____

   _____

3. Jean Jacques Rousseau, a French philosopher during the Enlightenment, introduced the notion of children as *noble savages*. Explain what he meant by this term. (p. 13)

   _____

   _____

   _____

4. Describe some of the key differences in the theories put forth by John Locke and Jean Jacques Rousseau. (p. 13)

_____

_____

_____

5. Cite two concepts included in Rousseau's theory that remain important to modern theories of child development. (p. 13)

   A. _____

   B. _____

Scientific Beginnings

1. Explain the two principles emphasized in Darwin's theory of evolution. (pp. 13–14)

   A. _____

   _____

   _____

   _____

   _____

   B. _____

   _____

   _____

   _____

2. Who is generally regarded as the founder of the child study movement? (p. 14)

   _____

3. The _____ approach to child development uses age-related averages to represent typical development. (p. 14)

4. Who constructed the first successful intelligence test? (p. 14)

   _____

5. Why did this test succeed, while previous efforts to create a useful intelligence test had failed? (p. 14)

   _____

   _____

6. A translated version of this test was developed for use with American children. What is the name of this instrument? (p. 14)

   _____

   _____

The Psychoanalytic Perspective

1. Summarize the basic concepts of the *psychoanalytic perspective*. (pp. 15–16)

   _____

   _____

   _____

2. Freud's _____ *theory* emphasized that how parents manage their child's sexual and aggressive drives in the first few years of life is crucial for healthy personality development. (p. 15)

3. Name and briefly describe the three components of personality outlined in Freud's theory. (pp. 15–16)

   A. _____

   _____

   B. _____

   _____

   C. _____

   _____

4. Match each of the following stages of psychosexual development with the appropriate description. (pp. 15–16)

   _____ Stage in which sexual instincts die down

   _____ Stage in which the infant desires sucking activities

   _____ Stage in which the Oedipal and Electra conflicts take place

   _____ Stage marked by mature sexuality

   _____ Stage in which toilet training becomes a major issue between parent and child

   1. Genital
   2. Anal
   3. Oral
   4. Latency
   5. Phallic

5. Cite one contribution and three limitations of Freud's theory. (pp. 17–18)

   Contribution: _____

   _____

   _____

   Limitation: _____

   _____

   _____

   Limitation: _____

   _____

   _____

   Limitation: _____

   _____

   _____

6. In what way did Erikson build upon and improve Freud's theory? (pp. 16–17)

_____

_____

_____

_____

7. Match each of Erikson's stages with the appropriate description. (pp. 16–17)

_____ Successful resolution of this stage depends on the adult's
success at caring for other people and productive work.

_____ The primary task of this stage is the development of a sense of self
and a sense of one's place in society.

_____ Successful resolution of this stage depends on a warm, loving
relationship with the caregiver.

_____ In this stage, children experiment with adult roles through make-
believe play.

_____ Successful resolution of this stage depends on parents granting
the child reasonable opportunities for free choice.

_____ In this stage, successful resolution involves reflecting on life's
accomplishments.

_____ The development of close relationships with others helps ensure
successful resolution of this stage.

_____ Children who develop the capacity for cooperation and productive
work will successfully resolve this stage.

1. Industry vs. inferiority
2. Autonomy vs. shame and doubt
3. Intimacy vs. isolation
4. Identity vs. identity diffusion
5. Basic trust vs. mistrust
6. Generativity vs. stagnation
7. Initiative vs. guilt
8. Ego integrity vs. despair

8. Cite two contributions of psychoanalytic theory. (p. 17)

A. _____

B. _____

9. Discuss two reasons why psychoanalytic theory is no longer in the mainstream of child development research.
(pp. 17–18)

A. _____

_____

B. _____

_____

Behaviorism and Social Learning Theory

1. True or False: Behaviorism focuses on the inner workings of the mind. (p. 18)

2. Watson's study of little Albert, an 11-month-old baby who was taught to fear a white rat by associating it with a loud
noise, supported Pavlov's concept of *conditioning*. (p. 18)

_____

3. Summarize B. F. Skinner's *operant conditioning theory*. (p. 18)

_____

_____

_____

4. Describe the concept of *observational learning*, as elaborated in Bandura's social learning theory. (p. 19)

_____

_____

_____

5. Summarize Bandura's revisions to his social learning theory, which stress the importance of cognition in the learning process. (p. 19)

_____

_____

_____

6. Behaviorism and social learning theory have had a major applied impact on the field of child development through the introduction of *behavior modification*. Explain this procedure. (p. 19)

_____

_____

_____

7. Discuss two limitations of behaviorism and social learning theory. (p. 19)

A. _____

_____

B. _____

_____

Piaget's Cognitive-Developmental Theory

1. True or False: Piaget's *cognitive-developmental theory* is consistent with the principles of behaviorism; that is, Piaget believed that knowledge is imparted to children through the use of reinforcement. Briefly explain your response. (p. 20)

_____

_____

2. Define Piaget's notion of *adaptation*. (p. 20)

_____

_____

3. Match each of Piaget's stages with the appropriate description. (p. 21)

_____ During this stage, thought becomes more complex, and children develop the capacity for abstract reasoning.

_____ This stage is characterized by the use of eyes, ears, and hands to explore the environment.

_____ During this stage, children develop the capacity for abstract thought.

_____ This stage is marked by the development of logical, organized reasoning skills.

1. Sensorimotor
2. Preoperational
3. Concrete operational
4. Formal operational

4. What did Piaget use as his chief method for studying child and adolescent thought? (p. 21)

_____

5. Cite three contributions of Piaget's theory. (pp. 21–22)

   A. _____

   _____

   B. _____

   _____

   C. _____

   _____

6. Describe three recent challenges to Piaget's theory. (p. 22)

   A. _____

   _____

   B. _____

   _____

   C. _____

   _____

Recent Theoretical Perspectives

Information Processing

1. Briefly describe the *information-processing view* of child development. (p. 23)

   _____

   _____

   _____

2. How are flow charts used by information-processing researchers? (p. 24)

   _____

   _____

3. In what basic way are information processing and Piaget's theory alike? In what basic way are they different? (p. 24)

   A. _____

   B. _____

4. Cite one strength and two limitations of the information-processing approach. (p. 24)

   Strength: _____

   Limitation: _____

   Limitation: _____

Ethology and Evolutionary Developmental Psychology

1. *Ethology* is the study of (p. 24)

   _____

   _____

2. Name the two European zoologists who laid the modern foundations of ethology. (p. 24)

   A. _____

   B. _____

3. Contrast the notion of a *critical period* with that of a *sensitive period*. (pp. 24–25)

   Critical period:

   _____

   _____

   _____

   Sensitive period:

   _____

   _____

   _____

4. Explain how John Bowlby used the principles of ethology to understand the infant-caregiver relationship. (p. 25)

   _____

   _____

   _____

5. Briefly explain what is studied in the field of *evolutionary developmental psychology.* (p. 25)

   _____

   _____

   _____

   _____

Vygotsky's Sociocultural Theory

1. Explain the importance of social interaction in Vygotsky's sociocultural theory. (p. 26)

   _____

   _____

   _____

2. Compare and contrast the theories of Piaget and Vygotsky. (p. 26)

   _____

   _____

   _____

   _____

3. True or False: Because cultures select tasks for children's learning, children in every culture develop unique strengths not present in others. (pp. 24–27)

4. Vygotsky's emphasis on culture and social experience led him to neglect _____ contributions to development. (p. 27)

Ecological Systems Theory

1. Summarize the core tenet of Bronfenbrenner's *ecological systems theory*. (p. 27)

_____

_____

2. Match each level of ecological systems theory with the appropriate description or example. (p. 28)

_____ Relationship between the child's home and school	1. Exosystem
_____ The influence of cultural values	2. Microsystem
_____ The parent's workplace	3. Mesosystem
_____ The child's interaction with parents	4. Macrosystem

3. Provide examples of factors in each system that can enhance development. (pp. 28–29)

Microsystem: _____

Mesosystem: _____

Exosystem: _____

Macrosystem: _____

4. Bronfenbrenner's _____-system refers to temporal changes that affect development, such as the timing of the birth of a sibling. (p. 29)

5. In ecological systems theory, development is controlled by (environmental circumstances / inner dispositions / the interaction of environmental circumstances and inner dispositions). (p. 29)

New Directions: Development as a Dynamic System

1. Describe the *dynamic systems perspective*. (p. 29)

_____

_____

_____

2. Based on dynamic systems theory, explain how individuals develop both universal traits and individual abilities. (pp. 29–30)

Universal traits: _____

_____

Individual abilities: _____

_____

Comparing Child Development Theories

1. Identify the stand that the following modern theories take on the three basic issues of childhood and child development: (p. 32)

Theory	One Course of Development versus Many Courses of Development	Continuous versus Discontinuous Development	Nature versus Nurture
Psychoanalytic theory	_____	_____	_____
Behaviorism and social learning	_____	_____	_____
Piaget's cognitive-developmental theory	_____	_____	_____
Information processing	_____	_____	_____
Ethology	_____	_____	_____
Vygotsky's sociocultural perspective	_____	_____	_____
Dynamic systems theory	_____	_____	_____

Studying the Child

1. Research usually begins with a _____ , or a prediction about behavior drawn from a theory. (p. 31)

Common Methods of Gathering Information

1. Compare and contrast *naturalistic* and *structured observation* techniques, noting one strength and one limitation of each approach. (pp. 33–34)

Naturalistic: _____

_____

_____

Strength: _____

_____

_____

Limitation: _____

_____

_____

Structured: _____

_____

_____

Strength: _____

_____

_____

Limitation: _____

_____

_____

2. Explain how *clinical interviews* differ from *structured interviews*, and note the benefits and limitations of each technique. (pp. 33, 35)

Clinical: _____

_____

_____

Benefits: _____

_____

_____

Limitations: _____

_____

_____

Structured: _____

_____

_____

Benefits: _____

_____

_____

Limitations: _____

_____

_____

3. _____ *methods* measure the relationship between physiological processes and behavior. (p. 35)

4. List several commonly used physiological measures that are sensitive to an individual's psychological state. (p. 35)

_____

_____

5. _____ , which yields three-dimensional pictures of brain activity, provide the most precise information about which brain regions are specialized for certain functions. (p. 36)

6. Describe two limitations of psychophysiological methods. (p. 36)

   A. _____

   B. _____

7. Cite the primary aim of the *clinical method*, and note the procedures often used to achieve this goal. (pp. 36–37)

   Aim: _____

   Procedures: _____

8. What are the drawbacks of using the clinical method? (p. 37)

   _____

   _____

   _____

9. Under what circumstances might a researcher employ the clinical method despite its limitations? (p. 37)

   _____

   _____

   _____

10. _____ is a research method aimed at understanding a culture or distinct social group. This goal is achieved through _____ , a technique in which the researcher lives with the cultural community and participates in all aspects of daily life. (p. 37)

11. Cite two limitations of the ethnographic method. (pp. 37–38)

    A. _____

    B. _____

Cultural Influences: Immigrant Youths: Amazing Adaptation

1. True or False: Students who are first-generation (foreign-born) and second-generation (American-born with immigrant parents) Americans achieve in school as well as or better than students of native-born parents. (p. 38)

2. Compared with their agemates, adolescents from immigrant families are (more / less) likely to commit delinquent and violent acts, to use drugs and alcohol, and to have early sex. (p. 39)

3. Discuss two ways in which family and community exert an influence on the academic achievement of adolescents from immigrant families. (pp. 38–39)

   A. _____

   _____

   B. _____

   _____

General Research Designs

1. Explain the basic features of the *correlational design*. (p. 39)

_____

_____

_____

2. True or False: The correlational design is preferred by researchers because it allows them to infer cause and effect. Explain your response. (pp. 39–40)

_____

_____

_____

3. Investigators examine the relationships among variables using a(n)_____ , a number that describes how two measures, or variables, are associated with one another. (p. 40)

4. A *correlation coefficient* can range from _____ to _____ . The magnitude of the number shows the (strength / direction) of the relationship between the two variables, whereas the sign indicates the (strength / direction) of the relationship. (p. 40)

5. For a correlation coefficient, a positive sign means that as one variable increases, the other (increases / decreases); a negative sign indicates that as one variable increases, the other (increases / decreases). (p. 40)

6. A researcher determines that the correlation between warm, consistent parenting and child delinquency is –.80. Explain what this indicates about the relationship between these two variables. (p. 40)

_____

_____

_____

7. If the same researcher had found a correlation of +.45, what would this have indicated about the relationship between warm, consistent parenting and child delinquency? (p. 40)

_____

_____

_____

8. What is the difference between a correlation of +1.00 and a correlation of –1.00? (p. 40)

_____

_____

9. What is the primary distinction between a *correlational design* and an *experimental design*? (p. 40)

_____

10. Describe the difference between an *independent* and a *dependent* variable. (p. 40)

Independent: _____

_____

Dependent: _____

_____

11. What is the feature of an experimental design that enables researchers to infer a cause-and-effect relationship between the variables? (p. 40)

_____

_____

12. _____ is a procedure which allows researchers to control for unknown characteristics of the participants which could reduce the accuracy of the findings. (p. 41)

13. In _____ *experiments,* researchers randomly assign people to treatment conditions in natural settings. (p. 41)

14. True or False: Natural experiments differ from correlational research in that groups of participants are carefully chosen to ensure that their characteristics are as much alike as possible. (p. 41)

15. Why might a researcher opt to use a field experiment or a natural experiment rather than conducting a laboratory experiment? (p. 41)

Field: _____

_____

Natural: _____

_____

Designs for Studying Development

1. In a _____ *design,* a group of participants is studied repeatedly at different ages, and changes are noted as the participants mature. (p. 41)

2. List two advantages of the longitudinal design. (p. 42)

   A. _____

   _____

   B. _____

   _____

3. Describe three problems in conducting longitudinal research. (p. 43)

   A. _____

   _____

   B. _____

   _____

   C. _____

   _____

4. Describe the *cross-sectional design.* (p. 43)

   _____

   _____

   _____

5. In cross-sectional designs, researchers (do / do not) need to worry about participant dropout and practice effects. (pp. 43, 45)

6. Summarize two drawbacks of the cross-sectional design. (p. 45)

A. _____

_____

B. _____

_____

7. In the _____ *design*, researchers merge longitudinal and cross-sectional research strategies. List two advantages of this design. (p. 45)

A. _____

_____

B. _____

_____

8. In a _____ design, researchers present children with a novel task and follow their mastery over a series of closely spaced sessions. (p. 46)

9. Microgenetic research is especially useful for studying (cognitive / physical) development. (p. 46)

10. List three reasons why microgenetic studies are difficult to carry out. (p. 46)

A. _____

_____

B. _____

_____

C. _____

_____

Social Issues: Health: Impact of Historical Times on Development: The Great Depression and World War II

1. Explain how the Great Depression impacted adolescent boys' and girls' long-term aspirations and adult lives. (p. 44)

Boys: _____

_____

Girls: _____

_____

2. Cite evidence suggesting that cultural-historic events have a differential impact on development, depending on the age at which they take place. (p. 44)

_____

_____

_____

Ethics in Research on Children

1. Discuss the special ethical concerns of conducting research on children. (p. 46)

   _____

   _____

   _____

2. Describe children's research rights. (pp. 46–47)

   A. Protection from harm:

   _____

   _____

   B. Informed consent:

   _____

   _____

   C. Privacy:

   _____

   _____

   D. Knowledge of results:

   _____

   _____

   E. Beneficial treatments:

   _____

   _____

3. For children _____ years and older, their own informed consent should be obtained in addition to parental consent prior to participation in research. (p. 47)

4. In _____ , the investigator provides a full account and justification of research activities to participants in a study in which deception was used. (p. 48)

ASK YOURSELF . . .

For *Ask Yourself* questions for this chapter, please log on to the Companion Website at *www.ablongman.com/berk.*

1. Select the Companion Website for *Infants, Children, and Adolescents*, Fifth Edition.

2. Use the "Jump to" menu to go directly to this chapter.

3. From the menu on the left side of your screen, select *Ask Yourself.*

4. Complete the questions and choose "Submit answers for grading" or "Clear answers" to start over.

SUGGESTED STUDENT READINGS

Goldhaber, D. (2000). *Theories of human development: Integrative perspectives.* Mountain View, CA: Mayfield Publishing Co. Presents an extensive review and critique of the most influential developmental theories, including coverage of classic theories and contemporary theories. The author also pays careful attention to the methodology for studying human development and how research methods contribute to and enhance our overall knowledge of the developmental process.

Greig, P. & Taylor, J. (1999). *Doing research with children.* London: Sage Publications Ltd. Reviews the various techniques and approaches, including the unique ethical and legal concerns, that are associated with child development research. This book provides a framework for studying children which can be utilized by students, researchers, practitioners, educators, and others working in the field of child development.

Moen, P., Elder, G. H., Jr., & Luscher, K. (Eds.). (1995). *Examining lives in context: Perspectives on the ecology of human development.* Washington, DC: American Psychological Association. Extends Bronfenbrenner's perspective, illustrating how ecological systems theory can be applied to a number of real-life problems. Explores how multiple contextual factors influence individuals, families, and communities across the lifespan.

Richardson, K. (1999). *The origins of human potential: Evolution, development, and psychology.* New York: Routledge. Presents a refreshing perspective on the development of cognitive competence. The author uses a dynamic systems approach in an attempt to illustrate the complexity of genetic and environmental factors and how these interactions contribute to cognitive development.

PUZZLE 1.1 TERM REVIEW

Across

3. Development as a process in which new ways of understanding and responding to the world emerge at specific times
4. In ecological systems theory, temporal changes in a child's environment
6. In ecological systems theory, social settings that do not contain the child but that affect their experiences in immediate settings
7. Development as gradually adding on more of the same types of skills that were there to begin with
8. Information-_____ approach: views the human mind as a symbol-manipulating machine
10. In ecological systems theory, cultural values, laws, customs, and resources that influence experiences and interactions at inner levels of the environment
12. Qualitative change characterizing a particular time period of development
14. Freud's theory focusing on early sexual and aggressive drives
16. Emphasizes the study of directly observable events
21. Theory that focuses on how social interaction contributes to development
22. Ability to adapt effectively in the face of threats to development
23. In ecological systems theory, activities and interaction patterns in the child's immediate surroundings

25. Unique combinations of personal and environmental circumstances that can result in different paths of change
26. Social _____ theory: emphasizes the role of observational learning in the development of behavior

Down

1. Theory that emphasizes the unique developmental history of each child
2. _____ savages: view of children as possessing an innate plan for healthy growth
5. In ecological systems theory, connections between the child's immediate settings
9. _____ systems perspective: the child's mind, body, and physical and social worlds form an integrated system
11. View of the child as a blank slate: tabula _____
13. _____ development: field of study devoted to understanding constancy and change from conception through adolescence and emerging adulthood
15. _____ systems theory: view of the child as developing within a complex system of relationships
17. Erikson's stage theory of development entailing resolution of psychological conflicts
18. Piaget's _____-developmental theory suggests that children actively construct knowledge as they manipulate and explore their world.
19. Nature-_____ controversy
20. Genetically determined, naturally unfolding course of growth
24. Theory concerned with the adaptive value of behavior

PUZZLE 1.2 TERM REVIEW

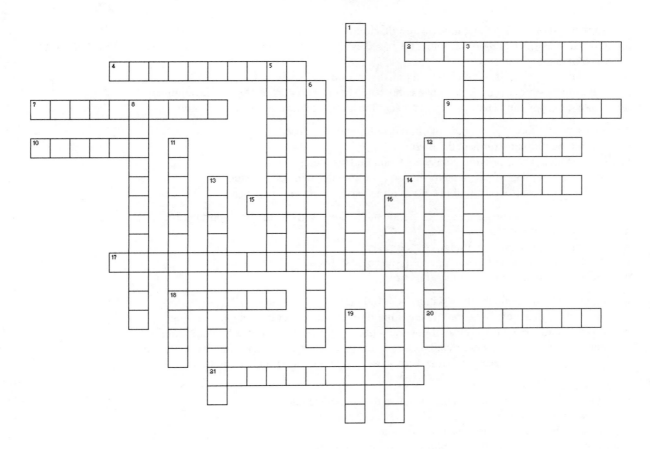

Across

2. Structured _____ : the researcher sets up a situation that evokes a behavior of interest and observes that behavior in a laboratory setting
4. _____ interview: each participant is asked the same questions in the same way
7. Longitudinal-_____ design: follows two or more age groups over time
9. _____ period: a time that is optimal for certain capacities to emerge
10. _____ effects refer to the impact of cultural historical change on the accuracy of findings.
12. In a _____ interview, the researcher uses a flexible, conversational style to probe for a participant's point of view.
14. Variable expected to be influenced by the experimental manipulations
15. The clinical method or _____ study approach
17. Method used to measure the relationship between physiological processes and behavior
18. Describes, explains, and predicts behavior
20. Approach that uses age-related averages to represent typical development
21. Variable manipulated by the researcher

Down

1. Design in which researchers gather information without altering the participants' experience
3. Design that permits inferences about cause and effect
5. Participant observation of a culture
6. Design in which groups of people differing in age are studied at the same point in time
8. _____ observation: observing a behavior of interest in the natural environment
11. Behavior _____ : procedures that combine conditioning and modeling to eliminate undesirable behaviors and increase desirable responses
12. A number describing how two variables are related is called a correlation _____ .
13. Design in which researchers present children with a novel task and follow their mastery over a series of closely spaced sessions
16. Design in which the same participants are studied repeatedly, at different ages
19. _____ assignment helps researchers control for characteristics of participants that could reduce the accuracy of their findings.

PRACTICE TEST #1

1. Our knowledge of child development is interdisciplinary. What does this mean? (p. 4)
   a. Our knowledge of child development is based exclusively on research conducted by people in the field of child development.
   b. Child development is not recognized as a distinct field of study.
   c. Individuals from diverse fields have contributed to our knowledge of child development.
   d. Child development is part of a larger discipline known as developmental psychology.

2. Theories are vital tools for the field of child development because they (p. 7)
   a. lay out the ultimate truths in the field.
   b. can be valuable for providing answers to applied problems.
   c. reduce the number of participants that an experimenter will need to study.
   d. lead to great control of possible confounding variables in an experiment.

3. Theorists who emphasize _____ are most likely to focus on the importance of _____ . (pp. 8–9)
   a. change; nurture.
   b. the concept of stages; continuous development.
   c. the distinct contexts of development; issues of stability.
   d. the many courses of development; nature.

4. During the sixteenth century, the Puritans believed that children were (p. 12)
   a. theoretically capable of becoming anything if given the proper training and rearing.
   b. innately endowed with a sense of goodness that would only be harmed by adult training.
   c. neither inherently good nor evil, but simply the product of their environment and upbringing.
   d. naturally inclined toward evil unless given the proper guidance and instruction.

5. John Locke's philosophy (p. 13)
   a. characterizes children as playing an active role in development.
   b. deals with the power of heredity to shape the child.
   c. regards child development as discontinuous.
   d. emphasizes the possibility of many courses of development.

6. Charles Darwin is considered the forefather of scientific child study because (pp. 13–14)
   a. he discovered that human prenatal growth differs markedly from that of other species.
   b. he constructed the first theory of human development.
   c. he was the first to conduct experiments on children.
   d. his theory prompted other researchers to study children and their development directly.

7. Both Rousseau and Hall (pp. 13–14)
   a. believed that children were born evil and stubborn and had to be civilized.
   b. likened children's minds to a blank slate.
   c. characterized children as naturally endowed with a plan for development.
   d. regarded development as a discontinuous process.

8. The primary purpose of the first successful intelligence test, developed by Binet and Simon, was to (p. 14)
   a. identify childhood geniuses.
   b. measure IQ.
   c. document children's intellectual functioning at various ages.
   d. identify children who needed special education services.

9. According to the behavioristic approach, the proper focus of study for psychology should be (p. 18)
    a. unconscious impulses and drives.
    b. directly observable events.
    c. adaptive evolutionary behavior patterns.
    d. each person's unique inner experience.

10. _____ theory emphasizes the role of _____ in children's learning. (p. 19)
    a. Bandura's; cognition
    b. Skinner's; classical conditioning
    c. Watson's; reinforcers and punishment
    d. Pavlov's; operant conditioning

11. According to _____ theory, as children develop their ways of thinking adapt to better fit with, or represent, the external world. (p. 19)
    a. social learning
    b. cognitive-developmental
    c. information processing
    d. evolutionary developmental

12. A major strength of the information processing approach is (p. 24)
    a. its commitment to rigorous research methods.
    b. the comprehensive theory of cognitive development that has been developed from computer simulations.
    c. its focus on children's thinking in real-life situations.
    d. its emphasis on the adaptive nature of children's cognition.

13. Observations of _____ led to the concept of the critical period in human development. (p. 24)
    a. human infant-caregiver attachment
    b. imprinting
    c. joint problem solving in chimpanzees
    d. stimulus-response associations learned by newborn mice

14. A(n) _____ psychologist would be MOST interested in examining the following research question: What role does the infant's capacity to imitate facial expressions play in survival? (p. 25)
    a. ecological systems
    b. sociocultural
    c. evolutionary developmental
    d. psychodynamic

15. Vygotsky believed that _____ produce development. (p. 26)
    a. bidirectional influences within the chronosystem
    b. cooperative dialogues between children and more knowledgeable members of society
    c. children's active, independent efforts
    d. environmental influences that occur during a sensitive period

16. _____ has risen to the forefront of the field because it provides the most differentiated and thorough account of contextual influences on children's development. (p. 27)
    a. Sociocultural theory
    b. Evolutionary developmental theory
    c. Social learning theory
    d. Ecological systems theory

17. A major advantage of structured observations is that they (p. 33)
    a. are useful for studying behaviors that investigators rarely have an opportunity to see in everyday life.
    b. permit participants to display their thoughts in terms that are as close as possible to the way they think in everyday life.
    c. yield richly detailed narratives that offer valuable insight into the many factors that affect development.
    d. allow researchers to see the behavior of interest as it occurs in natural settings.

18. Ethnographers strive to minimize their influence on the culture that they are observing by (p. 37)
    a. employing rigorous experimental procedures.
    b. minimizing the time spent with the cultural community they are studying.
    c. relying on unobtrusive techniques, such as surveillance cameras and one-way mirrors.
    d. becoming part of the cultural community they are studying.

19. An experimental design permits inferences about cause and effect because (p. 40)
    a. experiments take place in laboratory settings using sophisticated equipment.
    b. all participants are treated exactly alike except for changes in the independent variable.
    c. participants are chosen randomly from the population.
    d. the methods used must be both reliable and valid.

20. Imagine that a researcher concludes that 5-year-olds in the 1950s learn more slowly than the 5-year-olds of today. Which of the following poses a threat to the accuracy of such a finding? (p. 43)
    a. biased sampling
    b. investigator bias
    c. cohort effects
    d. selective attrition

PRACTICE TEST #2

1. The three major domains of development that operate through the lifespan are (p. 5)
   a. verbal, mathematical, and spatial.
   b. biological, environmental, and cognitive.
   c. theoretical, empirical, and applied.
   d. physical, cognitive, and social.

2. Child development theorists who emphasize the impact of _____ on individual development typically stress the importance of _____ . (p. 9)
   a. heredity; discontinuous change
   b. early experiences; environment
   c. stages; continuous change
   d. context; one course of development

3. Eighteenth-century philosopher Jean Jacques Rousseau (p. 13)
   a. viewed children as a tabula rasa or "blank slate."
   b. regarded children as miniature, already-formed adults.
   c. recommended restrictive parenting practices as the most efficient means for taming children.
   d. believed that children were naturally endowed with a sense of right and wrong.

4. The first successful intelligence test was developed by (p. 14)
   a. Gesell and Binet.
   b. Stanford and Binet.
   c. Hall and Gesell.
   d. Binet and Simon.

5. According to Freud's psychosexual theory, (pp. 15–16)
   a. overeating and smoking in later life is often the result of unmet oral needs during infancy.
   b. the superego works to reconcile id impulses and ego demands.
   c. id impulses transfer to the genitals during the latency stage.
   d. children develop a sexual desire for the other-sex parent during the genital stage.

6. According to _____ , children acquire behaviors that adults desire of them to ensure that their primary and secondary drives will be met. (p. 19)
   a. Watson
   b. Bandura
   c. Skinner
   d. Hull

7. An approach that emphasizes the role of modeling, or observational learning, in the development of behavior is known as (p. 19)
   a. traditional behaviorism.
   b. drive reduction theory.
   c. operant conditioning.
   d. social learning theory.

8. _____ researchers often use flowcharts to map the precise steps individuals take to solve problems and complete tasks. (p. 23)
   a. Psychoanalytic
   b. Information-processing
   c. Ecological systems
   d. Dynamic systems

9. Unlike Piaget, Vygotsky (p. 26)
   a. emphasized continuous change.
   b. focused on development throughout the lifespan.
   c. emphasized the role of bidirectional influences in development.
   d. viewed development as dependent on direct teaching by adults.

10. Before Bronfenbrenner's ecological systems theory, most researchers viewed the environment (pp. 27–29)
    a. as the primary force of development.
    b. as limited to events and conditions immediately surrounding the child.
    c. in terms of reinforcements and punishments.
    d. as less important than the influence of heredity.

11. To examine preschoolers' physical aggression, Dr. Imbroglio recorded naturally occurring instances of hitting, pushing, and kicking on a preschool playground. This study is an example of which of the following research methods? (p. 33)
    a. natural experiment
    b. structured observation
    c. field experiment
    d. naturalistic observation

12. Two major strengths of the clinical interview are that it (p. 35)
    a. eliminates the threats of observer bias and observer influence.
    b. provides data that is highly objective and that can be generalized.
    c. provides large amounts of information in a brief time period and exposes the way participants think in everyday settings.
    d. accurately assesses participants who have both low verbal ability and low expressiveness.

13. If a researcher asks a number of different people the same set of questions in the same way and in the same order, this technique is called (p. 35)
    a. naturalistic observation.
    b. laboratory experiment.
    c. structured interview.
    d. clinical interview.

14. One limitation of the ethnographic method is that (pp. 37–38)
    a. its findings cannot be applied to individuals and settings other than the ones studied.
    b. control over the treatment conditions is weaker than in the laboratory.
    c. observations may not be typical of the way participants behave in everyday life.
    d. age-related changes may be distorted because of participant dropout and cohort effects.

15. To reduce the chances that characteristics of participants will interfere with the accuracy of research findings in experimental studies, investigators (p. 41)
    a. directly manipulate changes in the independent variable.
    b. carefully choose participants to ensure that their characteristics are as much alike as possible.
    c. complement laboratory experiments with natural experiments.
    d. randomly assign participants to treatment conditions.

16. A researcher interested in the development of aggression in young children goes into a preschool classroom. She keeps a record of all aggressive acts occurring during her time in the classroom. This is an example of a (p. 33)
    a. naturalistic observation.
    b. structured observation.
    c. field experiment.
    d. case study.

17. If you test a group of 5-year-olds and a group of 7-year-olds on the same day, your study would be (p. 43)
    a. cross-sequential.
    b. longitudinal.
    c. time-lagged.
    d. cross-sectional.

18. According to the children's basic research right regarding beneficial treatments, if experimental treatments believed to be beneficial are under investigation, (p. 47)
    a. control groups without beneficial treatment cannot be used.
    b. all children in the study must receive the same beneficial treatment.
    c. children in control groups have the right to request the same treatment given to those in the experimental group.
    d. children in control groups have the right to available alternative beneficial treatments.

19. In an experiment on the effects of traditional classrooms versus open classrooms on peer relations, the independent variable would be (p. 40)
    a. type of classroom.
    b. measures of peer relations.
    c. the number of children in the experiment.
    d. measures of adjustment problems.

20. A researcher obtains consent from the parents of a 4-year-old to include their child in his study. During the experiment, the child becomes upset and does not want to participate any longer. Which of the following statements is true of this situation? (p. 48)
    a. The researcher obtained parental consent, so he can keep the child in the study.
    b. The researcher can keep the child in the study as long as he / she is debriefed at the end of the session.
    c. The researcher can only force the child to continue participation if he is certain that the experimental treatment will be beneficial.
    d. It would be ethically irresponsible for the researcher to force the child to finish the experiment.

CHAPTER 2
BIOLOGICAL AND ENVIRONMENTAL FOUNDATIONS

BRIEF CHAPTER SUMMARY

This chapter examines the complex contributions of heredity and environment to development. Principles of genetic transmission determine the characteristics that make us human and contribute to individual differences in appearance and behavior. Inheritance of harmful recessive genes and abnormalities of the chromosomes are major causes of serious developmental problems. Genetic counseling and prenatal diagnosis help people at risk for transmitting hereditary disorders assess their chances of giving birth to a healthy baby.

Environmental influences on development are equally as complex as hereditary factors. The family has an especially powerful impact, operating as a complex and dynamic social system in which members exert direct, indirect, and third-party effects on one another. Socioeconomic status influences child-rearing practices, and poverty and homelessness undermine effective family functioning and children's well-being. The quality of community life, from neighborhoods and schools to small towns and cities, also affects children's development. Cultural values, laws, and government programs shape experiences in all of these contexts.

Child development specialists view the relationship between genetic and environmental factors in different ways. Some believe that it is useful and possible to answer the question of "how much" each contributes to behavior. Others think that heredity and environment cannot be divided into separate influences. They want to discover "how" these two major determinants of development work together in a complex, dynamic interplay.

LEARNING OBJECTIVES

After reading this chapter, you should be able to:

2.1 Distinguish between genotypes and phenotypes. (p. 53)

2.2 Describe the structure and function of chromosomes and DNA molecules. (pp. 54–55)

2.3 Explain the process of mitosis. (p. 55)

2.4 Describe the process of meiosis, and explain how it leads to genetic variability. (pp. 55–56)

2.5 Describe the genetic events that determine the sex of the new organism. (pp. 55–57)

2.6 Identify two types of twins, and explain how each is created. (p. 57)

2.7 Explain how alleles influence the inheritance of traits, such as through dominant–recessive inheritance, codominance, X-linked inheritance, polygenic inheritance, and genetic imprinting. (pp. 58–62)

2.8 Describe the origins and consequences of Down syndrome and abnormalities of the sex chromosomes. (pp. 62–64)

2.9 Discuss reproductive options available to prospective parents. (pp. 64–70)

2.10 Describe family functioning from the ecological systems perspective, noting direct and indirect family influences and explaining the view of the family as a dynamic, changing system. (pp. 71–74)

2.11 Discuss the impact of socioeconomic status and poverty on family functioning. (pp. 74–76)

2.12 Summarize the role of neighborhoods and schools in the lives of children. (pp. 76–77)

2.13 Discuss how cultural values and public policies influence the well-being of children. (pp. 77–82)

2.14 Describe concepts that explain how heredity and environment work together to influence complex human characteristics. (pp. 83–89)

STUDY QUESTIONS

1. _____ are directly observable characteristics that depend in part on the _____ , the complex blend of genetic information transmitted from one generation to the next. (p. 53)

Genetic Foundations

1. Rodlike structures in the nuclei of cells that store and transmit genetic information are called _____ . (p. 54)

2. Humans have (23 / 46) pairs of chromosomes in each cell. (p. 54)

The Genetic Code

1. Chromosomes are made up of a chemical substance called _____ . It looks like a twisted ladder and is composed of segments called _____ . (p. 54)

2. The process through which DNA duplicates itself so that each new body cell contains the same number of chromosomes is called _____ . (p. 55)

The Sex Cells

1. Sex cells, or _____ , are formed through the process of (mitosis / meiosis). (p. 55)

2. True or False: Sex cells contain only half the number of chromosomes normally present in body cells. (p. 55)

3. During meiosis, the process of _____ , in which chromosomes next to each other break at one or more points and exchange segments, creates new hereditary combinations unique to the individual. (p. 55)

4. When the sperm and ova unite at fertilization, the cell that results is called a _____ . (p. 55)

Boy or Girl?

1. The twenty-two matching pairs of chromosomes are called _____ . (p. 57)

2. The twenty-third pair of chromosomes, also called the sex chromosomes, determine the sex of the child. In females, this pair is called _____ , whereas in males it is called _____ . (p. 57)

Multiple Births

1. Match each of the following terms with the appropriate description. (p. 57)

_____ This type of twinning may result from environmental influences such as temperature changes, variations in oxgen levels, or late fertilization of the ovum.

_____ This is the most common type of multiple birth.

_____ Older maternal age and use of fertility drugs and in vitro fertilization are major causes of twinning.

_____ These twins are genetically no more alike than ordinary siblings.

_____ These twins share the same genetic makeup.

1. Identical, or monozygotic, twins
2. Fraternal, or dizygotic, twins

2. True or False: Children of single births are often healthier and develop more rapidly than twins during the early years of life. (p. 57)

Patterns of Genetic Inheritance

1. Each of two forms of a gene located at the same place on the autosome is called a(n) _____ . (p. 58)

2. If the alleles from both parents are alike, the child is _____ and will display the inherited trait. If the alleles inherited from the mother and father are different, then the child is _____ , and the relationship between the alleles will determine the trait that will appear. (p. 58)

3. Explain the nature of *dominant–recessive inheritance*, and provide one example of this type of inheritance. (p. 58)

   _____

   _____

   _____

   _____

4. One of the most common recessive disorders is _____ , which affects the way the body breaks down proteins contained in many foods. (p. 58)

5. _____ *genes* enhance or dilute the effects of other genes. (p. 58)

6. True or False: Serious diseases typically result from dominant alleles. Briefly explain your response. (p. 58)

   _____

   _____

7. What is *codominance*? (p. 59)

   _____

   _____

   _____

   _____

8. Name one condition or trait that results from codominant inheritance. (p. 59)

   _____

9. (Males / Females) are more likely to be affected by X-linked inheritance. Why is this the case? (pp. 59, 61)

   _____

   _____

10. Name one X-linked disorder. (p. 60)

    _____

11. _____ occurs when alleles are chemically marked in such a way that one pair member is activated, regardless of its makeup. (p. 61)

12. List three conditions or diseases that are caused by genetic imprinting. (p. 61)

    A. _____   B. _____

    C. _____

13. Explain how harmful genes are created. (pp. 61–62)

_____

_____

14. Describe *polygenic inheritance*, and give an example of a trait that is determined by this pattern of inheritance. (p. 62)

_____

_____

_____

Chromosomal Abnormalities

1. Most chromosomal defects are the result of mistakes during _____ , when the ovum and sperm are formed. (p. 62)

2. _____ , the most common chromosomal abnormality, often results from a defect in the 21st chromosome. For this reason, the disorder is sometimes called Trisomy 21. (p. 62)

3. List the physical and behavioral characteristics of Down syndrome. (pp. 62–63)

    Physical: _____

    _____

    Behavioral: _____

    _____

4. True or False: The risk of Down syndrome rises with maternal age. (p. 63)

5. Disorders of the sex chromosomes result in (more / less) serious consequences than do disorders of the autosomes. (p. 63)

Reproductive Choices

Genetic Counseling

1. What is the purpose of genetic counseling, and who is most likely to seek this service? (p. 64)

_____

_____

_____

Prenatal Diagnosis and Fetal Medicine

1. _____ are medical procedures that permit detection of developmental problems before birth. (p. 65)

2. Cite four types of prenatal diagnostic methods. (p. 65)

    A. _____

    B. _____

    C. _____

    D. _____

3. True or False: The techniques used in fetal medicine rarely result in complications such as premature labor or miscarriage. (p. 68)

4. Summarize the goals of the Human Genome Project, and explain why this program offers hope for correcting hereditary defects. (pp. 68–69)

_____

_____

_____

_____

5. Describe three steps that prospective parents can take before conception to increase their chances of having a healthy baby. (p. 69)

A. _____

B. _____

C. _____

Social Issues: Health: The Pros and Cons of Reproductive Technologies

1. Explain the following reproductive technologies: (p. 66)

Donor insemination:

_____

_____

_____

_____

In vitro fertilization:

_____

_____

_____

_____

2. True or False: Children conceived through in vitro fertilization typically exhibit a variety of behavioral and adjustment problems and have insecure attachments to their parents. (p. 66)

3. Discuss some of the concerns surrounding the use of donor insemination and in vitro fertilization. (p. 66)

_____

_____

_____

_____

_____

4. Describe some of the risks involved with surrogate motherhood. (pp. 66–67)

_____

_____

_____

_____

_____

5. Briefly describe some of the new reproductive technologies that have been introduced in recent years. (p. 67)

_____

_____

_____

_____

The Alternative of Adoption

1. Adopted children and adolescents have (fewer / more) learning and emotional difficulties than do other children. Cite two possible reasons for this trend. (pp. 69–70)

   A. _____

   B. _____

2. True or False: Most adoptees have serious, long-term adjustment problems that are evident well into adulthood. (p. 70)

Environmental Contexts for Development

The Family

1. Distinguish between direct and indirect familial influences. (pp. 72–73)

   Direct: _____

   _____

   Indirect: _____

   _____

2. Discuss some of the ways in which the family system must adapt over time. (pp. 73–74)

   _____

   _____

   _____

Socioeconomic Status and Family Functioning

1. List the three variables that determine a family's socioeconomic status (SES). (p. 74)

   A. _____   B. _____

   C. _____

2. Compare child characteristics emphasized in lower-SES families with those emphasized in their higher-SES counterparts. (p. 74)

Lower-SES: _____

_____

Higher-SES: _____

_____

3. Describe the influence of SES on parenting practices and parent-child interaction. (p. 74)

_____

_____

_____

4. Summarize the factors that explain SES differences in family interaction. (p. 74)

_____

_____

_____

5. True or False: Higher-SES children show more advances in cognitive development and tend to perform better in school than their lower-SES peers. (p. 74)

The Impact of Poverty

1. What subgroups of the population are hardest hit by poverty? (pp. 74–75)

   A. _____   B. _____

   C. _____   D. _____

2. Describe how the constant stresses that accompany poverty gradually weaken the family system. (p. 75)

_____

_____

_____

3. Describe the developmental risks associated with homelessness in children. (pp. 75–76)

_____

_____

_____

_____

Beyond the Family: Neighborhoods and Schools

1. True or False: Dissatisfaction with one's community is associated with increased child abuse and neglect. (p. 76)

2. Neighborhood resources have a greater impact on children growing up in (disadvantaged / well-to-do) areas. Why is this the case? (p. 76)

_____

_____

_____

3. Summarize features of the Better Beginnings, Better Futures Project of Ontario, Canada, and note major outcomes of the program. (p. 77)

Features: _____

_____

_____

Outcomes: _____

_____

_____

4. List four broad features of the school environment that impact students' developmental outcomes. (p. 77)

A. _____

B. _____

C. _____

D. _____

5. Why are higher-SES parents more likely to have regular contact with teachers than are lower-SES parents? (p. 77)

_____

_____

The Cultural Context

1. What are *subcultures*? (p. 78)

_____

_____

2. The African _____ *household*, in which one or more adult relatives live with the parent-child nuclear family unit, is a vital feature of black family life. (p. 78)

3. Distinguish the characteristics of *collectivist* versus *individualistic* societies. (p. 78)

Collectivist: _____

_____

Individualistic: _____

_____

4. What are *public policies*? (p. 78)

_____

5. True or False: Among developed nations, the United States and Canada have served as forerunners in the development of public policies to safeguard children. (p. 78)

6. List some of the areas in which American and Canadian public policies regarding children are deficient. (pp. 78–80)

_____

_____

_____

7. Cite four reasons why attempts to help children and youth in the United States and Canada have been difficult to realize. (pp. 79–80)

   A. _____

   B. _____

   C. _____

   D. _____

8. The _____ is a legal agreement which commits each cooperating country to work toward guaranteeing environments that foster children's development, protect them from harm, and enhance their community participation and self-determination. The United States (is / is not) one of the two countries in the world that has not yet ratified this agreement. (pp. 80–81)

Cultural Influences: The African-American Extended Family

1. Describe three ways in which extended-family relationships benefit African-American families. (p. 79)

   A. _____

   B. _____
   _____

   C. _____
   _____

Social Issues: Health: Welfare Reform, Poverty, and Child Development

1. Summarize features of the welfare-to-work program. (p. 81)

   _____
   _____
   _____
   _____
   _____

2. True or False: To date, the welfare-to-work program has been successful in making all welfare recipients financially independent. (p. 81)

3. True or False: A welfare-work combination, in which individuals retain some welfare support while working, seems to have the greatest benefit for children and families. Elaborate on your response. (p. 81)

   _____
   _____
   _____

4. Explain how welfare policies in other Western nations, such as France and Canada, attempt to protect children from the damaging effects of poverty. (p. 81)

France:

_____

_____

Canada:

_____

_____

Understanding the Relationship Between Heredity and Environment

1. _____ is a field devoted to uncovering the contributions of nature and nurture as they relate to individual differences in human traits and abilities. (p. 83)

The Question, "How Much?"

1. Name the two methods used by behavioral geneticists to infer the role of heredity in human characteristics. (p. 83)

    A. _____   B. _____

2. What are *heritability estimates*? (p. 83)

    _____

    _____

    _____

    _____

3. Heritability estimates are obtained from _____ *studies*, which compare characteristics of family members. (pp. 83–84)

4. True or False: Heritability estimates for intelligence and personality are approximately .50, indicating that genetic makeup can explain half of the variance in these traits. (p. 84)

5. What is a *concordance rate*? (p. 84)

    _____

    _____

6. What do concordance rates of 0 and of 100 mean? (p. 84)

    0: _____

    100: _____

7. When a concordance rate is much higher for (identical / fraternal) twins, then heredity is believed to play a major role. (p. 84)

37

8. Discuss three limitations of heritability estimates and concordance rates. (pp. 84–85)

A. _____

_____

B. _____

_____

C. _____

_____

The Question, "How?"

1. The concept of _____ emphasizes that each person responds to the environment in a unique way because of his or her genetic makeup. (p. 85)

2. Define the term *canalization*. (p. 86)

_____

_____

_____

3. Which is more strongly canalized: infant perceptual and motor development or intelligence and personality? (p. 86)

4. According to the concept of _____ , our genes influence the environments to which we are exposed. (p. 86)

5. Describe passive, evocative, and active genetic–environmental correlations. (pp. 86–87)

Passive: _____

_____

Evocative: _____

_____

Active: _____

_____

6. The tendency to choose environments that complement our own heredity is called _____ . (p. 87)

7. Define the term *epigenesis*. (p. 88)

_____

_____

Biology and Environment: Uncoupling Genetic–Environmental Correlations for Mental Illness and Antisocial Behavior

1. True or False: Adopted children whose biological mothers have psychological disorders are more likely to develop mental illness when reared in maladaptive homes than when reared in healthy homes. (p. 88)

ASK YOURSELF . . .

For *Ask Yourself* questions for this chapter, please log on to the Companion Website at *www.ablongman.com/berk*.

1. Select the Companion Website for *Infants, Children, and Adolescents*, Fifth Edition.

2. Use the "Jump to" menu to go directly to this chapter.

3. From the menu on the left side of your screen, select *Ask Yourself*.

4. Complete the questions and choose "Submit answers for grading" or "Clear answers" to start over.

SUGGESTED STUDENT READINGS

Baker, D. L., Schuette, J. L., & Uhlmann, W. R. (Eds.). (1998). *A guide to genetic counseling*. New York: Wiley-Liss. A detailed presentation of the components, theoretical framework, goals, and unique approaches used in genetic counseling.

Children's Defense Fund (2000). *The state of America's children, 2000*. Washington, DC: Author. Provides a comprehensive analysis of the current condition of children in the United States, government-sponsored programs serving them, and proposals for improving child and family programs.

Jargowsky, P. A. (1997). *Poverty and place: Ghettos, barrios, and the American city*. New York: Russell Sage Foundation. Discusses the impact of growing up in impoverished inner city neighborhoods on a variety of developmental outcomes. Illustrates the notion of context as a powerful influence on child development.

Johnson-Powell, G., Yamamoto, J., Wyatt, G. E., & Arroyo, W. (Eds.). (1997). *Transcultural child development: Psychological assessment and treatment*. New York: John Wiley & Sons, Inc. Written primarily for professionals working with children from other cultures, this book focuses on the impact of culture on child development with particular emphasis on the development of psychological disorders.

Lamb, M. E. (Ed.). (1999). *Parenting and child development in "nontraditional" families*. Mahwah, NJ: Lawrence Erlbaum Associates, Inc., Publishers. A collection of chapters that examines how nontraditional patterns of child care affects development. Topics include dual-earner families, single parenthood, poverty, adoption, parents with gay or lesbian sexual orientations, and nonparental child care.

Segal, N. L. (1999). *Entwined lives: Twins and what they tell us about behavior*. New York: Dutton/Penguin Books. Presents a compelling account of the unique behavioral and physical development of twins. The author covers topics such as the unusual language patterns of twins, the role of fertility treatments in twin conceptions, the loss of a twin through death, and how conjoined twins interact on a daily basis.

PUZZLE 2.1 TERM REVIEW

Across

2. Genes that enhance or dilute the effects of other genes
6. A heterozygous individual who can pass a recessive trait to his or her children
11. Having two different alleles at the same place on a pair of chromosomes
13. The genetic makeup of an individual
15. _____ chromosomes: The 23rd pair of chromosomes; XX in females, XY in males
16. Long, double-stranded molecules that make up chromosomes (abbr.)
19. Dominant-_____ inheritance: in heterozygous pairings, only one allele affects the child's traits.
20. A segment of a DNA molecule that contains hereditary instructions
21. Directly observable characteristics
22. The process of cell duplication
23. Cell formed by the union of the sperm and the ovum at conception
24. A sudden but permanent change in a segment of DNA

Down

1. _____ inheritance: the recessive gene is carried on the X chromosome
3. Genetic _____: alleles are chemically marked in such a way that one pair member is activated, regardless of its makeup.
4. Having two identical alleles at the same place on a pair of chromosomes
5. An exchange of genes between chromosomes next to each other during meiosis (2 words)
7. _____ twins have the same genetic makeup.
8. Each of two forms of a gene located at the same place on the autosomes
9. Rodlike structures in the cell nucleus that store and transmit genetic information
10. Pattern of inheritance in which both alleles influence the person's characteristics
12. The 22 matching chromosome pairs in each human cell
14. Human sperm and ova
17. The process of cell division
18. Fraternal, or _____, twins
21. _____ inheritance: Many genes determine a characteristic

PUZZLE 2.2 TERM REVIEW

Across

6. _____ diagnostic methods are medical procedures that permit detection of problems before birth.

9. _____ rate: percentage of instances in which both members of a twin pair show a trait when it is present in one pair member

11. Tendency for individuals to actively choose environments that compliment their heredity (2 words; hyph)

12. Tendency of heredity to restrict the development of some characteristics to just one or a few outcomes

14. _____ genetics: field devoted to uncovering the contributions of nature and nurture to individual differences in human traits and abilities

15. _____ estimate: measure of the extent to which individual differences in complex traits in a specific population are due to genetic factors

17. In _____ societies, people define themselves as part of a group and stress group over individual goals.

Down

1. _____ studies compare the characteristics of family members to obtain heritability estimates.

2. Genetic _____ is designed to help couples assess their chances of giving birth to a baby with a hereditary disorder.

3. In _____ -family households, parent and child live with one or more adult relatives.

4. _____ -environmental correlation: the notion that heredity influences the environments to which an individual is exposed

5. Development resulting from ongoing, bidirectional exchanges between heredity and environment

7. Range of _____ : a person's genetically determined response to a range of environmental conditions

8. In _____ societies, people think of themselves as separate entities and are largely concerned with their own personal needs.

10. Group of people with beliefs and customs that differ from those of the larger culture

13. _____ policies: laws and government programs designed to improve the condition of children and families

16. A measure of a family's social position and economic well-being (abbr.)

PRACTICE TEST #1

1. Inside each human cell are rodlike structures called _____ that store and transmit genetic information. (p. 54)
    a. chromosomes
    b. nuclei
    c. genes
    d. DNA

2. A unique feature of DNA is that it can duplicate itself through a process called _____ . (p. 55)
    a. meiosis
    b. mitosis
    c. imprinting
    d. codominance

3. A person whose 23rd pair of chromosomes is xy (p. 57)
    a. has Turner syndrome.
    b. has Down syndrome.
    c. is male.
    d. is heterozygous.

4. Identical twins are created when (p. 57)
    a. one egg cell is fertilized by two different sperm cells.
    b. a fertilized egg divides into two separate clusters of cells.
    c. two different egg cells are fertilized by the same sperm cell.
    d. two different eggs are fertilized by two different sperm.

5. Allison has blonde hair and Albert has dark hair. If they have four children, which scenario is most likely? (p. 58)
    a. All four children will have dark hair.
    b. Two children will have blonde hair and two children will have dark hair.
    c. Three children will have dark hair, and one child will have blonde hair.
    d. All four children will have blonde hair.

6. Maya tested positive for PKU at birth. For Maya to have a normal lifespan, she will (p. 58)
    a. require hormone replacement therapy.
    b. have to be placed on a diet low in phenylalanine.
    c. need regular injections of insulin.
    d. require frequent blood transfusions.

7. _____ are more likely than _____ to be affected by X-linked diseases. (pp. 59–61)
    a. African Americans; European Americans
    b. First-born children; later-born children
    c. Males; females
    d. Singletons; twins or triplets

8. _____ helps explain why children are more likely to develop asthma if their mothers, rather than their fathers, suffer from it. (p. 61)
    a. Genetic imprinting
    b. X-linked inheritance
    c. Modifier genes
    d. Polygenetic inheritance

9. A child born with an extra 21st chromosome has (p. 62)
    a. sickle cell anemia.
    b. fragile X syndrome.
    c. hemophilia.
    d. Down syndrome.

10. Abnormalities of the sex chromosomes (p. 63)
    a. typically result in sexual dysfunctions during adulthood.
    b. are a leading cause of mental retardation.
    c. often are not recognized until adolescence.
    d. usually disrupt development so severely that miscarriage occurs.

11. Except for _____ and _____ , prenatal diagnosis should not be used routinely, since other methods have some chance of injuring the fetus. (p. 65)
    a. ultrasound; amniocentesis
    b. maternal blood analysis; ultrasound
    c. fetoscopy; chorionic villus sampling
    d. amniocentesis; maternal blood analysis

12. When a marriage is tense and hostile, parents are less responsive to their children's needs. This is an example of a(n) _____ influence between parents and their children. (p. 73)
    a. epigenetic
    b. direct
    c. niche-picking
    d. indirect

13. Which of the following is supported by research on SES? (p. 74)
    a. Lower-SES parents tend to place greater emphasis on psychological traits, whereas higher-SES parents tend to emphasize external characteristics.
    b. Lower-SES fathers tend to devote more time to parenting compared to higher-SES fathers.
    c. Commands to children, such as "You do that because I told you to," are more common in lower-SES than in higher-SES households.
    d. Within the first few days of life, higher-SES infants show higher IQ than lower-SES infants.

14. For single mothers with preschool children, the poverty rate is the United States is nearly (p. 75)
    a. 10 percent.
    b. 20 percent.
    c. 35 percent.
    d. 50 percent.

15. Nearly _____ of the homeless in the United States are families with children. (p. 75)
    a. 5 percent
    b. 15 percent
    c. 30 percent
    d. 40 percent

16. One important reason that the American people have been reluctant to accept the idea of publicly supported child care is (pp. 78–80)
    a. that few mothers of children under age 5 years work outside the home.
    b. American values that emphasize independence, self-reliance, and the privacy of family life.
    c. that most grandparents regularly participate in child rearing.
    d. the common wisdom that daily separation from the mother is harmful to young children.

17. Public policies safeguarding children and youth have been _____ in the United States than in other Western industrialized nations. (pp. 78–80)
    a. enacted earlier
    b. more protective
    c. more successful
    d. slower to emerge

18. Compared with other nations, how does the United States stand on indicators of child health and well-being? (p. 80)
    a. The United States is ahead of almost all other nations.
    b. The United States lags behind virtually all other nations.
    c. The United States is about the same as other nations.
    d. The United States lags behind other industrialized nations.

19. A concordance rate of 50 percent indicates that (p. 84)
    a. if one twin has the trait, the other one will have it half the time.
    b. half of the variation in the trait can be explained by individual differences in genetic makeup.
    c. the probability that one's offspring will have the trait is 50 percent.
    d. half of the variation in the trait is due to environmental factors.

20. The concept of range of reaction explains that children who are exposed to the same environmental conditions (pp. 85–86)
    a. may respond to them differently because of their genetic makeup.
    b. will tend to show the same pattern of responses over time.
    c. tend to overcome their inheritance, so their genes have no effect.
    d. will become genetically more similar than other children are.

PRACTICE TEST #2

1. A(n) _____ is a segment of DNA along the length of the chromosome. (p. 54)
    a. gene
    b. zygote
    c. gamete
    d. autosome

2. When sperm and ovum unite at conception, the resulting cell is called a _____ and contains _____ chromosomes. (p. 55)
    a. gamete; 23
    b. gamete; 46
    c. zygote; 23
    d. zygote; 46

3. Carriers of a trait that follows the rules of dominant–recessive inheritance are (p. 58)
    a. homozygous individuals with just one recessive gene.
    b. heterozygous individuals with two recessive genes.
    c. heterozygous individuals with just one recessive gene.
    d. homozygous individuals with two recessive genes.

4. When children inherit a single sickle cell gene, (p. 59)
    a. sickle cell anemia occurs in full form.
    b. they are completely unaffected by the disease.
    c. a mild form of sickle cell illness can occur at high altitudes or after intense physical exercise.
    d. they are more resistant to rubella than are individuals with two genes for normal red blood cells.

5. When a harmful gene is carried on the X chromosome, (pp. 59, 61)
    a. males are more likely to be affected than females.
    b. it faces an increased risk of mutation.
    c. the characteristic does not follow the rules of dominant–recessive inheritance.
    d. it responds differently based on which parent contributed the gene.

6. Research shows that children are more likely to develop asthma if their mother, rather than their father, suffers from it. _____ explains this pattern of genetic inheritance. (p. 61)
    a. Polygenetic inheritance
    b. Genetic imprinting
    c. X-linked inheritance
    d. Codominance

7. High-energy radiation is an established cause of (p. 62)
    a. mutation.
    b. crossing over.
    c. genetic imprinting.
    d. polygenic inheritance.

8. Most chromosomal defects are the result of (p. 62)
    a. recessive disorders.
    b. mistakes during meiosis.
    c. X-linked disorders.
    d. mistakes during mitosis.

9. Fetoscopy refers to a procedure in which (p. 65)
   a. high-frequency sound waves are beamed at the uterus and their reflection is translated into a picture on a video screen.
   b. a thin tube is inserted into the vagina and a small plug of tissue is removed from the end of one or more chorionic villi.
   c. a small tube with a light source at one end is inserted into the uterus to inspect the fetus for defects of the limbs and face.
   d. a hollow needle is inserted through the abdominal wall to obtain a sample of fluid in the uterus.

10. Children conceived through in vitro fertilization procedures. (p. 66)
   a. tend to develop a less secure attachment to their parents than those who are easily conceived
   b. are at high risk for prematurity and illness during infancy.
   c. are less well adjusted than those who were naturally conceived.
   d. may be genetically unrelated to the woman who gave birth to them.

11. When a marriage is tense and hostile, mothers and fathers are likely to express anger, criticize, and punish their children. This is an example of a(n) _____ influence on the interaction between parents and their children. (p. 73)
   a. direct
   b. microsystem
   c. indirect
   d. macrosystem

12. The strong emphasis on _____ in the United States is one reason why the American public has been slow to accept the idea of publicly supported health insurance and child care for children of employed parents. (p. 78)
   a. realism
   b. idealism
   c. collectivism
   d. individualism

13. Which of the following statements is true regarding employment leave for childbirth and parenting? (p. 81)
   a. The United States guarantees 3 months paid and an additional 9 months unpaid leave.
   b. The United States guarantees 12 months unpaid leave.
   c. The United States guarantees 12 weeks paid leave.
   d. Federal law in the United States does not mandate any paid leave.

14. Heritability estimates (pp. 83–84)
   a. provide no precise information about how traits develop.
   b. can be used to accurately estimate the extent to which ethnic differences are due to heredity.
   c. indicate that, in general, the heritability of traits decreases with age.
   d. refer to the percentage of instances in which both twins show a trait when it is present in one twin.

15. Which of the following is true of concordance rates? (p. 84)
   a. Concordance rates range from 0 to +1.00.
   b. A concordance rate of 1.00 means that if one twin has the trait, the other will always have it.
   c. A concordance rate of 0 indicates that if one twin has the trait, the other twin will never have it.
   d. A concordance rate of .50 means that if one twin has the trait, the other twin will have it half of the time.

16. The concept of _____ suggests that each person, due to his or her genetic makeup, responds differently as the quality of the environment changes. (p. 85)
   a. concordance rate
   b. range of reaction
   c. canalization
   d. genetic–environmental correlation

17. The acquisition of which of the following behaviors is MOST strongly canalized? (p. 86)
    a. reading
    b. skiing
    c. swimming
    d. walking

18. The concept of _____ helps explain why identical twins become somewhat more alike and fraternal twins less alike in intelligence. (p. 87)
    a. canalization
    b. niche-picking
    c. range of reaction
    d. epigenesis

19. _____ means the development of the individual resulting from ongoing, bidirectional exchanges between heredity and all levels of the environment. (p. 88)
    a. Range of reaction
    b. Niche-picking
    c. Canalization
    d. Epigenesis

20. According to the epigenetic framework, gene–environment influences (pp. 88–89)
    a. are driven entirely by genetics.
    b. restrict the development of some characteristics to a few outcomes.
    c. can be changed only by strong environmental forces.
    d. are bi-directional.

CHAPTER 3
PRENATAL DEVELOPMENT

BRIEF CHAPTER SUMMARY

This chapter begins with a discussion of motivations for parenthood and current changes in birth patterns. Today, men and women are more likely to weigh the pros and cons of having children than they did in previous generations. The American family has declined in size over time, a trend that has child-rearing benefits. Births to women over thirty have increased, a change associated with both advantages and disadvantages for children.

At no other time is change as rapid as it is before birth. Prenatal development takes place in three phases: (1) the period of the zygote, during which the newly fertilized ovum travels down the fallopian tube and attaches itself to the uterine wall; (2) the period of the embryo, during which the groundwork for all body structures is laid down; and (3) the period of the fetus, the "growth and finishing" phase. The prenatal period is a vulnerable time. Teratogens such as drugs, smoking, alcohol, radiation, environmental pollution, maternal disease, inadequate nutrition, maternal stress, and Rh blood incompatibility can damage the developing organism. Prenatal health care is vitally important to ensure the health of mother and baby.

For most expectant parents, the prenatal period is not a time of medical hazard. Instead, it is a time of major life change in which mothers and fathers prepare for parenthood.

LEARNING OBJECTIVES

After reading this chapter, you should be able to:

3.1 Cite advantages and disadvantages of having children mentioned by modern North American couples. (pp. 94–95)

3.2 Review current trends in family size and childbearing age, and discuss their impact on child development. (pp. 95–98)

3.3 List the phases of prenatal development, and describe the major milestones of each. (pp. 99–106)

3.4 Define the term *teratogen,* and summarize the factors that affect the impact of teratogens. (p. 106)

3.5 List agents known to be or suspected of being teratogens, and discuss evidence supporting the harmful impact of each. (pp. 108–116)

3.6 Discuss maternal factors other than exposure to teratogens that can affect the developing embryo or fetus. (pp. 116–120)

3.7 Discuss the importance of prenatal health care and cite some of the barriers to seeking such care. (pp. 120–121)

3.8 Explain the factors that contribute to personal adjustment as expectant mothers and fathers prepare for parenthood. (pp. 122–125)

Motivations for Parenthood

Why Have Children?

1. List five advantages and five disadvantages of parenthood mentioned by North American couples. (p. 95)

    Advantages:

    A. _____

    B. _____

    C. _____

    D. _____

    E. _____

    Disadvantages:

    A. _____

    B. _____

    C. _____

    D. _____

    E. _____

How Large a Family?

1. List two major reasons that family size has declined in industrialized nations. (p. 95)

    A. _____

    B. _____

2. Describe the benefits of growing up in a small family. (pp. 95–96)

    _____

    _____

    _____

3. True or False: Research supports the commonly held belief that only children are spoiled and selfish. (p. 96)

4. Discuss some of the pros and cons of living in a one-child family, including perspectives of both parents and children. (p. 97)

    Pros (children): _____

    _____

    Cons (children): _____

    _____

    Pros (parents): _____

    _____

Cons (parents): _____

_____

Is There a Best Time During Adulthood to Have a Child?

1. Cite reasons why many modern couples are delaying childbearing into their thirties and beyond. (p. 98)

    _____

    _____

2. True or False: Both males and females experience a decline in reproductive capacity with age. (p. 98)

Social Issues: Education: A Global Perspective on Family Planning

1. Discuss five reasons why poverty is linked to higher birth rates. (p. 97)

    A. _____

    B. _____

    C. _____

    D. _____

    E. _____

2. List two strategies that have been effective in breaking the cycle through which poverty and high birth rates perpetuate one another. (pp. 96–97)

    A. _____

    B. _____

Prenatal Development

Conception

1. Approximately once every 28 days, an ovum is released from one of a woman's two _____ , and it travels through one of the two _____ , which are long, thin structures that lead to the uterus. (p. 99)

2. The male produces vast numbers of sperm in the _____ , two glands located in the scrotum. (p. 99)

The Period of the Zygote

1. The period of the zygote lasts about _____ weeks, from fertilization until the tiny mass of cells drifts down and out of the fallopian tube and attaches itself to the uterus. (pp. 100, 101)

2. Match each term with the appropriate definition. (p. 101)

    _____ will become the structures that provide protective   1. Blastocyst
    covering and nourishment to the new organism   2. Embryonic disk
    _____ hollow, fluid filled ball that is formed by a   3. Trophoblast
    tiny mass of cells four days after fertilization
    _____ will become the new organism

3. List two functions of the amniotic fluid. (p. 101)

   A. _____

   B. _____

4. True or False: As many as 30 percent of zygotes do not make it through the first two weeks. (p. 101)

5. The _____ permits food and oxygen to reach the developing organism and waste products to be carried away. (p. 101)

6. The placenta is connected to the developing organism by the _____ . (p. 101)

The Period of the Embryo

1. The period of the embryo lasts from implantation through the _____ week of pregnancy. (p. 102)

2. True or False: The most rapid prenatal changes take place during the period of the embryo. (p. 102)

3. Why is the embryo especially vulnerable to interference with healthy development? (p. 102)

   _____

   _____

4. List the organs and structures which will be formed from each of the three layers of the embryonic disk. (p. 102)

   Ectoderm: _____

   Mesoderm: _____

   Endoderm: _____

5. Summarize the events that take place during the second month of pregnancy. (p. 103)

   _____

   _____

   _____

   _____

The Period of the Fetus

1. The period of the fetus is sometimes referred to as the _____ phase. (p. 103)

2. Prenatal development is divided into _____ , or three equal periods of time. (p. 104)

3. The white, cheeselike substance that protects the skin from chapping in the amniotic fluid is called _____ . (p. 104)

4. _____ is a white, downy hair that covers the entire body of the fetus. (p. 104)

5. The age at which the baby can first survive if born early is called the *age of* _____ . When does this typically occur? (p. 104)

   _____

6. Summarize research findings on the relationship between fetal activity patterns and temperament in early childhood. (p. 104)

_____

_____

_____

Prenatal Environmental Influences

Teratogens

1. Define the term *teratogen,* and describe four factors that affect the impact of teratogens on prenatal development. (p. 106)

   Teratogen: _____

   _____

   A. _____

   B. _____

   C. _____

   D. _____

2. A _____ *period* is a limited time span in which a part of the body or a behavior is biologically prepared to develop rapidly and is especially sensitive to its surroundings. (p. 107)

3. True or False: The fetal period is the time when teratogens are most likely to cause serious defects. (p. 107)

4. When taken by mothers 4 to 6 weeks after conception, _____ , a sedative widely available in some countries during the early 1960s, produced deformities of the embryo's developing arms and legs, and less frequently, caused damage to the ears, heart, kidneys, and genitals. (p. 108)

5. True or False: Heavy caffeine intake during pregnancy is associated with prematurity, miscarriage, and newborn withdrawal symptoms. (p. 110)

6. Describe the difficulties faced by babies who are prenatally exposed to heroine, methadone, or cocaine. (pp. 110–111)

   _____

   _____

   _____

   _____

7. Explain why it is difficult to isolate the precise damage caused by prenatal exposure to cocaine. (pp. 111–112)

   _____

   _____

   _____

   _____

8. Summarize physical and behavioral effects of maternal smoking during the prenatal period. (p. 112)

_____

_____

_____

_____

_____

9. True or False: If the mother stops smoking at any time during her pregnancy, even during the last trimester, she reduces the chances that her baby will be negatively impacted. (p. 112)

10. Explain the mechanisms through which smoking harms the fetus. (p. 112)

_____

_____

_____

_____

11. True or False: Passive smoking has not been linked with any adverse effects on the infant. (p. 112)

12. Infants who have a cluster of physical and behavioral abnormalities and whose mothers drank heavily throughout most or all of pregnancy are said to have _____ ; infants who show some, but not all, of these deficits and whose mothers drank in smaller quantities during pregnancy are said to suffer from _____ . (p. 113)

13. List some of the common impairments evidenced by children with fetal alcohol syndrome. (p. 113)

_____

_____

_____

14. True or False: The physical and mental impairments seen in babies with fetal alcohol syndrome typically abate by the time the individual reaches adolescence or early adulthood. (p. 113)

15. Describe two ways in which alcohol produces its devastating effects. (p. 113)

A. _____

_____

B. _____

_____

16. True or False: There is no precise dividing line between safe and dangerous drinking levels during pregnancy. (p. 113)

17. True or False: Low doses of radiation exposure, such as through medical x-rays, are believed to be safe for the developing fetus and have not been linked to any negative outcomes. (p. 114)

18. Match each of the following environmental pollutants with its effect on development. (p. 114)

_____ This teratogen, commonly found in paint chippings   1. Mercury
from old buildings and other industrial materials,   2. Lead
is related to low birth weight, prematurity, brain damage,   3. PCBs
and physical defects.

_____ In the 1950s, children prenatally exposed to this teratogen
in a Japanese community displayed mental retardation,
abnormal speech, and uncoordinated movements.

_____ Women who ate fish contaminated with this substance
gave birth to babies with slightly reduced birth weights,
smaller heads, more intense physiological reactions to stress,
less interest in their surrounings, and later memory and
intellectual deficits.

19. Describe the outcomes associated with embryonic and fetal exposure to maternal rubella. (p. 115)

Embryonic: _____

_____

_____

Fetal: _____

_____

_____

20. When women carrying the AIDS virus become pregnant, they pass on the disease to their baby approximately
_____ to _____ percent of the time. (p. 115)

21. True or False: Most infants prenatally exposed to the AIDS virus survive 8 to 10 years after the appearance of symptoms. (p. 115)

22. Pregnant women can become infected with _____, a parasitic disease found in many
animals, from eating raw or undercooked meat or from contact with the feces of infected cats. (p. 116)

Other Maternal Factors

1. Regular, moderate exercise during pregnancy is associated with (increased / decreased) birth weight. (pp. 116–117)

2. Summarize the behavioral and health problems of prenatally malnourished babies. (pp. 117–118)

_____

_____

3. List the vitamin and mineral supplements which have been found to reduce prenatal complications and birth defects. (p. 118)

A. _____   B. _____

C. _____   D. _____

E. _____

4. True or False: Prenatal malnutrition is currently limited to developing countries, and it has been entirely eradicated in the United States through government programs for low-income pregnant women. (p. 118)

5. Describe the mechanisms through which maternal stress affects the developing organism, and note outcomes associated with severe emotional stress during pregnancy. (pp. 118–119)

Mechanisms: _____

_____

_____

Outcomes: _____

_____

_____

6. Under what conditions can the Rh factor cause problems for the developing fetus? (p. 119)

_____

_____

_____

7. Problems resulting from the Rh factor are more likely to affect (first-born / later-born) children. (p. 119)

8. True or False: Healthy women in their late thirties and early forties experience far more prenatal difficulties than do women in their twenties. (p. 119)

9. The physical immaturity of teenage mothers (does / does not) lead to pregnancy complications. (p. 119)

The Importance of Prenatal Health Care

1. Describe some of the benefits of prenatal health care. (p. 120)

_____

_____

_____

_____

2. Name two groups of women who often do not receive adequate prenatal care, and note how this impacts their babies. (p. 120)

A. _____   B. _____

Impact: _____

_____

3. Discuss some of the barriers to obtaining prenatal health care mentioned by expectant mothers who delay or never seek such care. (pp. 120–121)

_____

_____

_____

_____

Biology and Environment: The Prenatal Environment and Health in Later Life

1. True or False: Across numerous cross-cultural studies, low birth weight has been consistently linked to serious health problems later in life, including heart disease, stroke, and diabetes. (p. 108)

2. What adulthood health condition has been linked to high birth weight in females? (pp. 108–109)

   _____

Social Issues: Health: Can a Thalidomide-Like Tragedy Occur Again? The Teratogenic Effects of Accutane

1. What is Accutane? (p. 110)

   _____

   _____

2. Summarize pregnancy complications and birth defects associated with use of Accutane. (p. 110)

   Pregnancy complications: _____

   _____

   Birth defects: _____

   _____

3. Describe barriers to preventing prenatal exposure to Accutane. (pp. 110–111)

   _____

   _____

   _____

4. Cite three strategies for preventing prenatal Accutane exposure. (p. 111)

   A. _____

   B. _____

   C. _____

Preparing for Parenthood

1. Over _____ percent of pregnancies in industrialized nations result in healthy newborn babies. (p. 122)

Seeking Information

1. Pregnant mothers regard _____ as an extremely valuable source of information, second in importance only to their doctors. (p. 123)

The Baby Becomes a Reality

1. What changes and experiences help expectant parents come to view the baby as a reality? (p. 123)

    _____

    _____

    _____

Models of Effective Parenthood

1. True or False: Men and women who have had good relationships with their own parents are more likely to develop positive images of themselves as parents during the pregnancy. (p. 123)

Practical Concerns

1. Describe the ways in which American culture and Japanese culture differ in their views of pregnancy. (p. 124)

    _____

    _____

    _____

    _____

The Parental Relationship

1. True or False: Having a baby typically improves a troubled marital relationship. (p. 125)

2. Describe some of the ways in which pregnancy changes a marital relationship. (p. 125)

    _____

    _____

    _____

ASK YOURSELF . . .

For *Ask Yourself* questions for this chapter, please log on to the Companion Website at *www.ablongman.com/berk.*

1. Select the Companion Website for *Infants, Children, and Adolescents*, Fifth Edition.

2. Use the "Jump to" menu to go directly to this chapter.

3. From the menu on the left side of your screen, select *Ask Yourself.*

4. Complete the questions and choose "Submit answers for grading" or "Clear answers" to start over.

SUGGESTED STUDENT READINGS

Kleinfeld, J., Morse, B., Wescott, S. (Eds.). (2000). *Fantastic Antone grows up: Adolescents and adults with fetal alcohol syndrome.* Fairbanks, AK: University of Alaska Press. Primarily written as a guide for parents and caregivers, presents real-life accounts of the unique experiences of adolescents and young adults living with fetal alcohol syndrome.

Russell, A., Sobo, E. J., & Thompson, M. S. (Eds.). (2000). *Contraception across cultures: Technologies, choices, constraints.* New York: Berg. A collection of chapters highlighting the social, economic, political, and cultural contexts of contraception use, family planning, and reproductive health.

Susser, E. S., Brown, A. S., & Gorman, J. M. (Eds.). (1999). *Prenatal exposure in schizophrenia.* Washington, DC: American Psychiatric Press, Inc. Explores the genetic and environmental causes of schizophrenia. The authors focus on prenatal infection, prenatal malnutrition, and obstetric complications which may contribute to mental disorders.

Zeanah, C. H. Jr. (Eds.). (2000). *Handbook of infant mental health* (2nd ed.). New York: The Guilford Press. Describes the psychological experience of pregnancy, with particular emphasis on the origin of the infant-parent relationship.

PUZZLE 3.1 TERM REVIEW

Across

1. Viral infection that destroys the immune system (abbr.)
4. Period of the _____: growth and finishing phase
5. White, cheeselike substance that covers the fetus and prevents chapping
10. _____ tube: primitive spinal cord
11. Sedative available in the early 1960s that caused deformities of the arms and legs when taken between the 4th and 6th week after conception
12. Period of the _____: lasts from implantation through the 8th week of pregnancy
13. Zygote four days after fertilization, when it forms a hollow, fluid-filled ball
16. Environmental agent that causes damage during the prenatal period
19. The blastocyst burrows deep into the uterine lining during _____.
21. Ring of cells which will become the structures that provide protective covering and nourishment to the new organism
22. Embroynic _____ : cluster of cells inside the blastocyst which will become the new organism
23. Illness marked by increased maternal blood pressure and swelling of the face, hands, and feet
24. Three equal periods of time in prenatal development

Down

2. Fetal Alcohol _____: mental retardation, slow growth, and facial abnormalities resulting from maternal alcohol consumption during pregnancy
3. German measles; causes a variety of prenatal abnormalities
6. Age of _____: age at which the fetus can first survive if born early
7. _____ fluid: keeps the temperature in the womb constant and provides a cushion against jolts
8. The _____ cord connects the prenatal organism to the placenta.
9. Fetal Alcohol _____: condition of children who display some, but not all, of the defects of fetal alcohol syndrome
11. Parasitic disease caused by eating raw or undercooked meat or by contacting the feces of infected cats
14. Separates the mother's bloodstream from that of the fetus while permitting the exchange of nutrients and waste products
15. Membrane that encloses the developing organism in amniotic fluid
17. Outer membrane that forms a protective covering and sends out villi from which the placenta emerges
18. White, downy hair that covers the fetus
20. When present in the fetus's blood but not in the mother's, the _____ factor may cause the mother to build up antibodies that destroy the fetus's red blood cells.

PRACTICE TEST #1

1. Which of the following is true? (p. 99)
   a. Males produce an average of 300 million sperm a day.
   b. Fertilization usually takes place in the uterus.
   c. Women can get pregnant only on the day of ovulation.
   d. Sperm survive for only one day after intercourse.

2. During the period of the zygote, the _____ will become the _____. (p. 101)
   a. trophoblast; brain and spinal cord
   b. amnion; amniotic fluid
   c. chorion; placenta and umbilical cord
   d. embryonic disk; embryo

3. The period of the zygote lasts about _____, beginning with _____. (p. 101)
   a. 3 months; fertilization
   b. 2 weeks; implantation
   c. 3 months; implantation
   d. 2 weeks; fertilization

4. The _____ encloses the developing organism in amniotic fluid. (p. 101)
   a. trophoblast
   b. amnion
   c. blastocyst
   d. chorion

5. The umbilical cord rarely tangles during pregnancy because the (p. 101)
   a. force of blood flowing through the cord keeps it firm.
   b. cord is simply too short to knot.
   c. thickness of the amniotic fluid does not allow the cord to float freely in the uterus.
   d. walls of the cord are much too rigid for it to knot.

6. The period of the embryo lasts from (p. 102)
   a. fertilization until the beginning of the second week of pregnancy.
   b. implantation until the eighth week of pregnancy.
   c. months four to six of pregnancy.
   d. the last three months of pregnancy.

7. During the period of the embryo, the _____ folds over to form the _____. (p. 102)
   a. chorion; placenta
   b. mesoderm; lungs
   c. blastocyst; digestive tract
   d. ectoderm; the neural tube

8. The most rapid prenatal changes take place during the period of the _____, whereas the rate of body growth is greatest during the period of the _____. (p. 102)
   a. zygote; fetus
   b. fetus; embryo
   c. embryo; fetus
   d. zygote; embryo

9. As early as the third month of pregnancy, (p.)103
   a. the fetus has a good chance of survival outside of the uterus if born prematurely.
   b. vernix covers the skin of the fetus.
   c. most of the brain's neurons are in place.
   d. the fetus can suck its thumb.

10. At the end of the second trimester, nearly all of the brain's _____ are in place. However the brain's _____ continue to increase at a rapid rate throughout pregnancy and after birth. (p. 104)
   a. glial cells; neurons
   b. neural tubes; neurons
   c. neurons; glial cells
   d. neurons; neural tubes

11. The age of viability occurs sometime between the _____ week of pregnancy. (p. 104)
   a. 19th and 23rd
   b. 22nd and 26th
   c. 25th and 29th
   d. 28th and 32nd

12. Research shows that _____ in the last weeks of pregnancy predicts a more active infant in the first month of life. (p. 104)
   a. caffeine use
   b. higher fetal activity
   c. vigorous exercise
   d. high maternal stress

13. The period of the _____ is the time when serious defects from teratogens are most likely to occur because _____ this time. (p. 107)
   a. fetus; birth takes place soon after
   b. zygote; implantation occurs during
   c. fetus; the prenatal organism is developing most rapidly during
   d. embryo; the foundations for all body parts are laid down during

14. Aspirin use during pregnancy (p. 109)
   a. is linked to low birth weight and infant death.
   b. has not been associated with any negative effects.
   c. is safe among healthy mothers under the age of 35 years.
   d. offers some protection against infections during the first few months of life.

15. The likelihood of negative effects due to smoking during pregnancy (p. 112)
   a. are reduced immediately if the mother decides to stop smoking.
   b. are reduced only if the mother stops before the period of the embryo.
   c. are not reduced unless the mother stops before the placenta begins carrying food and oxygen to the prenatal organism.
   d. are not reduced if the mother stops smoking, because the damage has likely already been done.

16. Research on fetal alcohol syndrome (FAS) indicates that (p. 113)
   a. the mental impairment done by heavy, regular alcohol use during pregnancy is reversible if the child is raised in an intellectually stimulating environment.
   b. all fetuses are equally vulnerable to the damaging effects of prenatal alcohol exposure.
   c. FAS babies catch up to agemates in physical size when provided with enriched diets.
   d. even mild drinking is associated with reduced head size and body growth.

17. Which of the following is true regarding HIV and AIDS? (p. 115)
    a. HIV-positive pregnant women invariably pass HIV to their babies.
    b. The number of women infected with HIV has decreased in the past decade.
    c. Drugs have not yet been successful in reducing the likelihood of prenatal AIDS transmission.
    d. In South Africa, one-fourth of all pregnant women are HIV-positive.

18. _____ supplementation during pregnancy greatly reduces the likelihood of _____. (p. 118)
    a. Vitamin C; maternal high blood pressure
    b. Folic acid; neural tube defects
    c. Iron; premature birth
    d. Calcium; skeletal abnormalities

19. Problems during pregnancy are most likely to occur if an Rh-negative mother is carrying her (p. 119)
    a. first Rh-positive baby.
    b. first Rh-negative baby.
    c. second Rh-positive baby.
    d. second Rh-negative baby.

20. The more information a pregnant woman seeks about pregnancy, childbirth, and parenting (p. 123)
    a. the less likely she is to view her obstetrician or her child's pediatrician as a valuable source of information.
    b. the more confident she tends to feel about her own ability to be a good mother.
    c. the more likely she is to form an emotional attachment to her fetus during pregnancy.
    d. the less likely she is to consult her own parents for advice on pregnancy and child rearing.

PRACTICE TEST #2

1. Compared to children in smaller families, children in larger families tend to (pp. 95–96)
   a. be healthier.
   b. be more well off economically.
   c. have less patient and more punitive parents.
   d. have somewhat higher intelligence test scores.

2. Which of the following two strategies are effective in reducing population growth in poor regions of developing countries? (pp. 96–97)
   a. having government subsidized health care; increasing job opportunities
   b. increasing job opportunities; having public transportation
   c. making labor-saving technologies available; making family planning services available
   d. emphasizing education and literacy; making family planning services available

3. Implantation occurs (p. 101)
   a. at fertilization.
   b. about 30 hours after conception.
   c. between the third and fourth day.
   d. between the seventh and ninth day.

4. The organ that separates the mother's bloodstream from the embryonic or fetal bloodstream but permits exchange of nutrients and waste is called the (p. 101)
   a. amnion.
   b. chorion.
   c. placenta.
   d. umbilical cord.

5. The prenatal organism forms eyes, ears, fingers, and toes during the (p. 103)
   a. second month of pregnancy.
   b. period of the zygote.
   c. fourth month of pregnancy.
   d. third trimester.

6. Most of the neurons that will ever be produced in the brain are present by the end of the (p. 104)
   a. period of the zygote.
   b. period of the embryo.
   c. first trimester.
   d. second trimester.

7. As neurological organization improves during the last 3 months of pregnancy, (p. 104)
   a. the fetus is awake about 30 percent of the time.
   b. the fetus's physical activity declines.
   c. the fetus's lungs begin to expand and contract in preparation for breathing air.
   d. the fetus starts to bend its arms, form a fist, curl its toes, open its mouth, and suck its thumb.

8. In one study, mothers who read aloud *The Cat in the Hat* during the last 6 weeks of pregnancy had newborns who preferred to hear (p. 106)
   a. their mother, rather than a stranger read *The Cat in the Hat*.
   b. their mother read *The Cat in the Hat* over her reading other rhyming stories.
   c. any rhyming story over non-rhyming stories.
   d. their mother read new stories rather than the familiar *The Cat in the Hat*.

9. The effects of teratogens have the most serious impact (p. 107)
   a. before implantation.
   b. during the embryonic period.
   c. as the placenta and umbilical cord are forming.
   d. during the fetal period.

10. Daughters of mothers who took _____ during pregnancy show unusually high rates of _____. (p. 109)
    a. thalidomide; infant death around the time of birth
    b. aspirin; mental retardation
    c. diethylstilbestrol; vaginal cancer and uterine malformations
    d. sugar substitutes; heart deformities

11. Which of the following is supported by research on tobacco use during pregnancy? (p. 112)
    a. If a pregnant woman stops smoking during the third trimester, she reduces the chances that her baby will be born underweight and suffer from future problems.
    b. Smoking during pregnancy is harmful to the prenatal organism only if the mother smokes a pack or more a day.
    c. In the United States, about 2 to 3 percent of pregnant women smoke regularly.
    d. Exposure to passive smoke during pregnancy is not associated with any harmful effects to the developing organism.

12. Pregnant women should not eat undercooked meat or clean a cat's litter box due to the danger of acquiring (p. 116)
    a. rubella.
    b. cytomegalovirus.
    c. toxoplasmosis.
    d. tuberculosis.

13. Which of the following infectious diseases causes the MOST severe effects on the baby during pregnancy? (p. 115)
    a. rubella
    b. malaria
    c. mumps
    d. chicken pox

14. _____ babies are associated with excessive maternal estrogen exposure during pregnancy and are at risk for _____ in adulthood. (pp. 108–109)
    a. High-birth-weight; stroke
    b. Low-birth-weight; heart disease
    c. High-birth-weight female; breast cancer
    d. Low-birth-weight; diabetes

15. Which form of exercise would be most highly recommended for a healthy, physically fit pregnant woman? (pp. 116–117)
    a. regular swimming at a moderate pace
    b. frequent high-intensity aerobics
    c. infrequent walking
    d. regular running

16. Infants of teenagers are born with a higher rate of problems because (p. 119)
    a. a teenager's body is not physically strong enough to fully support pregnancy.
    b. the uterus of a teenager is not developed enough to maintain a pregnancy for the full 38 to 40 weeks.
    c. the uterus of a teenager is too small to maintain a pregnancy for the full 38 to 40 weeks.
    d. many pregnant teenagers do not have access to medical care or are afraid to seek it.

17. Women who receive late or no prenatal care (p. 120)
    a. are more likely than those who receive adequate prenatal care to have low-birth-weight infants or infants who die before birth or during the first year of life.
    b. are no more likely than those who received adequate prenatal care to experience birth complications.
    c. are not more likely than those who receive adequate prenatal care to engage in high-risk behaviors, such as smoking and drug use.
    d. make up less than 15 percent of pregnant women in the United States.

18. A serious illness of pregnancy in which the mother's blood pressure increases sharply and her face, hands, and feet swell is called (p. 120)
    a. toxemia.
    b. phyloric stenosis.
    c. ectopic pregnancy.
    d. Rh blood incompatibility.

19. Japan has one of the lowest rates of pregnancy and birth complications in the world because (p. 125)
    a. Japan has the greatest medical advances and the broadest knowledge base for intervening effectively with infants and children.
    b. Japanese women tend to have children at a significantly earlier age than women from other countries.
    c. of the superior social programs and federal policies protecting children's health and well being.
    d. cultural values hold the maternal role in high esteem and place the safety of the infant first.

20. Expectant couples who are unhappy in their marriages during pregnancy (p. 125)
    a. often are brought closer by the birth of their child.
    b. tend to have more children than those who are satisfied with their marriage.
    c. are as effective parents as those who are happy in their marriages.
    d. tend to be dissatisfied after the baby is born.

CHAPTER 4
BIRTH AND THE NEWBORN BABY

BRIEF CHAPTER SUMMARY

Childbirth takes place in three stages: (1) dilation and effacement of the cervix; (2) delivery of the baby; and (3) birth of the placenta. Production of stress hormones helps the infant withstand the trauma of childbirth. The Apgar Scale permits assessment of the baby's physical condition immediately after birth. Natural or prepared childbirth and delivery in a birth center or at home are increasingly popular alternatives to traditional hospital delivery. Social support during labor and delivery can lead to more successful childbirth experiences. Nevertheless, childbirth in the United States is often accompanied by a variety of medical interventions. Although they help save the lives of many babies, these procedures can cause problems of their own when used routinely.

Although most births proceed normally, serious complications sometimes occur. Among the most common are oxygen deprivation and prematurity. Fortunately, many babies who experience severe birth trauma recover with the help of favorable child-rearing environments.

Infants begin life with a remarkable set of skills for relating to the surrounding world. Newborns display a wide variety of reflexes. In the early weeks, babies frequently move in and out of different states of arousal, although they spend the most time asleep, including important REM sleep, which stimulates the brain. Crying is the first way that babies communicate. With experience, parents become better at interpreting the meaning of the infant's cries. Newborns' senses of touch, taste, smell, and sound are well developed. Vision is the least mature sensory capacity. The baby's many capacities have been put together into tests that permit the behavioral assessment of the newborn.

The baby's arrival is exciting, but it brings with it profound changes. Special interventions exist to ease the transition to parenthood. Husbands and wives who support each other in their new roles typically adjust well.

LEARNING OBJECTIVES

After reading this chapter, you should be able to:

4.1   Describe the events leading up to childbirth and the three stages of labor. (pp. 130–133)

4.2   Discuss the baby's adaptation to labor and delivery, and describe the appearance of the newborn. (p. 133)

4.3   Explain the purpose and main features of the Apgar Scale. (pp. 133–134)

4.4   Discuss the concept of natural childbirth, noting the typical features of a natural childbirth program, the benefits of the natural childbirth experience, and the role of social support in the natural childbirth process. (pp. 135–136)

4.5   Discuss the benefits and concerns associated with home delivery. (p. 136–137)

4.6   Explain several medical techniques commonly used by doctors during labor and delivery, including fetal monitoring, labor and delivery medication, instrument delivery, induced labor, and cesarean delivery. Additionally, describe the circumstances that justify the use of each technique, and discuss the risks that each procedure may pose for mothers and babies. (pp. 137–140)

4.7   Discuss the risks associated with oxygen deprivation, preterm, small-for-date, low birth weight, and postterm births, and review the developmental outlook for infants born under such circumstances. (pp. 140–143)

4.8   Describe several interventions for preterm infants, including infant stimulation and parent training. (pp.143–146)

4.9   Summarize the findings of the Kauai Study relating to the long-term consequences of birth complications. (p. 146)

4.10   Discuss parents' feelings of involvement with their newborn babies, including the findings on bonding. (p. 147)

4.11 Name and describe major newborn reflexes, noting the functions served by each, and discuss the importance of assessing newborn reflexes. (pp. 148–150)

4.12 Describe the five infant states of arousal, with particular attention to sleep and crying. (pp. 150–154)

4.13 Describe the newborn baby's responsiveness to touch, taste, smell, sound, and visual stimulation. (pp. 154–156)

4.14 Describe Brazelton's Neonatal Behavioral Assessment Scale (NBAS), and explain its usefulness. (pp. 156–157)

4.15 Describe some common changes in the family system associated with the birth of a child, and discuss the impact of intervention programs on the transition to parenthood. (pp. 157–160)

STUDY QUESTIONS

The Stages of Childbirth

1. Describe three signs that indicate that labor is near. (p. 130)

   A. _____

   B. _____

   C. _____

2. Name and describe the three stages of labor. (pp. 130–133)

   A. _____

   _____

   _____

   B. _____

   _____

   _____

   C. _____

   _____

   _____

3. The climax of Stage 1 is called _____ , in which the frequency and strength of contractions are at their peak and the cervix opens completely. (p. 131)

The Baby's Adaptation to Labor and Delivery

1. True or False: The infant's production of stress hormones is especially harmful during childbirth. Elaborate on your response. (p. 133)

   _____

   _____

The Newborn Baby's Appearance

1. The average newborn baby is _____ inches long and weighs _____ pounds. (p. 133)

2. At birth, the head is very (small / large) in relation to the trunk and legs. (p. 133)

Assessing the Newborn's Physical Condition: The Apgar Scale

1. List the five characteristics assessed by the Apgar Scale, and note which is the least reliable of these measures. (pp. 133–134)

   A. _____

   B. _____

   C. _____

   D. _____

   E. _____

   Least reliable: _____

2. On the Apgar Scale, a score of _____ or better indicates that the infant is in good physical condition; a score between _____ and _____ indicates that the baby requires special assistance; a score of _____ or below indicates a dire emergency. (p. 134)

Biology and Environment: What Controls the Timing of Birth?

1. Name the placental hormone believed to initiate the complex hormonal system that controls the timing of birth. (p. 132)

   _____

2. Explain how the "CRH-cortisol circuit" helps to ensure that labor will occur only when the fetus is ready to survive outside of the womb. (pp. 132–133)

   _____

   _____

Approaches to Childbirth

Natural, or Prepared, Childbirth

1. What is the goal of *natural childbirth*? (p. 135)

   _____

2. List and describe the three activities that comprise a typical natural childbirth program. (p. 135)

   A. _____

   _____

   B. _____

   _____

   C. _____

   _____

3. Mothers who go through natural childbirth have (more / less) favorable attitudes toward the childbirth experience than those who do not. (pp. 135–136)

4. Research suggests that social support (is / is not) an important part of the success of natural childbirth techniques. (p. 136)

5. Name the childbirth position favored by research findings, and cite the benefits of using this position. (p. 136)

Position: _____

Benefits: _____

_____

Home Delivery

1. Discuss some of the reasons why increasing numbers of American women are opting for home delivery. (p. 136)

_____

_____

_____

2. Home births are typically handled by *certified* _____ , who have degrees in nursing and additional training in childbirth management. (p. 136)

3. True or False: For healthy women assisted by a trained professional, it is just as safe to give birth at home as in a hospital. (p. 137)

Medical Interventions

Fetal Monitoring

1. Explain the purpose of *fetal monitoring*. (p. 137)

_____

_____

2. Cite four reasons why fetal monitoring is a controversial procedure. (p. 137)

A. _____

B. _____

C. _____

D. _____

Labor and Delivery Medication

1. True or False: Some form of medication is used in 85 to 90 percent of births in the United States. (p. 138)

2. Discuss three problems with the routine use of labor and delivery medication. (p. 138)

A. _____

_____

B. _____

_____

C. _____

_____

Instrument Delivery

1. In what circumstance is delivery with forceps or a vacuum extractor appropriate? (p. 138)

    _____

    _____

2. Summarize the risks associated with instrument delivery using forceps and vacuum extraction. (pp. 138–139)

    Forceps: _____

    _____

    Vacuum extractor: _____

    _____

Induced Labor

1. Briefly explain how labor is induced. (p. 139)

    _____

    _____

2. Describe two ways in which an induced labor proceeds differently than a naturally occurring one. (p. 139)

    A. _____

    _____

    B. _____

    _____

Cesarean Delivery

1. What is a *cesarean delivery*? (p. 139)

    _____

    _____

2. In what circumstances is a cesarean delivery warranted? (p. 139)

    _____

    _____

3. How can cesarean delivery affect the adjustment of the newborn baby, and consequently, the early infant-caregiver relationship? (pp. 139–140)

    _____

    _____

    _____

Oxygen Deprivation

1. Describe the physical difficulties associated with *cerebral palsy.* (p. 140)

   _____

   _____

2. _____ refers to oxygen deprivation during the birth process. (p. 140)

3. Placenta _____ refers to a premature separation of the placenta, whereas placenta _____ refers to a detachment of the placenta resulting from implantation of the blastocyst low in the uterus so that the placenta covers the cervical opening. (p. 140)

4. True or False: The vast majority of children who experience anoxia display a life-long impairment in cognitive and linguistic skills. (p. 141)

5. Infants born more than six weeks early are at risk for _____ , a condition in which the baby's lungs are so poorly developed that the air sacs collapse, causing serious breathing difficulties. (p. 141)

Preterm and Low-Birth-Weight Infants

1. Babies are considered premature if they are born _____ weeks or more before the end of a full 38-week pregnancy or if they weigh less than _____ pounds. (p. 141)

2. True or False: Birth weight is the best available predictor of infant survival and healthy development. (pp. 141–142)

3. List the problems associated with low birth weight. (p. 142)

   _____

   _____

   _____

   _____

4. Distinguish between *preterm* and *small-for-date* babies. (p. 142)

   Preterm: _____

   _____

   Small-for-date: _____

   _____

5. Of the two types of babies, (preterm / small-for-date) infants usually have more serious problems. (p. 142)

6. Describe the characteristics of preterm infants, and explain how those characteristics may influence the behavior of parents. (p. 142)

   _____

   _____

   _____

   _____

   _____

7. Discuss several methods of stimulation used to foster the successful development of preterm infants. (pp. 143–145)

_____

_____

_____

_____

8. True or False: Research suggests that all preterm children, regardless of family characteristics, require continuous, high-quality interventions well into the school years in order to maintain developmental gains. (pp. 144–145)

Birth Complications, Parenting, and Resilience

1. Summarize important findings from the Kauai study regarding the development of infants who experienced birth complications. (p. 146)

_____

_____

_____

_____

_____

Social Issues: Health: A Cross-National Perspective on Health Care and Other Policies for Parents and Newborn Babies

1. _____ *mortality* refers to the number of deaths in the first year of life per 1,000 live births. (p. 144)

2. True or False: Black infants are more than twice as likely as white infants to die in the first year of life. (p. 144)

3. _____ *mortality*, the rate of death in the first month of life, accounts for 67 percent of the infant death rate in the United States and 80 percent in Canada. (p. 144)

4. List the two leading causes of neonatal mortality. (p. 144)

   A. _____

   B. _____

5. Discuss the factors largely responsible for the relatively high rates of infant mortality in the United States. (pp. 144–145)

_____

_____

_____

_____

6. Discuss factors linked to lower infant mortality rates. (pp. 144–145)

_____

_____

_____

_____

Precious Moments After Birth

1. True or False: Fathers provide their infants with as much stimulation and affection as mothers do. (p. 147)

2. True or False: The parent–infant relationship is highly dependent on close physical contact in the hours after birth in order for bonding to develop. (p. 147)

3. _____ is an arrangement in which the infant stays in the mother's hospital room all or most of the time. (p. 147)

The Newborn Baby's Capacities

Reflexes

1. What is a *reflex*? (p. 148)

    _____

2. Match each reflex with the appropriate response or function descriptor. (p. 148)

_____ Spontaneous grasp of adult's finger	1. Eye blink
_____ When the sole of the foot is stroked, the toes fan out and curl	2. Tonic neck
	3. Palmar grasp
_____ Helps infant find the nipple	4. Babinski
_____ Prepares infant for voluntary walking	5. Rooting
_____ Permits feeding	6. Sucking
_____ Infant lies in a "fencing position"	7. Swimming
_____ Protects infant from strong stimulation	8. Stepping
	9. Moro
_____ In our evolutionary past, may have helped infant cling to mother	
_____ Helps infants survive if dropped in water	

3. Briefly explain the adaptive value of several newborn reflexes. (pp. 148–149)

    A. _____

    B. _____

    C. _____

4. Discuss research findings concerning how early reflexive stimulation contributes to motor control. (p. 149)

    _____

    _____

    _____

    _____

5. When do most newborn reflexes disappear? (p. 150)

    _____

6. Explain the importance of assessing newborn reflexes. (p. 150)

_____

_____

_____

States

1. Name and describe the five infant states of arousal. (pp. 150–151)

   A. _____

   B. _____

   C. _____

   D. _____

   E. _____

2. Describe the characteristics of *REM* and *NREM sleep*. (pp. 150–151)

   REM: _____

   _____

   NREM: _____

   _____

3. Why do infants spend so much time in REM sleep? (p. 150)

   _____

   _____

4. What is the most effective way to soothe a crying baby when feeding and diaper changing do not work? (p. 153)

   _____

5. How do the cries of brain-damaged babies and those who have experienced prenatal and birth complications differ from those of healthy infants, and how might this difference affect parental responding? (p. 154)

   _____

   _____

   _____

Sensory Capacities

1. True or False: Infants are born with a poorly developed sense of touch, and consequently, they are not sensitive to pain. (p. 154)

2. True or False: Infants not only have taste preferences, but they are also capable of communicating these preferences to adults through facial expressions. (pp. 154–155)

3. True or False: Certain odor preferences are innate. (p. 155)

4. True or False: Newborn infants are attracted to the scent of a lactating woman, but they are unable to discriminate the smell of their own mother's breast from that of an unfamiliar lactating woman. (p. 155)

5. At birth, infants prefer (pure tones / complex sounds). (p. 155)

6. True or False: Infants can discriminate almost all of the speech sounds of any human language. (p. 155)

7. Cite the characteristics of human speech preferred by infants. (p. 156)

_____

_____

8. Vision is the (most / least) mature of the newborn baby's senses. (p. 156)

9. Describe the newborn baby's *visual acuity*. (p. 156)

_____

_____

10. True or False: Infants have well-developed color vision at birth, and they are immediately capable of discriminating colors. (p. 156)

Neonatal Behavioral Assessment

1. Which areas of behavior does the Neonatal Behavioral Assessment Scale (NBAS) evaluate? (p. 156)

_____

_____

2. Since the NBAS is given to infants all around the world, researchers have been able to learn a great deal about individual and cultural differences in newborn behavior and the ways in which various childbearing practices affect infant behavior. Briefly discuss these findings. (p. 156)

_____

_____

_____

_____

3. Why is a single NBAS score not a good predictor of later development, and what should be used in place of a single score? (pp. 156–157)

_____

_____

4. How are NBAS interventions beneficial for the early parent–infant relationship? (p. 157)

_____

Social Issues: Health: The Mysterious Tragedy of Sudden Infant Death Syndrome

1. What is *Sudden Infant Death Syndrome (SIDS)*? (p. 152)

_____

_____

2. True or False: In industrialized countries, SIDS is the leading cause of infant mortality between one week and twelve months of age. (p. 152)

3. True or False: Researchers have recently determined the precise cause of SIDS. (p. 152)

4. Describe some early physical problems that are common among SIDS victims. (p. 152)

_____

_____

_____

5. Explain how impaired brain functioning might cause SIDS. (p. 152)

_____

_____

_____

6. Describe four environmental factors associated with SIDS. (p. 152)

A. _____

_____

B. _____

_____

C. _____

_____

D. _____

_____

The Transition to Parenthood

1. Discuss several changes in the family system following the birth of a new baby. (pp. 157–158)

_____

_____

_____

_____

Changes in the Family System

1. True or False: For most new parents, the arrival of a baby causes significant marital strain. (p. 158)

2. In what ways does postponing childbearing until the late twenties or thirties ease the transition to parenthood? (p. 158)

_____

_____

_____

Parent Interventions

1. Describe four strategies that couples can use to ease the transition to parenthood. (p. 160)

   A. _____

   _____

   B. _____

   _____

   C. _____

   _____

   D. _____

   _____

2. Discuss the ways in which interventions for parents who are not at risk differ from those for high-risk parents. (p. 160)

   Not at risk: _____

   _____

   _____

   High risk: _____

   _____

   _____

Biology and Environment: Postpartum Depression and the Parent–Child Relationship

1. Differentiate between postpartum blues and postpartum depression, noting the prevalence rate of each. (p. 159)

   Postpartum blues: _____

   _____

   Postpartum depression: _____

   _____

2. Describe how the mother's depressed mood affects her newborn infant in the first months of life. (p. 159)

   _____

   _____

3. Describe parenting practices associated with persistent maternal depression, and note how these parenting behaviors impact the development of the child. (p. 159)

   Parenting practices: _____

   _____

   _____

Impact on child: _____

_____

_____

4. Briefly summarize treatments for postpartum depression. (p. 159)

_____

_____

ASK YOURSELF . . .

For *Ask Yourself* questions for this chapter, please log on to the Companion Website at *www.ablongman.com/berk*.

1. Select the Companion Website for *Infants, Children, and Adolescents*, Fifth Edition.

2. Use the "Jump to" menu to go directly to this chapter.

3. From the menu on the left side of your screen, select *Ask Yourself*.

4. Complete the questions and choose "Submit answers for grading" or "Clear answers" to start over.

SUGGESTED STUDENT READINGS

Barr, R. G., St James, Roberts, I., & Keefe, M. R. (Eds.). (2001). *New evidence on unexplained early infant crying: Its origins, nature, and management.* Columbia, SC: Johnson & Johnson Pediatric Institute. Written by some of the world's most prominent researchers and health care professionals, this book explores various causes of infant crying and the effects of crying on parents and caregivers. The authors also provide strategies to help parents and caregivers cope with excessive and unexplained infant crying.

Curtis, G. B. & Schuler, J. (2003). *Your pregnancy for the father-to-be.* New York: Perseus Publishing. Written for a general audience, this book provides information to expectant fathers about physical changes during pregnancy, medical tests and procedures, and the importance of social support during the pregnancy and after the baby arrives. Other topics include: costs of having a baby, childcare expenses, planning for the future, and the impact of pregnancy on the couple's relationship.

Tracey, N. (Ed.). (2000). *Parents of premature infants: Their emotional world.* London: Whurr Publishers, Ltd. A series of in-depth interviews which focuses on the emotions, thoughts, and fantasies of parents of premature infants.

PUZZLE 4.1 TERM REVIEW

Across

2. Positioning of the baby in the uterus such that the buttocks or feet would be delivered first
4. A strong pain-killing drug that blocks sensation
6. A mild pain-relieving drug
7. _____ delivery: a surgical delivery in which the doctor makes an incision in the mother's abdomen and lifts the baby out of the uterus
10. _____ and effacement of the cervix: widening and thinning of the cervix during the first stage of labor
11. Infants whose birth weight is below normal when length of pregnancy is taken into account (3 words)
14. _____ distress syndrome: disorder of preterm infants in which the lungs are so immature that the air sacs collapse, causing breathing difficulties
16. _____ monitors: electronic instruments that track the baby's heart rate during labor

Down

1. Natural, or _____ , childbirth: approach designed to overcome the idea that birth is a painful ordeal requiring extensive medical intervention
3. Inadequate oxygen supply
5. General term for a variety of problems that result from brain damage before, during, or just after birth (2 words)
8. The _____ Scale is used to assess the newborn immediately after birth.
9. Metal clamps placed around the baby's head; used to pull the baby from the birth canal
12. Climax of the first stage of labor; the frequency and strength of contractions peak and the cervix opens completely
13. _____ extractor: a plastic cup attached to a suction tube; used to assist in delivering the baby
15. _____ labor: a labor started artificially by breaking the amnion and giving the mother a hormone that stimulates contractions

PUZZLE 4.2 TERM REVIEW

Across

1. An "irregular" sleep state in which brain wave activity is similar to that of the waking state (abbr.)
4. A "regular" sleep state in which the heart rate, breathing, and brain wave activity are slow and regular (abbr.)
6. Arrangement in which the baby stays in the mother's hospital room all or most of the time (2 words)
9. The unexpected death of an infant younger than one year of age that remains unexplained after thorough investigation (abbr.)
11. States of _____: different degrees of sleep and wakefulness
12. Visual _____: fineness of visual discrimination

Down

1. An inborn, automatic response to a particular form of stimulation
2. Infants born several weeks or months before their due date
3. Parents' feelings of affection and concern for the newborn baby
5. _____ depression: feelings of sadness and withdrawal that appear shortly after childbirth and continue for weeks or months
7. Test developed to assess the behavior of the infant during the newborn period (abbr.)
8. _____ mortality: the number of deaths in the first month of life per 1,000 live births
10. _____ mortality: the number of deaths in the first year of life per 1,000 live births

PRACTICE TEST #1

1. Bloody show occurs when the (p. 130)
   a. amniotic sac is ruptured.
   b. mucus plug is released from the cervix.
   c. fetus' head drops low into the uterus.
   d. first uterine contractions take place.

2. Which of the following is true about transition? (pp. 130–131)
   a. The mother feels an urge to push with her abdominal muscles during transition.
   b. Transition is the least painful part of labor and delivery.
   c. The placenta is delivered during transition.
   d. Transition occurs for a relatively brief period of time.

3. The infant's production of stress hormones during childbirth (pp. 132–133)
   a. helps the baby withstand oxygen deprivation by sending a rich supply of blood to the brain and heart.
   b. causes the placenta to separate from the wall of the uterus prematurely.
   c. floods the lungs with amniotic fluid thereby making it difficult for the newborn to breathe effectively.
   d. leads to the dilation and effacement of the cervix.

4. Baby Saul received a score of 1 on his 1-minute Apgar and a 3 on his 5-minute Apgar. Saul (p. 134)
   a. is in serious danger and requires emergency medical attention.
   b. needs immediate assistance establishing breathing and possibly other vital functions.
   c. was born in good physical condition.
   d. had trouble adjusting to conditions outside of the uterus at first.

5. Which of the following positions is MOST effective for delivery? (p. 136)
   a. sitting upright
   b. lying on one side
   c. supporting oneself on hands and knees
   d. lying on the back with feet in stirrups

6. Which of the following mothers should have their baby in a hospital rather than at home? (p. 137)
   a. Elizabeth, a healthy 25-year-old whose baby is in a breech position
   b. Michelle, a 40-year-old, assisted by a well-trained midwife
   c. Debra, a 19-year-old, with a family history of sickle cell anemia
   d. Alexandra, a 30-year-old who had a previous miscarriage

7. Fetal monitoring (p. 137)
   a. reduces the rates of infant brain damage and death in healthy pregnancies.
   b. is usually reserved for babies at risk for birth complications.
   c. is linked to an increased number of cesarean deliveries.
   d. does not prevent the mother from moving around during labor.

8. Epidural analgesia (p. 138)
   a. interferes with pushing during the second stage of labor.
   b. limits pain reduction to the pelvic region.
   c. blocks the mother's ability to feel the pressure of uterine contractions.
   d. numbs the lower half of the body.

9. Research suggests that forceps and vacuum extractors (pp. 138–139)
   a. are applied too freely in North American hospitals.
   b. should be used in most births to speed the delivery of the baby.
   c. do not increase the risk of brain damage during delivery.
   d. interfere with the movement of the baby through the birth canal.

10. Cerebral palsy results from (p. 140)
    a.   brain damage before, during, or just after birth.
    b.   a recessive disorder involving a harmful allele.
    c.   a failure of the 21st pair of chromosomes to separate during meiosis.
    d.   an extra X chromosome.

11. _____ is the best available predictor of infant survival and healthy development. (pp. 141–142)
    a.   Apgar score
    b.   Birth weight
    c.   Adequacy of prenatal care
    d.   Gestational age

12. "Kangaroo care" of preterm infants (p. 143)
    a.   is often used by mothers who do not feel confident about handling a fragile preterm baby.
    b.   refers to the practice of supporting infants in a sling that straps to the chest of the mother.
    c.   is rarely used in industrialized countries where surgery is possible.
    d.   fosters improved breathing, feeding, and alertness.

13. Research on bonding suggests skin-to-skin contact between a mother and her baby in the minutes after birth (p. 147)
    a.   is the best available predictor of emotional closeness between the new mother and the newborn.
    b.   is especially important for mothers who have had difficult or surgical births.
    c.   provides a short window of opportunity during which a newborn will spontaneously latch on to the mother's breast and begin sucking.
    d.   is not essential for the development of a lasting mother-child bond.

14. Which of these reflexes has immediate survival value to a newborn baby? (p. 148)
    a.   rooting
    b.   moro
    c.   palmar grasp
    d.   tonic neck

15. Newborn reflexes that persist beyond the point in development when they should normally disappear (p. 150)
    a.   can signal brain damage.
    b.   indicate that the baby is unusually intelligent and persistent.
    c.   suggest that the baby will learn motor skills more quickly than average.
    d.   indicate nothing as far as modern science can tell.

16. REM sleep in newborns (p. 150)
    a.   is associated with dreaming.
    b.   accounts for approximately 20 percent of sleep time.
    c.   safeguards the central nervous system.
    d.   reflects a state where brain-wave activity is slow and even.

17. Research on pain during infancy shows that (p. 154)
    a.   newborn males do not perceive pain during circumcision.
    b.   offering a nipple that delivers a sugar solution reduces discomfort in young babies.
    c.   local anesthetics cannot be used during newborn circumcisions because they can elevate the heart rate to dangerous levels.
    d.   newborns not given a local anesthetic during circumcision react less intensely to later routine vaccinations.

18. Research on newborn infants' sense of smell indicates that (p. 155)
    a.   infants do not have a well-developed sense of smell until several months after birth.
    b.   newborn infants recognize the smell of their own mothers' breast and amniotic fluid.
    c.   odor preferences are gradually developed through environmental exposure to a variety of scents.
    d.   infants can distinguish pleasant and unpleasant odors but cannot defend themselves from unpleasant odors by turning their head away.

19. Which of the following senses is LEAST developed at birth? (p. 156)
    a. touch
    b. taste
    c. vision
    d. smell

20. A single Neonatal Behavioral Assessment Scale (NBAS) score is a poor predictor of later development because (pp. 156–157)
    a. changes in parenting style can quickly change NBAS scores.
    b. different examiners often give the same child widely varying scores.
    c. of the day-to-day variability in newborns' behavior.
    d. the capacities tapped by the NBAS do not correlate with measures of later intellectual functioning.

PRACTICE TEST #2

1. Lightening refers to (p. 130)
    a. rupturing of the amniotic sac.
    b. release of a mucus plug from the cervix.
    c. the fetus's head dropping low into the uterus.
    d. irregular contractions that occur during false labor.

2. Which of the following takes place during Stage 1 of childbirth? (p. 130)
    a.   dilation and effacement of the cervix
    b.   birth of the placenta
    c.   crowning of the baby's head
    d.   prelabor

3. During the _____ stage of labor, the mother pushes with each contraction and the baby is born. (p. 131)
    a.   first
    b.   second
    c.   third
    d.   fourth

4. Which part of a newborn is very large in comparison to the rest of the baby's body? (p. 133)
    a.   the head
    b.   the trunk
    c.   the arms and legs
    d.   the hands and feet

5. An Apgar score of _____ indicates that the newborn is in good physical condition. (p. 134)
    a.   4 to 6
    b.   3 or below
    c.   5 or above
    d.   7 or above

6. Mothers who experience natural, or prepared, childbirth (p. 136)
    a.   feel less pain than those who do not experience natural childbirth.
    b.   have longer labors compared to women who opt for labor and delivery medication.
    c.   receive support from a nurse-midwife during childbirth.
    d.   feel less in control of their labor and delivery than do women who use pain-relieving drugs during childbirth.

7. Home delivery (pp. 136–137)
    a.   is recommended for women who are at risk for birth complications.
    b.   commonly leads to birth complications, and therefore, should not be considered a safe option under any circumstances.
    c.   accounts for approximately 15 percent of all births.
    d.   is a safe option for healthy, well-assisted women.

8. Fetal monitors (p. 137)
    a.   do not reduce the likelihood of brain damage and death in healthy pregnancies.
    b.   measure the infant's heart rate through a thin needle that is inserted through the mother's abdomen during childbirth.
    c.   are associated with a decreased rate of emergency cesarean delivery.
    d.   measure the fetus' oxygen supply through a recording device that is strapped across the mother's abdomen throughout labor.

9. Forceps (pp. 138–139)
   a. measure the fetus' oxygen supply through a recording device that is strapped across the mother's abdomen throughout labor.
   b. are less likely to tear the mother's tissue than vacuum extractors.
   c. are seldom used to pull the baby through most or all of the birth canal.
   d. are used at about the same rate in both North America and Europe.

10. Which country has the highest cesarean delivery in the world? (p. 139)
    a. Canada
    b. Sweden
    c. Japan
    d. the United States

11. A disorder of preterm infants in which the immaturity of the lungs results in the collapse of the air sacs, leading to breathing difficulties and sometimes death is (p. 141)
    a. cystic fibrosis.
    b. respiratory distress syndrome.
    c. anoxia.
    d. gauze membrane disease.

12. _____ babies usually have more serious birth complications than _____ infants. (p. 142)
    a. Preterm; small-for-date
    b. Postterm, preterm
    c. Small-for-date; preterm
    d. Postterm; small-for-date

13. In the Kauai study, a few children with both serious birth complications and troubled families grew into competent adults. These children (p. 146)
    a. were adopted by high-SES families during infancy.
    b. participated in a high number of extracurricular school-based activities during the school years.
    c. were enrolled in high-quality child care during the first year of life.
    d. relied on factors outside the family and within themselves to overcome stress.

14. For new parents in the United States, the federal government mandates 12 weeks of (p. 144)
    a. paid leave.
    b. unpaid leave.
    c. paid leave for employees in businesses with at least 50 workers.
    d. unpaid leave for employees in businesses with at least 50 workers.

15. Research suggests skin-to-skin contact between a mother and her baby in the minutes after birth (p. 147)
    a. guarantees immediate emotional closeness between the new mother and the newborn.
    b. is only important for mothers who have had difficult or surgical births.
    c. may be harmful for preterm infants because they cannot adjust to the extra stimulation.
    d. helps parents feel more confident about meeting their infants' needs and offers numerous physical benefits to babies.

16. The absence of newborn reflexes is indicative of (p. 150)
    a. fetal alcohol syndrome.
    b. brain damage.
    c. prenatal malnutrition.
    d. exposure to cocaine, heroin, or methadone during pregnancy.

17. Who spends the greatest portion of their time asleep in REM sleep? (p. 150)
    a. fetuses
    b. full-term newborns
    c. toddlers
    d. preschool-aged children

18. Newborns (p. 155)
    a. prefer salty water to regular water.
    b. purse their lips when they taste something sour.
    c. use longer sucks with more pauses when given a sweet liquid instead of water.
    d. tend to reject or react indifferently to sweet tastes.

19. Which of the following is true regarding Brazelton's Neonatal Behavioral Assessment Scale (NBAS)? (pp. 156–157)
    a. The NBAS evaluates the baby's heart rate, breathing, reflexes, muscle tone, and color.
    b. A single NBAS score obtained after the newborn has gone home from the hospital is the best estimate of the baby's ability to recover from the stress of birth.
    c. The NBAS is used to teach parents about their newborn baby's capacities.
    d. The NBAS is given twice—the first immediately after birth and the second at five minutes after birth.

20. Which of the following is true regarding treatment for maternal depression? (p. 159)
    a. Antidepressant medication is rarely prescribed.
    b. Children of depressed mothers are typically involved in therapy sessions with the mother.
    c. Long-term treatment is usually necessary.
    d. When mothers do not respond to treatment, a warm relationship with another caregiver can safeguard children's development.

CHAPTER 5
PHYSICAL DEVELOPMENT IN INFANCY
AND TODDLERHOOD

BRIEF CHAPTER SUMMARY

Body size increases dramatically during the first 2 years of life, following organized patterns of growth. Fat increases faster than muscle, and the skull expands rapidly to accommodate the rapidly growing brain. Neurons form intricate connections and their fibers myelinate, causing a rapid increase in brain weight. Already, the two hemispheres of the cortex have begun to specialize, although the brain retains considerable plasticity during the first few years. In addition, specific sensitive periods in brain development are now recognized, when the brain must receive appropriate stimulation for it to reach its full potential.

A variety of factors affect early physical growth. Heredity contributes to height, weight, and rate of physical maturation. Nutrition is essential for rapidly growing babies, and breast milk is especially suited to meet their needs. Malnutrition during the early years can result in permanent stunting of physical growth and of brain development. Affection and stimulation are also essential for healthy physical growth.

Infants are marvelously equipped to learn immediately after birth. Classical conditioning, operant conditioning, habituation and recovery, and imitation are important early learning capacities that assist infants in finding out about their physical and social worlds. Although motor development follows the same organized sequences as physical growth, it does not follow a fixed maturational timetable. According to dynamic systems theory, previously learned skills are combined in increasingly complex ways to result in new abilities. Central nervous system development, movement possibilities of the body, the task the child has in mind, and environmental supports combine to influence the development of motor skills.

Hearing and vision undergo major advances during the first 2 years as infants organize stimuli into complex patterns, improve their perception of depth and objects, and combine information across sensory modalities. The Gibsons' differentiation theory helps us understand the course of perceptual development.

LEARNING OBJECTIVES

After reading this chapter, you should be able to:

5.1 Describe changes in body size, body proportions, and muscle–fat makeup during the first 2 years of life. (pp. 166–167)

5.2 Discuss skeletal growth during the first 2 years of life, including the growth of the skull and the appearance of teeth. (pp. 168–169)

5.3 Describe brain development during infancy and toddlerhood at the level of individual brain cells and at the level of the cerebral cortex. (pp. 169–171)

5.4 Explain the concepts of brain lateralization and brain plasticity. (pp. 171–174)

5.5 Describe research findings related to the existence of sensitive periods in brain development, and note the evidence of brain growth spurts and need for appropriate stimulation. (pp. 174–176)

5.6 Discuss the changes in the organization of sleep and wakefulness between birth and 2 years of age. (p. 176)

5.7 Discuss the impact of heredity on early physical growth. (p. 178)

5.8 Discuss the nutritional needs of infants and toddlers, the advantages of breastfeeding, and the extent to which chubby babies are at risk for later overweight and obesity. (pp. 178–180)

5.9 Discuss the impact of severe malnutrition on the development of infants and toddlers, and cite two dietary diseases associated with this condition. (pp. 180–181)

5.10 Describe the growth disorder known as nonorganic failure to thrive, noting common symptoms and family circumstances surrounding the disorder. (pp. 181–182)

5.11 Describe how infants learn through classical conditioning, operant conditioning, habituation, and imitation. (pp. 182–186)

5.12 Describe the sequence of motor development in the first 2 years of life. (pp. 187–188)

5.13 Explain the dynamic systems theory of motor development, and discuss the support for this approach stemming from microgenic and cross-cultural research. (pp. 188–189)

5.14 Describe the development of reaching and grasping, and explain how early experiences affect these skills. (pp. 189–191)

5.15 Summarize the development of hearing in infancy, giving special attention to speech perception. (pp. 193–194)

5.16 Summarize the development of vision in infancy, with particular attention to depth perception and pattern perception. (pp. 194–199)

5.17 Discuss the development of object perception during the first year of life. (pp. 200–201)

5.18 Explain the concept of intermodal perception. (pp. 201–202)

5.19 Explain the differentiation theory of perceptual development. (pp. 202–203)

STUDY QUESTIONS

Body Growth

Changes in Body Size and Muscle–Fat Makeup

1. Infant and toddler growth is marked by (steady gains / little spurts). (p. 166)

2. Summarize changes in muscle–fat makeup during the first 2 years of life. (p. 166)

_____

_____

_____

3. There (are / are not) sex and ethnic differences in body size and muscle–fat makeup during infancy. (pp. 166–167)

Changes in Body Proportions

1. Briefly explain the *cephalocaudal* and *proximodistal* trends, which represent two growth patterns used to describe changes in body proportions. (p. 167)

Cephalocaudal: _____

_____

Proximodistal: _____

_____

Skeletal Growth

1. The best way of estimating a child's physical maturity is to use _____, a measure of the development of the bones of the body. Explain how this estimate is obtained. (p. 168)

    _____

    _____

    _____

2. At birth, the bones of the skull are separated by six gaps, or soft spots, called _____. Explain their function. (pp. 168–169)

    _____

    _____

    _____

3. At approximately what age do infants get their first tooth? (p. 169)

    _____

4. True or False: Almost all infants display physical symptoms while teething, and therefore, it is generally safe for parents to conclude that signs of illness are due to teething during this time. (p. 169)

Brain Development

Development of Neurons

1. The human brain has 100 to 200 billion _____, or nerve cells, that store and transmit information. Between them are tiny gaps, or _____, across which messages pass. (p. 169)

2. Explain the process of *synaptic pruning.* (p. 170)

    _____

    _____

    _____

3. About one-half the brain's volume is made up of _____, which do not carry messages, but instead are responsible for _____, the coating of neural fibers with an insulating fatty sheath that improves the efficiency of message transfer. (p. 170)

Development of the Cerebral Cortex

1. True or False: The cerebral cortex is the largest, most complex brain structure, accounting for 85 percent of the brain's weight and containing the greatest number of neurons and synapses. (p. 171)

2. Name the regions of the cerebral cortex, and describe the function of each. (p. 171)

    A. _____

    B. _____

    C. _____

    D. _____

3. Describe the different functions controlled by the left and right hemispheres of the brain. (pp. 171–172)

Left: _____

_____

Right: _____

_____

4. Explain the concepts of *lateralization* and *brain plasticity,* noting how the two are related. (pp. 171–172)

Lateralization: _____

_____

Plasticity: _____

_____

_____

Relationship: _____

_____

_____

5. The brain is (more / less) plastic during the early years than during later years in life. (p. 174)

Sensitive Periods in Brain Development

1. Summarize evidence that appropriate stimulation is essential for healthy brain development. (p. 174)

_____

_____

_____

2. True or False: Overstimulation of infants and toddlers threatens their interest in learning and may create conditions similar to those of stimulus deprivation. (p. 175)

3. Distinguish between *experience-expectant* and *experience-dependent* brain growth. (p. 175)

Experience-expectant: _____

_____

_____

Experience-dependent: _____

_____

_____

4. Evidence (does / does not) exist for a sensitive period in the first 5 or 6 years of life for mastering skills that depend on extensive training, such as musical performance or gymnastics. (pp. 175–176)

Changing States of Arousal

1. Describe major changes in the organization of sleep and wakefulness during the first 2 years of life, and discuss how the social environment impacts these changing arousal patterns. (p. 176)

_____

_____

_____

_____

Biology and Environment: Brain Plasticity: Insights from Research on Brain-Damaged Children and Adults

1. Adults who suffered brain injuries in infancy and early childhood show (fewer / more) cognitive impairments than do adults with later occurring injuries. (p. 172)

2. Describe the impact of brain injury on childhood language development and spatial skills, noting how this relates to brain plasticity. (p. 172)

   Language: _____

   _____

   Spatial skills: _____

   _____

3. Describe the negative consequences of high brain plasticity. (pp. 172–173)

   _____

   _____

4. True or False: Brain plasticity is restricted to childhood and is no longer evident by the time individuals reach adulthood. Provide research evidence to support your response. (p. 173)

   _____

   _____

   _____

Cultural Influences: Cultural Variations in Infant Sleeping Arrangements

1. True or False: Although rare in the United States, parent–infant cosleeping is common in many other countries around the world. (p. 177)

2. Explain the role of collectivist versus individualistic cultural values in determining infant sleeping arrangements. (p. 177)

   _____

   _____

   _____

3. Discuss the criticisms and concerns surrounding infant cosleeping. (p. 177)

   _____

   _____

   _____

Influences on Early Physical Growth

Heredity

1. True or False: When diet and health are adequate, height and rate of physical growth are largely determined by heredity. (p. 178)

2. Describe the phenomenon of *catch-up growth*. (p. 178)

   _____

   _____

Nutrition

1. Describe four nutritional and health benefits of breast milk. (pp. 178–179)

   A. _____

   _____

   B. _____

   _____

   C. _____

   _____

   D. _____

   _____

2. Discuss the benefits of breastfeeding as they relate to mothers and infants in poverty-stricken regions of the world. (pp. 178–179)

   _____

   _____

   _____

   _____

3. Rapid weight gain in infancy (is / is not) related to obesity at older ages. (p. 180)

4. Cite two ways in which parents can prevent infants and toddlers from becoming overweight at later ages. (p. 180)

   A. _____

   B. _____

Malnutrition

1. Describe the causes of *marasmus* and *kwashiorkor,* two dietary diseases associated with severe malnutrition, and summarize the developmental outcomes associated with these extreme forms of malnutrition. (pp. 180–181)

   Marasmus: _____

   _____

   _____

   _____

Kwashiorkor: _____

_____

_____

_____

Outcomes: _____

_____

_____

_____

2. True or False: Malnutrition is largely confined to developing countries and recent surveys indicate that it is almost nonexistent in the United States and Canada. (p. 181)

Emotional Well-Being

1. What is *nonorganic failure to thrive,* and what are some common symptoms? (p. 181)

_____

_____

_____

_____

2. Discuss the family circumstances surrounding nonorganic failure to thrive. (pp. 181–182)

_____

_____

_____

Learning Capacities

1. Define *learning.* (p. 182)

_____

Classical Conditioning

1. Briefly explain how learning takes place through *classical conditioning.* (p. 182)

_____

_____

_____

2. Why is classical conditioning of great value to infants? (p. 182)

_____

_____

_____

3. Match the following terms to the appropriate definitions. (pp. 182–183)

    _____ A neutral stimulus that leads to a new response once learning
    has occurred
    _____ A learned response exhibited toward a previously
    neutral stimulus
    _____ A reflexive response
    _____ A stimulus that automatically leads to a reflexive response

    1. Unconditioned stimulus (UCS)
    2. Conditioned stimulus (CS)
    3. Unconditioned response (UCR)
    4. Conditioned response (CR)

4. Using the above definitions as a guide (see question 3), outline the three steps involved in classical conditioning. (pp. 182–183)

    A. _____
    _____

    B. _____
    _____

    C. _____
    _____

5. In classical conditioning, if the CS is presented alone enough times, without being paired with the UCS, the CR will no longer occur. This is referred to as _____. (p. 183)

Operant Conditioning

1. Briefly explain how learning takes place through *operant conditioning.* (pp. 183–184)

    _____
    _____
    _____

2. Define the terms *reinforcer* and *punishment* as they relate to operant conditioning. (p 184)

    Reinforcer: _____
    _____
    _____

    Punishment: _____
    _____
    _____

3. Describe how operant conditioning plays a role in the development of infant–caregiver attachment. (p. 184)

    _____
    _____
    _____

Habituation

1. Define the terms *habituation* and *recovery*. (p. 184)

   Habituation: _____

   _____

   Recovery: _____

   _____

2. As infants get older, they habituate to stimuli more (slowly / quickly). What does this indicate about their cognitive development? (pp. 184–185)

   _____

   _____

Imitation

1. Summarize what infants are able to learn through the process of *imitation*. (pp. 185–186)

   _____

   _____

   _____

Motor Development

The Sequence of Motor Development

1. Distinguish between gross and fine motor development, and provide examples of each. (p. 187)

   Gross: _____

   _____

   Examples: _____

   Fine: _____

   _____

   Examples: _____

2. True or False: Although the *sequence* of motor development is fairly uniform, large individual differences exist in the *rate* of development. (p. 187)

3. Discuss the organization and direction of motor development in relation to the cephalocaudal and proximodistal trends. (p. 188)

   _____

   _____

   _____

Motor Skills as Dynamic Systems

1. According to the *dynamic systems theory of motor development,* mastery of motor skills involves acquisition of increasingly complex *systems of action.* Explain what this term means. (p. 188)

    _____

    _____

    _____

    _____

2. List four factors that contribute to the development of each new motor skill. (p. 188)

    A. _____

    B. _____

    C. _____

    D. _____

3. True or False: Dynamic systems theory regards motor development as a genetically determined process. Briefly explain your response. (p. 188).

    _____

    _____

    _____

Dynamic Motor Systems in Action

1. What did Esther Thelen's microgenetic studies reveal about infant motor development? (pp. 188–189)

    _____

    _____

    _____

Cultural Variations in Motor Development

1. Give at least one example of how cultural variations in infant-rearing practices affect motor development. (p. 189)

    _____

    _____

    _____

Fine Motor Development: Reaching and Grasping

1. Match each of the following terms to the appropriate definition. (pp. 189–191)

    ____ Well-coordinated movement in which infants use the thumb and forefinger opposably

    ____ Poorly coordinated swipes or swings toward an object

    ____ Clumsy motion in which the fingers close against the palm

    1. Prereaching
    2. Ulnar grasp
    3. Pincer grasp

2. Voluntary reaching (is / is not) affected by early experience. (p. 191)

Bowel and Bladder Control

1. At what age should parents typically begin toilet training their children, and why is this the case? (p. 192)

   Age: _____

   Reason: _____

   _____

   _____

2. Name three effective toilet training techniques. (pp. 192–193)

   A. _____

   B. _____

   C. _____

Perceptual Development

Hearing

1. What is the greatest change in hearing that takes place over the first year of life? (p. 193)

   _____

2. Describe the changes in auditory perception over the first year of life which prepare infants for language acquisition. (pp. 193–194)

   By 6 months: _____

   _____

   _____

   6–12 months: _____

   _____

   _____

Vision

1. What is *depth perception,* and why is it important in infant development? (p. 194)

   _____

   _____

   _____

2. Describe Gibson and Walk's studies using the visual cliff, and cite the limitations of this approach for the study of infant depth perception. (p. 195)

   _____

   _____

   _____

   _____

3. Name and describe the three cues for depth. (p. 195)

A. _____

_____

B. _____

_____

C. _____

_____

4. Summarize research on the relationship between crawling and depth perception. (p. 196)

_____

_____

_____

_____

5. Provide an example from adult experience which helps to explain why crawling plays such an important role in the infant's knowledge and understanding of the three-dimensional world. (pp. 196–197)

_____

_____

6. The principle of _____, which accounts for early pattern preferences, states that if infants can detect a difference in contrast between two or more patterns, they will prefer the one with more contrast. (p. 197)

7. Summarize the development of face perception across the first year of life. (pp. 198–199)

Birth–1 month: _____

_____

_____

2–4 months: _____

_____

5–12 months: _____

_____

Object Perception

1. True or False: Size and shape constancy appear to emerge gradually over time as infants acquire more advanced knowledge of objects in the environment. (p. 200)

2. True or False: When two objects are touching, whether moving in unison or standing still, infants younger than 4 months of age do not perceive the boundary between the two objects, and therefore, cannot distinguish them. (p. 201)

Intermodal Perception

1. What is *intermodal perception*? (p. 201)

    _____

    _____

2. True or False: From birth, infants are capable of combining information from multiple sensory systems. Cite research evidence supporting your response. (p. 201)

    _____

    _____

    _____

    _____

Understanding Perceptual Development

1. Explain the *differentiation theory of perceptual development.* (p. 202)

    _____

    _____

    _____

    _____

2. Explain how acting on the environment plays a vital role in perceptual differentiation. (p. 202)

    _____

    _____

    _____

Biology and Environment: Development of Infants with Severe Visual Impairments

1. True or False: Children with severe visual impairments show delays in motor, cognitive, and social development. (p. 196)

2. Discuss how severe visual impairments impact motor exploration and spatial understanding. (p. 196)

    _____

    _____

    _____

    _____

3. How do severe visual impairments affect the caregiver–infant relationship? (pp. 196–197)

    _____

    _____

    _____

4. Cite four intervention techniques that can help infants with severe visual impairments become aware of their physical and social surroundings. (p. 197)

A. _____

_____

B. _____

_____

C. _____

_____

D. _____

_____

ASK YOURSELF . . .

For *Ask Yourself* questions for this chapter, please log on to the Companion Website at *www.ablongman.com/berk*.

SUGGESTED STUDENT READINGS

Black, R. E., & Michaelsen, K. F. (Eds.). (2002). *Public health issues in infant and child nutrition, vol. 48.* Philadelphia, PA: Lippincott Williams & Wilkens. A collection of chapters focusing on infant and child nutrition in both industrialized and developing regions of the world. Topics include: the relationship between malnutrition and infectious diseases, the benefits of breastfeeding, and public health strategies for reducing infant and child mortality.

Huttenlocher, P. R. (2002). *Neural plasticity: The effects of the environment on the development of the cerebral cortex.* Cambridge, MA: Harvard University Press. A compelling look at the positive and negative aspects of brain plasticity, including the brain's response to normal developmental processes and trauma, and the extent of plasticity beyond the first 3 years of life.

Shonkoff, J. P., & Phillips, D. A. (Eds.). (2000). *From neurons to neighborhoods: The science of early childhood development.* New York: National Academy Press. A multidisciplinary approach to child development, this book examines how early experiences contribute to neurological, social, and cultural aspects of development. An excellent resource for those interested in working with children.

Silberg, J., & D'Argo, L. (2000). *125 brain games for toddlers and twos: Simple games to promote early brain development.* Beltsville, MD: Gryphon House, Inc. Drawing from decades of brain research, this book provides parents and educators with age-appropriate games and activities that can be used to foster brain development in the first 3 years.

PUZZLE 5.1 TERM REVIEW

Across

1. In classical conditioning, an originally reflexive response that is produced by a CS after learning has occurred (abbr.)
4. In classical conditioning, a stimulus that leads to a reflexive response (abbr.)
10. Growth centers in the bones
13. Nerve cells that store and transmit information
15. Experience-_____ brain growth: early organization of the brain depends on ordinary experiences with the environment
18. Specialization of functions of the two hemispheres of the cerebral cortex
19. In classical conditioning, a reflexive response that is produced by an UCS (abbr.)
21. _____ age: an estimate of physical maturity based on development of the bones of the body
22. Cells that serve the function of myelination

Down

2. An increase in responsiveness to a new stimulus following habituation
3. The gaps between neurons across which messages are sent
5. Soft spots that separate the bones of the skull at birth
6. Process in which neural fibers are coated with an insulating fatty sheath which improves the efficiency of message transfer
7. Experience-_____ brain growth: growth and refinement of brain structures result from specific learning experiences
8. _____ conditioning: form of learning in which spontaneous behavior is followed by a stimulus that changes the probability that the behavior will occur again
9. In operant conditioning, a stimulus that increases the occurrence of a response
11. Brain _____: ability of other parts of the brain to take over functions of damaged regions
12. In operant conditioning, a stimulus that decreases the occurrence of a response
14. _____ conditioning: form of learning that involves associating a neutral stimulus with a stimulus that leads to a reflexive response
16. Synaptic _____: loss of connective fibers by seldom-stimulated neurons
17. The largest, most complex brain structure is the _____ cortex.
20. In classical conditioning, a neutral stimulus that through pairing with an UCS leads to a new response (abbr.)

PUZZLE 5.2 TERM REVIEW

Across

3. Contrast _____: if babies can detect a difference in contrast between two or more patterns, they will prefer the one with more contrast
7. A disease usually appearing between 1 and 3 years of age that is caused by a diet low in protein
8. _____ trend: pattern of physical growth that proceeds from head to tail
9. The poorly coordinated, primitive reaching movements of newborn infants
10. A gradual reduction in the strength of a response as a result of repeated stimulation
11. The action possibilities that a situation offers an organism with certain motor capabilities
14. _____ trend: pattern of physical growth that proceeds from the center of the body outward
17. In the differentiation theory of perceptual development, _____ features are those that remain stable in a constantly changing perceptual world.

Down

1. _____ failure to thrive: growth disorder caused by a lack of affection and stimulation
2. _____ perception combines information from more than one sensory system.
4. A disease usually appearing in the first year of life that is caused by a diet low in all essential nutrients
5. _____ theory: view that perceptual development involves detection of increasingly fine-grained, invariant features of the environment
6. Learning by copying another person
12. _____ constancy: perception of an object's size as the same, despite changes in the size of its retinal image
13. Clumsy grasp in which the fingers close against the palm
14. Well-formed grasp involving thumb and forefinger opposition
15. _____ systems theory of motor development: views new motor skills as a reorganization of previously mastered skills that lead to more effective ways of exploring and controlling the environment
16. _____ constancy: perception of an object's shape as the same, despite changes in the shape projected on the retina

PRACTICE TEST #1

1. During the first 2 years of life, physical growth (p. 166)
   a. is slow and steady.
   b. is more rapid than it was during the prenatal period.
   c. is faster than at any other time after birth.
   d. occurs in a uniform manner, regardless of the child's sex and ethnicity.

2. Which of the following is the best example of the proximodistal trend in development? (p. 167)
   a. Control of the toes develops before control of the legs.
   b. Control of the head develops before control of the trunk.
   c. Control of the arms develops before control of the legs.
   d. Control of the arms develops before control of the fingers.

3. At birth, the bones of the skill are separated by six gaps, or "soft spots," called (p. 168)
   a. epiphyses.
   b. marasmus.
   c. affordances.
   d. fontanels.

4. Research on teething demonstrates that (p. 169)
   a. nearly all teething babies show increased irritability and sleeplessness.
   b. on average, an African-American baby's first tooth appears at about 4 months, and a Caucasian baby's around 6 months.
   c. most infants do not get their first teeth until around 1 year of age.
   d. babies who get their first teeth early are likely to be delayed in physical maturity.

5. Synaptic pruning is the process by which (p. 169)
   a. new synapses are formed as the result of stimulation by input from the surrounding environment.
   b. seldom-used neurons die during the peak period of synaptic growth in any brain area.
   c. neural fibers become myelinated as a result of stimulation of the brain.
   d. seldom-stimulated neurons are returned to an uncommitted state so they can support the development of future skills.

6. An important function of _____ is to coat neural fibers with myelin to improve the efficiency of message transfers. (p. 170)
   a. neurons
   b. synapses
   c. glial cells
   d. neurotransmitters

7. The cerebral cortex (p. 171)
   a. is the largest, most complex brain structure.
   b. accounts for about half of the brain's weight.
   c. is the brain structure that is responsible for producing newborn reflexes.
   d. is the first part of the brain to stop growing.

8. Once the hemispheres lateralize, damage to a particular region (p. 172)
   a. can be compensated for by other regions of the brain.
   b. can be compensated for only if the damage occurred in the left hemisphere.
   c. can be compensated for only if the damage occurred in the right hemisphere.
   d. means that the abilities controlled by it will be lost forever.

9. Experience-expectant brain growth depends on (p. 175)
   a. specific learning experiences that vary widely across individuals and cultures.
   b. surges in frontal lobe activity.
   c. ordinary experiences that the brains of all children expect to encounter.
   d. early encounters with the environment that occur during sensitive periods.

10. Research on sleep during infancy reveals that (p. 176)
    a. the practice of isolating infants to promote sleep is rare in non-Western cultures.
    b. infants who nurse often during the night are at an increased risk for SIDS.
    c. mothers' total sleep time is decreased by cosleeping with their infants.
    d. infants who cosleep with their parents are at increased risk for developing later emotional problems.

11. Research on physical growth reveals that (p. 178)
    a. height and rate of physical growth are largely determined by environmental factors.
    b. physical growth is a strongly canalized process.
    c. catch-up growth is rare among children who have experienced early poor nutrition or illness.
    d. the weights of adopted children correlate more strongly with those of their adoptive than biological parents.

12. The World Health Organization recommends (p. 178)
    a. breastfeeding until 2 years of age.
    b. using breastfeeding as a method of birth control.
    c. that mothers in developing countries give their babies commercial formula.
    d. introducing solid foods no earlier than 1 year of age.

13. Research has revealed that (p. 180)
    a. infants and toddlers can eat nutritious foods freely, without risk of becoming overweight.
    b. most chubby babies are at risk for later overweight.
    c. less than half of American 12-month-olds eat candy daily.
    d. foods high in sugar or salt are relatively harmless to active infants and toddlers.

14. _____ is caused by a diet very low in _____. (p. 180)
    a. Kwashiorkor; protein
    b. Marasmus; iron
    c. Kwashiorkor; iron
    d. Marasmus; protein

15. In classical conditioning, the _____ must consistently produce a reflexive reaction before learning can take place. (p. 182)
    a. conditioned stimulus (CS)
    b. unconditioned stimulus (UCS)
    c. conditioned response (CR)
    d. unconditioned response (UCR)

16. In classical conditioning, if the conditioned stimulus (CS) is presented enough times without being paired with the unconditioned stimulus (UCS), the conditioned response (CR) will no longer occur. This is known as (p. 185)
    a. dishabituation.
    b. termination.
    c. disassociation.
    d. extinction.

17. A 2-month-old baby who learns to hit a mobile with her arms before she learns to kick it with her legs is exhibiting evidence of (p. 187)
    a. fine motor skills.
    b. prereaching.
    c. the cephalocaudal trend.
    d. the proximodistal trend.

18. A skill that is acquired by revising and combining earlier accomplishments into a more complex system is an example of a _____ behavior. (p. 188)
    a. softly assembled
    b. hardwired
    c. genetically predetermined
    d. canalized

19. Which behavior suggests that babies are biologically prepared for eye-hand coordination? (p. 189)
    a. prereaching
    b. the ulnar grasp
    c. the pincer grasp
    d. voluntary reaching

20. Research using the visual cliff suggests that _____ promotes sensitivity to depth information. (p. 196)
    a. an early preference for patterned as opposed to plain stimuli
    b. a built-in capacity to orient to depth cues
    c. infants' tendency to search for structure in patterned stimuli
    d. the crawling experience

PRACTICE TEST #2

1. During growth spurts in the first year of life, infants can grow as much as _____ in a 24-hour period. (p. 166)
   a. ½ inch
   b. ⅟₁₆ inch
   c. 1 inch
   d. ¼ inch

2. "Baby fat" peaks around _____ and muscle tissue peaks during _____. (p. 166)
   a. 3 months; middle childhood
   b. 9 months; adolescence
   c. 9 months; middle childhood
   d. 3 months; adolescence

3. The best way of estimating a child's physical maturity is to use (p. 168)
   a. skeletal age.
   b. growth charts.
   c. current body size.
   d. the rate of physical growth.

4. Research suggests that the brain growth that occurs around 8 months of age is closely tied to (p. 174)
   a. rapid gains in language acquisition.
   b. the development of voluntary reaching.
   c. the onset of crawling and searching for hidden objects.
   d. the emerging of walking and advanced object search behaviors.

5. A lateralized brain is adaptive because it permits (p. 172)
   a. increasing brain plasticity with age.
   b. the ability of the cortex to recover functions following brain injury throughout the lifespan.
   c. a far greater variety of talents than if both sides of the cortex served exactly the same functions.
   d. neurons seldom stimulated to return to an uncommitted state so they can support future development.

6. Which of the following provides evidence for early brain plasticity? (p. 172)
   a. In brain-injured adults, cognitive experiences often lead stimulated cortical structures to compensate for other, damaged areas.
   b. Most children who sustain brain injuries as infants show cognitive impairments throughout childhood.
   c. Adults have a greater capacity than infants and children to recover function following brain injury.
   d. Deficits in preschoolers with brain injuries sustained during infancy tend to be milder than those observed in brain-injured adults.

7. Brain plasticity refers to (p. 174)
   a. the specialization of functions of the two hemispheres of the brain.
   b. the extent of neural development at a particular period of development.
   c. the loss of neural connections resulting from inadequate stimulation.
   d. the ability of other parts of the brain to take over the functions of damaged regions.

8. The greatest change in the organization of sleep and wakefulness during the first 2 years of life is that (p. 170)
   a. with age, infants require more naps.
   b. there is a dramatic decrease in total sleep time.
   c. by the end of the first year, infants no longer have night wakings.
   d. periods of sleep and wakefulness become fewer but longer and the sleep-wake pattern increasingly conforms to a night-day schedule.

9. Cross-cultural research on infant sleeping practices has shown that (p. 177)
   a. Mayan mothers react with shock and disbelief when told that American infants sleep by themselves.
   b. sleep problems are more common in cultures that permit infant–parent cosleeping compared to those in which infants sleep in a separate room.
   c. most cultures that practice infant–parent cosleeping fail to take appropriate safety precautions that protect infants from suffocation due to entrapment in soft bedding.
   d. parents who practice cosleeping typically view babies as dependent beings who must be urged toward independence.

10. Bottle-fed infants _____ than breastfed infants. (p. 179)
   a. accept new foods more easily
   b. have fewer respiratory and intestinal illnesses
   c. are more likely to become constipated or have diarrhea
   d. receive greater protection against tooth decay

11. _____ is a dietary disease caused by an unbalanced diet very low in protein. (p. 180)
   a. Nonorganic failure to thrive
   b. Deprivation dwarfism
   c. Kwashiorkor
   d. Marasmus

12. Classical conditioning is of great value to babies because it helps them to (p. 182)
   a. anticipate what is about to happen next.
   b. manipulate their parents' actions.
   c. elicit positive reinforcements from their parents.
   d. regulate their reactions to new stimuli.

13. When baby Madeline babbles to her mother, her mother talks back, and then Madeline babbles again. This is an example of (p. 184)
   a. habituation.
   b. recovery.
   c. operant conditioning.
   d. classical conditioning.

14. Research on infants' habituation and recovery allows researchers to explore early (p. 184)
   a. perception and cognition.
   b. motor development.
   c. imitation skills.
   d. extinction responses.

15. According to the _____ theory of motor development, new motor skills are a matter of combining existing skills into increasingly complex systems of action. (p. 188)
   a. dynamic systems
   b. skill suites
   c. differentiation
   d. coordinated trends

16. Of all motor skills, _____ is believed to play the greatest role in infant cognitive development. (p. 189)
   a. voluntary reaching
   b. sitting alone
   c. crawling
   d. walking

17. Which of the following is vital to the development of depth perception? (p. 197)
    a.   crawling
    b.   opportunities to look at photographs and picture books
    c.   holding babies over dropoffs
    d.   repeated practice with a visual cliff

18. At which of the following stimuli would a newborn prefer to look? (p. 197)
    a.   a blue and red checkerboard with many squares
    b.   a black circle
    c.   a black-and-white drawing of the human face
    d.   a black-and-white checkerboard with many squares

19. _____is / are necessary for most 2- to 4-month-olds to infer object unity. (p. 201)
    a.   Motion
    b.   Binocular depth cues
    c.   Pictorial depth cues
    d.   Invariant features

20. According to the Gibson's differentiation theory, infants have a built-in tendency to search for (p. 202)
    a.   familiar environmental conditions.
    b.   invariant features in the environment.
    c.   intermodal associations in the environment.
    d.   aspects of the environment that are continually changing.

CHAPTER 6
COGNITIVE DEVELOPMENT IN INFANCY AND TODDLERHOOD

BRIEF CHAPTER SUMMARY

According to Piaget, from earliest infancy children actively build psychological structures, or schemes, as they manipulate and explore their world. The vast changes that take place in Piaget's sensorimotor stage are divided into six substages. By acting on the world, infants make strides in intentional behavior, mastery of object permanence, and physical reasoning. In the final substage, they transfer their action-based schemes to a mental level, and representation appears. Research indicates that a variety of sensorimotor milestones emerge earlier than Piaget believed and that cognitive development in infancy does not follow distinct, even stages. Debate continues concerning the degree to which cognitive development depends on motor, perceptual, or innate capacities.

Information processing, an alternative to Piaget's theory, focuses on the development of mental strategies for storing and interpreting information. With age, infants' attention becomes more effective and flexible, and memory improves and is supported by mental representation. Findings on infant categorization support the view that young babies structure experience in adultlike ways. Vygotsky's sociocultural theory stresses that cognitive development is socially mediated as adults help infants and toddlers master challenging tasks.

A variety of infant intelligence tests have been devised to measure individual differences in early mental development. Although most predict later performance poorly, those that emphasize speed of habituation and recovery to visual stimuli and object permanence show better predictability. Home, child care, and early intervention for at-risk infants and toddlers are powerful influences on intellectual progress.

Behaviorist and nativist theories provide contrasting accounts of language development. The interactionist view emphasizes that innate abilities and environmental influences combine to produce children's extraordinary language achievements. During the first year, infants prepare for language in many ways. First words appear around 12 months, 2-word utterances between 18 months and 2 years. At the same time, substantial individual differences exist in rate and style of early language progress. Conversational give-and-take and child-directed speech (a simplified form of parental language) support infants' and toddlers' efforts to become competent speakers.

LEARNING OBJECTIVES

After reading this chapter, you should be able to:

6.1   Describe Piaget's view of development, noting key concepts of his theory. (pp. 208–209)

6.2   Describe the major cognitive achievements of Piaget's six sensorimotor substages. (pp. 209–212)

6.3   Discuss recent research on sensorimotor development and its implications for the accuracy of Piaget's sensorimotor stage. (pp. 212–216)

6.4   Describe the alternate views of cognitive development, including the core knowledge perspective. (pp. 216–219)

6.5   Describe the structure of the information-processing system, as elaborated in information-processing theory, discuss how this approach differs from Piaget's perspective, and review the strengths and limitations of the information-processing theory of cognitive development. (pp. 220–226)

6.6   Discuss the advancements in attention, memory, and categorization taking place during infancy and toddlerhood. (pp. 221–226)

6.7   Explain how Vygotsky's concept of the zone of proximal development expands our understanding of early cognitive development. (pp. 226–227)

6.8   Describe the mental testing approach, the meaning of intelligence test scores, and the extent to which infant tests predict later performance. (pp. 229–230)

6.9   Discuss environmental influences on early mental development, including home, child care, and early interventions for at-risk infants and toddlers. (pp. 231–234)

6.10   Describe three major theories of language development, indicating the emphasis each places on innate and environmental influences. (pp. 235–238)

6.11   Describe how infants prepare for language and explain how adults support their emerging capacities. (pp. 238–239)

6.12   Describe the characteristics of infants' first words and two-word phrases, and explain why language comprehension develops ahead of language production. (pp. 240–241)

6.13   Describe individual and cultural differences in early language development and the factors that influence these differences. (pp. 241–242)

6.14   Explain how child-directed speech and conversational give-and-take support early language development. (pp. 242–244)

STUDY QUESTIONS

Piaget's Cognitive-Developmental Theory

1.   During Piaget's _____ stage, which spans the first 2 years of life, infants and toddlers "think" with their eyes, ears, and hands. (p. 208))

Piaget's Ideas About Cognitive Change

1.   According to Piaget, specific psychological structures, or organized ways of making sense of experience called _____, change with age. (p. 208)

2.   Match the following terms with the appropriate description. (pp. 208–209)

_____ Creating new schemes or adjusting old ones to produce a better fit with the environment

_____ Taking new schemes, rearranging them, and linking them with other schemes to create an interconnected cognitive system

_____ Using current schemes to interpret the external world

_____ Building schemes through direct interaction with the environment

1. Adaptation
2. Accommodation
3. Assimilation
4. Organization

The Sensorimotor Stage

1.   True or False: Piaget believed that infants already know a great deal about their world from the time they are born. (p. 210)

2. Match each of the following sensorimotor substages with its appropriate description. (pp. 209–212)

    ____ Infants' primary means of adapting to the environment is through reflexes   1. Substage 1
    ____ Infants engage in goal-directed behavior and begin to attain object permanence   2. Substage 2
    ____ Toddlers repeat behaviors with variation, producing new effects   3. Substage 3
    ____ Infants' adaptations are oriented toward their own bodies   4. Substage 4
    ____ Infants' attention begins to turn outward toward the environment   5. Substage 5
    ____ Toddlers gain the ability to create mental representations   6. Substage 6

3. Explain the differences between primary, secondary, and tertiary circular reactions. (pp. 210–211)

Primary: _____

_____

Secondary: _____

_____

_____

Tertiary: _____

_____

4. The understanding that objects continue to exist when out of sight is called
_____. (p. 211)

5. Describe the *A-not-B search error.* (p. 211)

_____

_____

6. Describe three new capacities that result from the ability to create mental representations. (pp. 211–212)

A. _____

_____

B. _____

_____

C. _____

_____

Follow-Up Research on Infant Cognitive Development

1. Many studies show that infants understand concepts (earlier / later) than Piaget believed. (p. 212)

2. Explain the *violation-of-expectation method,* which is often used by researchers to identify infants' grasp of object permanence and other aspects of physical reasoning. (p. 212)

_____

_____

_____

_____

3.   Explain why the violation-of-expectation method is controversial. (pp. 212–213)

_____

_____

_____

4.   Summarize the controversial new evidence on object permanence in infancy, including Renée Baillageon's studies, as well as those seeking to confirm or refute her findings. (pp. 213–216)

_____

_____

_____

_____

5.   True or False: Infants demonstrate the A-not-B search error because of memory deficits; that is, they cannot remember an object's new location after it has been hidden in more than one place. (p. 214))

6.   True or False: Laboratory research on deferred imitation supports Piaget's conclusion that infants cannot mentally represent experience until about 18 months of age. Provide evidence to support your response. (pp. 214–215)

_____

_____

_____

7.   By 10 to 12 months of age, infants can solve problems by _____, meaning that they take a strategy from one problem and apply it to other relevant problems. (p. 215)

Evaluation of the Sensorimotor Stage

1.   True or False: Recent research indicates that the cognitive attainments of infancy do, in fact, follow the neat, stepwise progression that Piaget postulated. (p. 216)

2.   According to the _____ perspective, babies are born with a set of innate knowledge systems, or core domains of thought. (p. 217)

3.   Cite four domains of thought studied by core knowledge theorists to assess infants' cognitive knowledge. (p. 217)

   A.   _____   B.   _____

   C.   _____   D.   _____

4.   Summarize criticisms of the core knowledge perspective. (p. 217)

_____

_____

_____

5.   Cite Piaget's contributions to our knowledge of infant cognition. (pp. 217, 219)

_____

_____

_____

Biology and Environment: Do Infants Have Built-In Numerical Knowledge?

1. What do research findings on infants' knowledge of numbers reveal? Why are these findings controversial? (p. 218)

   A. _____

   _____

   B. _____

   _____

Information Processing

Structure of the Information-Processing System

1. Describe the three basic parts of the information-processing system, noting ways in which mental strategies can facilitate storage and retrieval at each level. (pp. 220–221)

   Sensory Register: _____

   _____

   _____

   Working Memory: _____

   _____

   _____

   Long-term Memory: _____

   _____

   _____

2. Explain the role of the *central executive* in managing the complex activities of the working memory system. (p. 221)

   _____

   _____

3. True or False: Long-term memory has a limitless capacity. (p. 221)

4. Information-processing researchers believe that the (structure / capacity) of the human mental system is similar throughout life. (p. 221)

Attention

1. List three ways in which attention improves during infancy. (p. 221)

   A. _____

   B. _____

   C. _____

2. Cite one change in attention that occurs during the toddler years. (p. 222)

   _____

Memory

1. Habituation research greatly (underestimates / overestimates) infants' memory skills when compared to methods that rely on their active exploration of objects. (p. 222)

2. True or False: From the first few months of life, infant memory is independent of context, meaning that infants apply learned responses to relevant new situations. (p. 222)

3. Distinguish between *recognition* and *recall* memory. (p. 223)

   Recognition: _____

   Recall: _____

Categorization

1. The earliest categories are _____, or based on similar overall appearance or prominent object part. By the end of the first year, more categories are _____, or based on common function and behavior. (pp. 223–224)

2. Briefly explain how the perceptual-to-conceptual change takes place. (pp. 224–226)

   _____

   _____

   _____

Evaluation of Information-Processing Findings

1. Information-processing research underscores the (continuity / discontinuity) of human thinking from infancy into adulthood. (p. 226)

2. In what ways does information-processing research challenge Piaget's view of early cognitive development? (p. 226)

   _____

   _____

   _____

3. What is the greatest drawback of the information-processing approach to cognitive development? (p. 226)

   _____

   _____

   _____

Biology and Environment: Infantile Amnesia

1. What is *infantile amnesia*? (p. 224)

   _____

   _____

2. Describe two theories of infantile amnesia. (p. 224)

   A. _____

   _____

B. _____

3. Explain how the phenomenon of infantile amnesia can be reconciled with infants' and toddlers' remarkable memory skills. (p. 224)

_____

_____

_____

4. _____ memory refers to representations of special, one-time events that are long-lasting because they are imbued with personal meaning. (p. 224)

5. Discuss two developments that are necessary for memories to become autobiographical. (p. 224)

A. _____

_____

B. _____

The Social Context of Early Cognitive Development

1. According to Vygotsky's sociocultural theory, how do children learn to master activities and think in culturally meaningful ways? (pp. 226–227)

_____

_____

2. Explain Vygotsky's concept of the *zone of proximal development,* emphasizing the role of adults in fostering children's cognitive development. (p. 227)

_____

_____

_____

3. Explain how cultural variations in social experiences influence children's mental strategies. (p. 227)

_____

_____

_____

Cultural Influences: Social Origins of Make-Believe Play

1. Briefly summarize Vygotsky's view of make-believe play. (p. 228)

_____

_____

2. Explain why adults' participation in toddlers' make-believe play is so important. (p. 228)

_____

_____

_____

Individual Differences in Early Mental Development

1. How does the mental testing approach differ from the cognitive theories discussed earlier in this chapter? (p. 229)

_____

_____

_____

Infant Intelligence Tests

1. What types of responses are tapped by most infant intelligence tests? (p. 229)

_____

_____

2. One commonly used infant test is the _____ *Scales of Infant Development,* designed for children between 1 month and 3½ years. (p. 229)

3. Describe how intelligence scores are computed. (p. 230)

_____

_____

_____

4. Explain the difference between an *intelligence quotient,* or *IQ,* and a *developmental quotient,* or *DQ.* (p. 230)

_____

_____

_____

5. True or False: Scores on infant intelligence tests are excellent predictors of later intelligence. Why or why not? (p. 230)

_____

_____

_____

6. For what purpose are infant intelligence tests largely used? (p. 230)

_____

_____

7. Why does habituation and recovery predict later IQ more effectively than traditional infant intelligence tests? (p. 230)

_____

_____

Early Environment and Mental Development

1. What is the *Home Observation for Measurement of the Environment* (HOME)? What factors does the HOME measure? (p. 231)

   A. _____

   _____

   B. _____

   _____

2. Describe how HOME scores are related to early mental development. (p. 231)

   _____

   _____

   _____

3. Cite ways in which both heredity and home environment contribute to mental test scores. (p. 231)

   Heredity: _____

   _____

   Home environment: _____

   _____

4. Today, more than _____ percent of North American mothers with children under age 2 are employed. (p. 232)

5. Discuss the impact of low versus high quality child care on mental development. (p. 232)

   Low quality: _____

   _____

   High quality: _____

   _____

6. Describe the overall condition of child care for infants and toddlers in the United States and Canada. (pp. 232–233)

   _____

   _____

   _____

7. List and describe at least four signs of developmentally appropriate infant and toddler child care. (p. 233)

   A. _____

   B. _____

   C. _____

   D. _____

Early Intervention for At-Risk Infants and Toddlers

1. Describe the goals of center- and home-based interventions for infants and toddlers. (pp. 233–234)

    Center-based: _____

    _____

    _____

    Home-based: _____

    _____

    _____

2. Discuss the effectiveness of early intervention programs with relation to infant and toddler mental development. (p. 234)

    _____

    _____

3. Briefly describe the Carolina Abecedarian Project, and summarize the outcomes of this program. (p. 234)

    A. _____

    _____

    B. _____

    _____

Language Development

1. On average, children say their first word at _____ months of age. (p. 235)

Three Theories of Language Development

1. According to the behaviorist perspective, what two processes account for early language acquisition, and how do they do so? (pp. 235–236)

    A. _____

    _____

    B. _____

    _____

2. Why is the behaviorist perspective an incomplete explanation of early language development? (p. 236)

    _____

    _____

3. Discuss Chomsky's nativist perspective of language acquisition, noting how this approach differs from the behaviorist perspective. Be sure to explain the *language acquisition device* (LAD) in your response. (p. 236)

    _____

    _____

    _____

    _____

4. Provide evidence supporting Chomsky's view that human infants are biologically primed to acquire language. (p. 236)

_____

_____

_____

5. Name the two language-specific areas of the brain, and cite the function of each. (p. 236)

A. _____

_____

B. _____

_____

6. Broca's and Wernicke's areas (do / do not) offer conclusive support for a language acquisition device. Elaborate on your response. (p. 236)

_____

_____

7. True or False: Research supports the idea that there is a sensitive period for language development. (pp. 236–237)

8. List two challenges to Chomsky's theory. (p. 237)

A. _____

B. _____

9. Summarize the basic tenets of the interactionist perspective of language development. (pp. 237–238)

_____

_____

_____

10. True or False: The interactionist perspective predicts a universal pattern of language learning, with few individual differences. (p. 238)

Getting Ready to Talk

1. At around 2 months of age, infants begin to make vowel-like noises called _____. At around 4 months of age, _____ appears, in which infants repeat consonant-vowel combinations in long strings. (pp. 238–239)

2. Describe evidence that the timing of early babbling is due to brain maturation. (p. 238)

_____

_____

_____

3. Describe *joint attention,* and indicate how it impacts early language development. (p. 239)

_____

_____

_____

First Words

1. Briefly describe the nature of toddlers' first words (for example, to which subjects do these words commonly refer?) (p. 240)

    _____

    _____

    _____

2. When young children learn new words, they tend to make two types of errors. Name and describe each error, and provide an example of each. (p. 240)

    A. _____

    _____

    _____

    B. _____

    _____

    _____

3. True or False: Toddlers' overextensions are typically random, showing little sensitivity to categorical relations. (p. 240)

The Two-Word Utterance Phase

1. Explain the nature of *telegraphic speech*. (p. 241)

    _____

    _____

    _____

Comprehension versus Production

1. Distinguish between language *comprehension* and language *production*. (p. 241)

    Comprehension: _____

    _____

    _____

    Production: _____

    _____

2. (Comprehension / Production) is more well-developed at all ages. Why is this the case? (p. 241)

    _____

    _____

Individual and Cultural Differences

1. True or False: Early language development proceeds at about the same rate for boys and girls. (p. 241)

2. Distinguish between *referential* and *expressive* styles of early language learning, and indicate which style is associated with faster vocabulary development. (p. 242)

Referential: _____

_____

Expressive: _____

_____

3. Cite factors that influence the development of referential and expressive styles. (p. 242)

_____

_____

Supporting Early Language Development

1. Describe three ways in which caregivers can support early language learning. (p. 242)

   A. _____

   B. _____

   C. _____

2. Describe the characteristics of *child-directed speech*, noting how it promotes language development. (p. 242)

_____

_____

_____

3. True or False: Conversational give-and-take between parent and toddler is one of the best predictors of early language development and academic competence during the school years. (p. 242)

ASK YOURSELF . . .

For *Ask Yourself* questions for this chapter, please log on to the Companion Website at *www.ablongman.com/berk*.

SUGGESTED STUDENT READINGS

Erickson, M. F., Kurz-Riemer, K., Kurz-Riemer, K. M. (2002). *Infants, toddlers, and families: A framework for support and intervention.* New York: Guilford. A multidisciplinary approach to early intervention, the authors examine ways to foster healthy development during the first 3 years of life. In addition to providing services to children, high-quality early intervention programs should focus on promoting positive family relationships, enhancing parental knowledge of child development, and linking families with community support systems.

Hirsh-Pasek, K., Golinick, R. M., & Eyer, D. (2003). *Einstein never used flash cards: How our children really learn they need to play more and memorize less.* New York: Rodale. Based on research conducted by leading child development experts, this book explores the benefits of play for young children's development. The authors argue that programs emphasizing academics do not help infants, toddlers, and preschoolers learn better; rather, they can actually have a negative impact on learning and achievement. An excellent resource for parents, caregivers, and anyone interested in working with young children.

McGuinness, D. (2003). *Growing a reader from birth: Your child's path from language to literacy.* New York: Norton, W. W. & Company, Inc. Using up-to-date research on early language development, this book examines ways parents and caregivers can support developing language skills. In addition, the author highlights milestones in language development, including creative ways to read to and communicate with young children.

PUZZLE 6.1 TERM REVIEW

Across

2. In Piaget's theory, a specific structure, or organized way of making sense of experience, that changes with age
5. Object _____: understanding that objects still exist even when they are out of sight
8. ___-___ memory: contains our permanent knowledge base
9. _____ knowledge perspective: babies are born with a set of innate knowledge systems
10. Mental _____: procedures that operate on and transform information, thereby increasing the efficiency of thinking and the chances that information will be retained
14. _____, or goal-directed, behavior is a sequence of actions in which schemes are deliberately combined to solve a problem.
15. Piaget's first stage, during which infants and toddlers "think" with their eyes, ears, and hands
17. Violation-of-_____ method: researchers habituate infants to an event and then determine whether they recover to a possible event or an impossible event
19. The internal arrangement and linking together of schemes so that they form a strongly interconnected cognitive system
20. The external world is represented in terms of current schemes
21. New schemes are created and old ones adjusted to produce a better fit with the environment.

Down

1. The ability to remember and copy the behavior of a model who is not immediately present is known as _____ imitation.
3. Physical _____: the causal action one object exerts on another object through contact
4. Type of memory that involves noticing whether a new experience is identical to or similar to a previous one
6. _____ , or short-term. memory: conscious part of memory where we actively work on a limited amount of information
7. The _____ register is the part of the mental system in which sights and sounds are held until they decay or are transferred to short-term memory.
11. Process of building new schemes through direct contact with the environment
12. Mental _____: internal image of an absent object or past event
13. When infants stumble onto a new experience caused by their own motor activity and then try to repeat the event again and again, they are exhibiting a _____ reaction.
16. Type of memory that involves remembering something in the absence of perceptual support
18. __-___-__ search error: if an object is moved from hiding place A to hiding place B, 8- to 12-month-old infants will search only in the first hiding place

123

PUZZLE 6.2 TERM REVIEW

Across

5. Area of the brain that controls language production
7. _____ speech: toddlers' two-word utterances that leave out smaller and less important words
10. Early language error in which words are applied too narrowly
11. ____ quotient: a score on an infant intelligence test; based primarily on perceptual and motor responses
12. In language development, the words and word combinations that children understand
14. Early language error in which words are applied too narrowly, to a wider collection of objects and events than is appropriate
15. Form of speech marked by high-pitched, exaggerated expression, clear pronunciations, and distinct pauses between speech segments (2 words, hyph.)
16. Type of play involving pleasurable motor activity with or without objects
18. Standards devised by NAEYC that specify program characteristics that meet the developmental and individual needs of young children are called _____ appropriate practice.
21. Pleasant vowel-like noises made by infants
22. In language development, the words and word combinations that children use

Down

1. Area of brain responsible for interpreting language
2. _____ quotient: a score that permits an individual's performance on an intelligence test to be compared to the performances of other same-age individuals
3. Type of play in which children pretend, acting out everyday and imaginary images
4. Style of early language learning in which toddlers use language mainly to talk about feelings and needs
6. Style of early language learning in which toddlers use language mainly to label objects
8. Checklist for gathering information about the quality of children's home lives (abbr.)
9. _____ memory: narrative accounts of significant, one-time events that are long-lasting because they are imbued with personal meaning
13. _____ attention: the child attends to the same object or event as the caregiver, who offers verbal information
17. Repetition of consonant-vowel combinations in long strings
19. Zone of _____ development: range of tasks that a child cannot yet handle independently but can accomplish with the help of more skilled partners
20. Innate system that permits children to speak in a rule-oriented fashion as soon as they learn enough words (abbr.)

PRACTICE TEST #1

1. On a trip to a farm, 2-year-old Liam sees a horse for the first time. Noticing the horse's four legs, tail, and fur, Liam integrates it into his "animal" schema. This is an example of (p. 208)
   a. organization.
   b. accommodation.
   c. assimilation.
   d. equilibrium.

2. In Piaget's theory, when children are in a state of disequilibrium, (p. 209)
   a. they shift away from accommodation toward assimilation.
   b. they realize that new information does not match their current schemes.
   c. they are likely to construct inefficient schemes.
   d. their existing schemes are not likely to change very much.

3. According to Piaget's theory, which of the following behaviors is characteristic of infants in substage 2 of the sensorimotor period? (p. 210)
   a. a baby who accidentally hits a toy hung in front of her and then tries to repeat this effect
   b. a baby who can push aside a cover to retrieve a hidden toy
   c. a baby who drops toys down the steps in varying ways
   d. a baby who learns to open her mouth differently for a nipple than for a spoon

4. In substage 6 of the sensorimotor period, the ability to create mental representations enables toddlers to _____ and _____. (pp. 211–212)
   a. solve invisible displacement problems; engage in make-believe play
   b. understand object permanence; engage in goal-directed behavior
   c. engage in deferred imitation; understand object permanence
   d. engage in functional play; solve invisible displacement problems

5. In the violation-of-expectation method, _____ suggests that the infant is surprised at a deviation from physical reality. (p. 212)
   a. recovery to the impossible event
   b. habitation to the possible event
   c. recovery to the possible event
   d. habituation to the impossible event

6. Follow-up research indicates that babies make the A-not-B search error because they (p. 214)
   a. have trouble inhibiting a previously rewarded reaching response.
   b. have trouble remembering an object's new location after it is hidden in more that one place.
   c. have not yet developed the motor skills necessary for intentional reaching and grasping.
   d. believe that objects taken out of sight no longer exist.

7. Follow-up research on infant cognitive development suggests that (p. 212)
   a. problem solving by analogy emerges later than Piaget expected.
   b. babies have less built-in cognitive equipment than granted by Piaget.
   c. the cognitive attainments of infancy develop in the stepwise fashion Piaget predicted.
   d. infants comprehend a great deal before they are capable of the motor behaviors Piaget assumed led to those understandings.

8. The core knowledge perspective emphasizes the role of _____ in cognitive development. (p. 217)
   a. native endowment
   b. social interaction
   c. independent exploration
   d. culture

9. According to the information-processing perspective, _____ direct(s) the flow of information in the mental system. (p. 220)
   a. mental strategies
   b. the sensory register
   c. working memory
   d. the central executive

10. In the information-processing perspective, automatic cognitive processing (p. 221)
   a. expands working memory.
   b. increases the chances that information will be retained in the sensory register.
   c. interferes with recognition memory.
   d. leads to the offset of infantile amnesia.

11. Information-processing research reveals that with the transition to toddlerhood (p. 221)
   a. attraction to novelty declines.
   b. attention becomes less flexible.
   c. memory becomes increasingly context dependent.
   d. sustained attention decreases.

12. Information-processing research demonstrates that recall emerges (p. 223)
   a. during the first few weeks of life.
   b. between 4 to 6 months of age.
   c. between 1 and 2 years of age.
   d. between 3 and 4 years of age.

13. Information-processing theorists believe that changes in _____ make possible more complex forms of thinking with age. (p. 221)
   a. the capacity of the mental system
   b. the speed of habituation
   c. the structure of the mental system
   d. the speed of operant learning

14. Infants' earliest categories are _____, whereas categories become increasingly _____ during toddlerhood. (p. 224)
   a. functional; conceptual
   b. conceptual; perceptual
   c. perceptual; functional
   d. perceptual; conceptual

15. Compared with Piaget's theory, the information-processing approach to development has more difficulty with (p. 226)
   a. breaking down children's thoughts into precise procedures.
   b. reducing changes in thoughts into manageable proportions.
   c. counting the number of stages children's thoughts go through.
   d. integrating information into a broad comprehensive theory.

16. In Vygotsky's theory, _____ produce(s) cognitive development. (pp. 226–227)
   a. joint activities with more competent others
   b. independent interaction with the physical environment
   c. the biological unfolding of genetic structures
   d. the physical world acting on the child

17. Infant intelligence test scores (p. 230)
    a. are effective predictors of IQ during the school years.
    b. remain relatively stable throughout the first year of life.
    c. are used largely to identify babies who are likely to have future developmental problems.
    d. tap basic cognitive processes that underlie intelligent behavior at all ages.

18. Child care in the United States (p. 232)
    a. is nationally regulated to ensure its quality.
    b. must meet certain standards for developmentally appropriate practice.
    c. is mostly funded by the national government.
    d. is often substandard.

19. Two-year-old Noah uses the word "fish" for whales, dolphins, and sharks. Noah's error is known as an (p. 240)
    a. underextension.
    b. overextension.
    c. underregularization.
    d. overregularization.

20. Which of the following is supported by research on babbling? (p. 238)
    a. Deaf babies start babbling at the same age as hearing babies.
    b. Hearing babies who have deaf parents do not babble.
    c. Deaf infants begin babbling several months later than hearing infants.
    d. Infants must be able to hear human speech to begin babbling.

PRACTICE TEST #2

1. According to Piaget, during periods of rapid cognitive development, (p. 209)
    a. children are in a constant state of equilibrium.
    b. children tend to assimilate new experiences.
    c. children modify their schemes to achieve a steady, comfortable condition.
    d. adaptation predominates over organization.

2. Four-month-old Nick accidentally kicked a button on his crib toy that caused it to light up and spin. Over the next several days, Nick tried to repeat this effect by kicking his legs. When he succeeded in kicking the button again, he continued to repeat the motion. Nick's behavior is an example of a (p. 210)
    a. reflexive scheme.
    b. primary circular reaction.
    c. secondary circular reaction.
    d. tertiary circular reaction.

3. _____ emerges during Substage 6 of the sensorimotor period. (p. 211)
    a. Object permanence
    b. An appreciation for physical causality
    c. Intentional behavior
    d. An ability to create mental representations

4. Recent research suggests that the reason infants make errors in finding hidden objects is that they (p. 214)
    a. cannot remember the spatial locations of the hidden objects.
    b. cannot translate their knowledge into plans for finding objects.
    c. believe that objects taken out of sight no longer exist.
    d. have not yet developed the fine motor skills necessary for voluntary reaching and grasping.

5. Studies of deferred imitation have shown that infants as young as 6 weeks of age (p. 214)
    a. have the capacity to construct mental representations.
    b. appreciate physical causality.
    c. understand object permanence.
    d. can engage in goal-directed behavior.

6. Information-processing theorists believe that_____is / are responsible for gains in information-processing capacity. (p. 221)
    a. the ability to hold more and more items in working memory
    b. improvements in mental strategies
    c. the emergence of new, more complex mental structures
    d. increases in processing efficiency

7. In the information-processing system, long-term memory (p. 221)
    a. stores information permanently.
    b. is limited in capacity.
    c. is the conscious part of the mental system.
    d. is the central processing resource pool.

8. Which of the following activities is within a child's zone of proximal development? (p. 227)
    a. A puzzle that a toddler has just learned how to do by herself.
    b. A puzzle that a toddler can teach to other same-age peers.
    c. A puzzle that a toddler can do only with the assistance of an adult.
    d. A puzzle that a toddler cannot yet do, even with the help of an adult.

9. According to Vygotsky, the force that drives a child's cognitive development is (pp. 226–227)
   a. joint activities with more competent others.
   b. interaction with the physical environment.
   c. the biological unfolding of genetic structures.
   d. the physical world acting on the child.

10. What factors seem to be most important in the development of make-believe play in toddlers? (p. 228)
    a. the maturation of the frontal lobes and the cerebellum
    b. the child's readiness to engage in such play and social experiences that promote it
    c. time spent alone and time spent with other toddlers
    d. explicit instruction in play from parents and from teachers

11. Categorization research demonstrates that (p. 223)
    a. infants' earliest categories are conceptual rather than perceptual.
    b. babies can categorize emotional expressions within the first few days of life.
    c. babies begin to categorize people by voices and gender within the first month of life.
    d. infants' brains are set up from the start to represent and organize experience in adultlike ways.

12. Which of the following is the BEST infant predictor of childhood IQ? (p. 230)
    a. speed of habituation and recovery
    b. the Bayley Scales of Infant Development
    c. speed of operant conditioning
    d. the Wechsler Intelligence Scale for Infants

13. Research has shown that family living conditions, such as those measured by the HOME, (p. 231)
    a. predict children's IQ scores beyond the effects of parental intelligence and education.
    b. show equally strong correlations with IQ for both adopted and biological children.
    c. are not associated with IQ for ethnic minority children.
    d. predict children's school performance better than their IQ scores.

14. Infants exposed to poor-quality child care score lower on a measure of cognitive and social skills (p. 232)
    a. only if they come from poverty-stricken households.
    b. only in single-parent families.
    c. regardless of whether they are from low- or middle-SES families.
    d. only if they entered child care before six months of age.

15. The Carolina Abecedarian Project shows that _____ is an effective way to reduce the negative effects of poverty on children's mental development. (p. 234)
    a. furnishing free nutrition and health services
    b. providing children a special resource teacher during the early elementary school years
    c. an early intervention approach that focuses on parental involvement
    d. continuous high-quality child care from infancy throughout the preschool years

16. In Chomsky's theory, LAD refers to (p. 236)
    a. an innate speech-analyzing mechanism that enables young children to acquire the language to which they are exposed.
    b. language acquisition drills that are used to foster preverbal children's language development.
    c. the process by which parents provide children assistance in learning language.
    d. computer programs that attempt to generate the linguistic rules and cognitive processes that are needed for language acquisition.

17. Research suggests that children _____ because they have difficulty recalling or have not acquired a suitable word. (p. 240)
    a. underextend
    b. overregularize
    c. underregularize
    d. overextend

18. In which of the following cases should the parents be concerned about their child's language development? (pp. 238, 242)
    a. a 6-month-old infant who has not yet begun to coo
    b. a 12-month-old who has not yet said her first recognizable word
    c. an 18-month-old who has a vocabulary of only 50 words
    d. a 24-month-old who has not yet combined two words

19. Compared with other perspectives on language development, the interactionist perspective puts much more emphasis on (p. 237)
    a. innate language abilities.
    b. environmental influences.
    c. the child's strong desire to communicate with people.
    d. the sensitive period in language acquisition.

20. The most effective child-directed speech (p. 244)
    a. creates a zone of proximal development.
    b. fosters the development of children's autobiographical memory.
    d. promotes metalinguistic awareness.
    d. engages children in referential communication.

CHAPTER 7
EMOTIONAL AND SOCIAL DEVELOPMENT
IN INFANCY AND TODDLERHOOD

BRIEF CHAPTER SUMMARY

Erikson's psychoanalytic theories provide an overview of the emotional and social tasks of infancy and toddlerhood. For Erikson, trust and autonomy grow out of warm, supportive parenting and reasonable expectations for impulse control during the second year.

Emotions play an important role in the organization of relationships with caregivers, exploration of the environment, and discovery of the self. Infants' ability to express basic emotions, such as happiness, anger, sadness, and fear, and respond to the emotions of others expands over the first year. As toddlers become more self-aware, self-conscious emotions, such as shame, embarrassment, and pride, begin to emerge. Emotional self-regulation improves with brain maturation, gains in cognition and language, and sensitive child rearing.

Children's unique temperamental styles are apparent in early infancy. Heredity influences early temperament, but child-rearing experiences determine whether a child's temperament is sustained or modified over time.

Ethological theory is the most widely accepted view of the development of the infant–caregiver relationship. According to this perspective, attachment evolved over the history of our species to promote survival. Research shows that responding promptly, consistently, and appropriately to infant signals supports secure attachment, whereas insensitive caregiving is linked to attachment insecurity. Because children and parents are embedded in larger contexts, family circumstances influence attachment quality. Cultural factors also affect attachment patterns. Infants form attachment bonds with a variety of familiar people, including mothers, fathers, and siblings. Although quite limited, peer sociability is present in the first 2 years, and it is fostered by the early caregiver–child bond. Continuity of caregiving seems to be involved in the relationship of attachment security to later development.

Once self-awareness develops over the first and second year, it supports a diverse array of social and emotional achievements. Empathy, the ability to categorize the self, compliance, and self-control are by-products of toddlers' emerging sense of self.

LEARNING OBJECTIVES

After reading this chapter, you should be able to:

7.1   Discuss the first two stages of Erikson's psychosocial theory, noting the personality changes that take place at each stage. (p. 251)

7.2   Describe the development of basic emotions, including happiness, anger, sadness, and fear, throughout the first two years of life. (pp. 252–255)

7.3   Summarize the changes in infants' ability to understand and respond to the emotions of others, with particular attention to the emergence of social referencing. (pp. 255–256)

7.4   Explain the nature of self-conscious emotions, noting why they emerge during the second year and indicating their role in development. (p. 256)

7.5   Trace the development of emotional self-regulation during the first 2 years. (pp. 256–257)

7.6   Discuss the three underlying components of temperament, and identify the three temperamental styles elaborated by Thomas and Chess. (pp. 258–259)

7.7 Compare and contrast Thomas and Chess's model of temperament with that of Rothbart. (p. 259)

7.8 Explain how temperament is measured, and discuss the stability of temperament over time. (pp. 259–262)

7.9 Summarize the genetic and environmental influences on temperament, and describe the goodness-of-fit model. (pp. 262–264)

7.10 Describe and compare drive reduction, psychoanalytic, and ethological theories of attachment. (pp. 265–266)

7.11 Describe the Strange Situation procedure for measuring attachment, and discuss the four patterns of attachment that have been identified using this technique. (pp. 266–268)

7.12 Discuss the factors that affect attachment security. (pp. 269–274)

7.13 Discuss infants' attachment relationships with fathers and siblings, noting the factors that impact these relationships. (pp. 274–276)

7.14 Describe the link between infant–mother attachment and later cognitive, emotional, and social development, and explain how continuity of caregiving affects this link. (pp. 276–277)

7.15 Trace the emergence of self-awareness, and explain how it influences early emotional and social development, categorization of the self, and development of self-control. (pp. 278–281)

STUDY QUESTIONS

Erikson's Theory of Infant and Toddler Personality

Basic Trust versus Mistrust

1. How did Erikson expand upon Freud's view of development during the oral stage? (pp. 250–251)

_____

_____

2. Based on Erikson's theory, summarize the psychological conflict of the first year, *basic trust versus mistrust*, and explain how it can be positively resolved. (pp. 250–251)

Conflict: _____

_____

Resolution: _____

_____

_____

Autonomy versus Shame and Doubt

1. In what way did Erikson expand upon Freud's view of development during the anal stage? (p. 251)

_____

_____

2. Explain how the psychological conflict of toddlerhood, *autonomy versus shame and doubt,* is resolved favorably. (p. 251)

_____

_____

Development of Basic Emotions

1. Define the term *basic emotions,* and provide several examples. (p. 252)

   Definition: _____

   _____

   Examples: _____

   _____

2. True or False: Infants come into the world with the ability to express all of the basic emotions. (p. 252)

3. At approximately what age do infants' emotional expressions become well organized and specific? (p. 253)

   _____

4. What is a *social smile,* and when does it develop? (p. 254)

   _____

   _____

   _____

5. Laughter, which appears around _____ to _____ months, reflects (faster / slower) processing of information than does smiling. (p. 254)

6. How do expressions of happiness change between early infancy and the middle of the first year? (p. 254)

   _____

   _____

7. The frequency and intensity of infants' angry reactions (increase / decrease) with age. (p. 254)

8. Explain how cognitive and motor development affect infants' angry reactions. (p. 254)

   _____

   _____

   _____

   _____

9. Describe the circumstances in which infants are likely to express sadness. (p. 254)

   _____

   _____

10. Fear reactions (increase / decrease) during the second half of the first year. (p. 254)

11. The most frequent expression of fear in infancy is to unfamiliar adults, a response called _____ *anxiety.* (p. 254)

12. Cite several factors that influence infants' and toddlers' reactions to strangers. (pp. 254–255)

_____

_____

_____

_____

Understanding and Responding to the Emotions of Others

1. Early on, babies respond to others' emotions through the fairly automatic process of *emotional* _____
   _____, in which they smile, laugh, or feel sad in response to sensing these emotions in others.
   (p. 255)

2. Define *social referencing,* and explain its role in infant development. (p. 255)

   Definition: _____

   _____

   Role: _____

   _____

   _____

3. At what age do infants understand that others' emotional reactions may differ from their own? (p. 255)

   _____

Emergence of Self-Conscious Emotions

1. What are *self-conscious emotions*? (p. 256)

   _____

   _____

2. Cite several examples of self-conscious emotions. (p. 256)

   _____

3. Besides self-awareness, what ingredient is required in order for children to experience self-conscious emotions?
   (p. 256)

   _____

4. True or False: The situations in which adults encourage children's expressions of self-conscious emotions vary from
   culture to culture. (p. 256)

Beginnings of Emotional Self-Regulation

1. Define *emotional self-regulation.* (p. 256)

   _____

   _____

2. Explain how a caregiver's responses to an infant's emotional cues impact the infant's development of self-regulation.
   (p. 257)

   _____

   _____

3. By the end of the second year, gains in representation and language lead to new ways of regulating emotion. Explain how this occurs. (p. 257)

_____

_____

_____

Development of Temperament

1. Define *temperament*. (p. 258)

_____

_____

2. Cite two important findings from the New York longitudinal study of temperament. (p. 258)

A. _____

_____

B. _____

_____

The Structure of Temperament

1. List and describe five of the nine dimensions of personality outlined in Thomas and Chess's model of temperament. (p. 259)

A. _____

_____

B. _____

_____

C. _____

_____

D. _____

_____

E. _____

_____

2. List and describe the three temperamental types that have emerged from the work of Thomas and Chess. (p. 258)

A. _____

_____

B. _____

_____

C. _____

_____

3. True or False: All children fit into one of the three temperament categories described above. (p. 258)

4. Of the three styles of temperament, the _____ pattern places children at highest risk for adjustment problems. (p. 258)

5. Name the three components of temperament represented by Mary Rothbart's six dimensions. (pp. 258–259)

   A. _____

   B. _____

   C. _____

Measuring Temperament

1. Discuss the advantages and disadvantages of using parent reports to assess children's temperament. (pp. 259–260)

   Advantages: _____

   _____

   _____

   Disadvantages: _____

   _____

   _____

2. Most physiological assessments of temperament have focused on _____ children, who react negatively to and withdraw from novel stimuli, and _____ children, who display positive emotion to and approach novel stimuli. (p. 260)

Stability of Temperament

1. True or False: Temperamental stability from one age period to the next is generally low to moderate. (p. 261)

2. Long-term predictions about early temperament are best achieved after the _____ year of life, when styles of responding are better established. (p. 262)

3. True or False: Many children show little or no change in biologically-based temperamental traits, suggesting that such traits cannot be modified through environmental experiences. (p. 262)

Genetic Influences

1. Research shows that identical twins (are / are not) more similar than fraternal twins in temperament and personality. (p. 262)

2. True or False: Lack of consistent ethnic and sex differences in early temperament have called into question the role of heredity. (p. 262)

Environmental Influences

1. Describe how parental behaviors contribute to ethnic and sex differences in temperament. (pp. 262–263)

   _____

   _____

   _____

2. Explain how children reared in the same family develop distinct temperament styles. (p. 263)

_____

_____

_____

Temperament and Child Rearing: The Goodness-of-Fit Model

1. Describe the *goodness-of-fit* model. (p. 263)

_____

_____

2. How does the goodness-of-fit model help to explain why Western middle-class children with difficult temperaments are at high risk for future adjustment problems? (p. 263)

_____

_____

_____

3. Describe how cultural variations in values and life conditions affect the fit between parenting and child temperament. (p. 264)

_____

_____

Biology and Environment: Biological Basis of Shyness and Sociability

1. What percentage of children identified as displaying extremes in shyness and sociability retain their temperament style as they get older? (p. 260)

_____

2. Kagan, a researcher who studies shyness and sociability in children, believes that individual differences in arousal of the _____, an inner brain structure that controls avoidance reactions, contributes to these contrasting temperamental styles. (p. 260)

3. Discuss four physiological correlates of approach–withdrawal behavior. (pp. 260–261)

   A. _____

   B. _____

   C. _____

   D. _____

4. Heritability research indicates that genes contribute (modestly / substantially) to shyness and sociability. (p. 261)

5. Explain how child-rearing practices affect the chances that an emotionally reactive baby will become a fearful child. (p. 261)

_____

_____

_____

1. Define *attachment*. (p. 264)

_____

_____

2. True or False: Both psychoanalytic and behaviorist theories emphasize feeding as an important context in which infants and caregivers build a close emotional bond. (p. 265)

3. How did Harlow's research on rhesus monkeys challenge the idea that attachment depends on hunger satisfaction? (p. 265)

_____

_____

Bowlby's Ethological Theory

1. True or False: The ethological theory of attachment, which recognizes attachment as an evolved response that promotes survival, is the most widely accepted view of the infants' emotional tie to the caregiver. (p. 265)

2. According to Bowlby, the attachment bond has strong (biological / environmental) roots. It can best be understood within an evolutionary framework in which survival of the species is of utmost importance. (pp. 265–266)

3. Match each phase of attachment with the appropriate description. (pp. 265–266)

_____ Attachment to the familiar caregiver is evident, and infants display separation anxiety.
_____ Infants are not yet attached to their mother and do not mind being left with an unfamiliar adult.
_____ Separation anxiety declines as children gain an understanding of the parent's comings and goings and can predict his/her return.
_____ Infants start to respond differently to a familiar caregiver than to a stranger.

1. The preattachment phase
2. The attachment-in-the-making phase
3. The phase of "clear-cut" attachment
4. Formation of a reciprocal relationship

4. According to Bowlby, children develop an *internal working model* based on their experiences during the four phases of attachment. Define and explain this term. (p. 266)

_____

_____

_____

Measuring the Security of Attachment

1. The _____ technique, designed by Mary Ainsworth, is the most widely used technique for measuring the quality of attachment between 1 and 2 years of age. (p. 266)

2. Provide a brief description of the *Strange Situation* technique. (pp. 266–267)

_____

_____

_____

_____

3. Match each of the following attachment classifications with the appropriate description. (p. 267)

_____ Before separation, these infants seek closeness to the parent and fail to explore. When she returns, they display angry behaviors, may continue to cry after being picked up, and cannot be easily comforted.

_____ Before separation, these infants use the parent as a base from which to explore. They are upset by the parent's absence, and they seek contact and are easily comforted when she returns.

_____ Before separation, these infants seem unresponsive to the parent. When she leaves, they react to the stranger in much the same way as to the parent. Upon her return, they are slow to greet her.

_____ When the parent returns, these infants show confused, contradictory behaviors, such as looking away while being held.

1. Secure
2. Avoidant
3. Resistant
4. Disorganized/disoriented

4. The *Attachment* _____ is a more efficient alternative to the Strange Situation for measuring attachment in children ages 1–5. Briefly describe this method. (p. 267)

_____

_____

_____

Stability of Attachment

1. Explain how socioeconomic conditions impact children's attachment security. (p. 268)

_____

_____

2. (Securely / Insecurely) attached babies are more likely to maintain their attachment status. Cite one exception to this trend. (p. 268)

_____

Cultural Variations

1. Cite at least one example of how cultural variations in child rearing affect attachment security. (pp. 268–269)

_____

_____

Factors That Affect Attachment Security

1. List four important influences that affect attachment security. (p. 269)

A. _____

B. _____

C. _____

D. _____

2. True or False: Research on adopted children reveals that children can develop a first attachment bond as late as 4 to 6 years of age. (p. 269)

3. Describe the behavioral and emotional difficulties evidenced by children and adolescents who do not have the opportunity to develop a close attachment bond with a caregiver. (p. 269)

_____

_____

_____

4. Describe differences in caregiving experienced by securely attached and insecurely attached infants. (p. 269)

Securely attached: _____

_____

_____

Insecurely attached: _____

_____

_____

5. Describe several adjustment problems evidenced by children and adolescents who lacked the opportunity to develop attachment bonds during infancy and childhood. (p. 269)

_____

_____

_____

6. How does the child care experienced by avoidant and resistant infants differ from that experienced by securely attached infants? (pp. 269–270)

Avoidant: _____

_____

_____

Resistant: _____

_____

_____

7. True or False: Research findings consistently show that infant temperament exerts an extremely powerful influence on attachment security. (p. 270)

8. True or False: Style of caregiving can override the impact of infant characteristics on attachment security. (p. 270)

9. Discuss why goodness-of-fit is essential to attachment security. (p. 271)

_____

_____

_____

10. Explain how family circumstances, such as job loss, a failing marriage, or financial difficulties, affect infant attachment. (p. 271)

_____

_____

_____

11. Summarize the relationship between parents' childhood experiences and the quality of attachment with their own children. (pp. 271–272)

_____

_____

_____

12. True or False: The way parents *view* their childhood experiences is more influential than the actual experiences themselves in determining how parents rear their own children. (p. 273)

Multiple Attachments

1. Describe how mothers and fathers differ in the way they relate to and interact with babies, and discuss how these patterns are changing due to the revised work status of women. (p. 274)

_____

_____

_____

_____

2. List two conditions associated with increased paternal involvement with caregiving. (p. 274)

    A. _____

    B. _____

3. When a new baby arrives, how is a preschool-age sibling likely to respond? Include both positive and negative reactions in your answer. (pp. 274–275)

    Positive: _____

    _____

    Negative: _____

    _____

4. Discuss three ways in which mothers can promote positive relationships between infants and their preschool-age siblings. (p. 276)

    A. _____

    _____

    B. _____

    _____

    C. _____

    _____

From Attachment to Peer Sociability

1. Explain the link between attachment to a sensitive caregiver and early peer relationships. (p. 277)

   _____

   _____

   _____

Attachment and Later Development

1. Which attachment pattern is consistently related to high hostility and aggression during the preschool and school years? (p. 277)

   _____

2. Some researchers have suggested that *continuity of caregiving* determines whether attachment is linked to later development. Briefly explain this relationship. (p. 277)

   _____

   _____

   _____

Social Issues: Health:
Does Child Care in Infancy Threaten Attachment Security and Later Adjustment?

1. True or False: American infants placed in full-time child care before 12 months of age are more likely than home-reared infants to display insecure attachments. (p. 272)

2. Discuss several reasons why we must be cautious about concluding that child care is harmful to infants' attachment security. (pp. 272–273)

   A. _____

   _____

   B. _____

   _____

   C. _____

   _____

3. Based on findings from the NICHD Study of Early Child Care, cite two factors that influence the impact of child care experiences on attachment security. (pp. 272–273)

   A. _____

   B. _____

4. True or False: Research suggests that early, extensive child care has a far stronger impact on preschoolers' problem behavior than does parenting. (pp. 272–273)

Cultural Influences: The Powerful Role of Paternal Warmth in Development

1. True or False: Fathers' affectionate behavior toward their children predicts later cognitive, emotional, and social competencies as strongly as does mothers' warm behavior. (p. 275)

2. Describe two factors that promote paternal warmth. (p. 275)

   A. _____

   _____

   B. _____

   _____

Self-Understanding

Self-Awareness

1. The earliest aspect of the self to emerge is the _____-self, or sense of self as agent, involving awareness that the self is separate from the surrounding world and can control its own thoughts and actions. (p. 278)

2. A second aspect of the self, the _____-self, is a sense of self as an object of knowledge and evaluation. What qualities make up this component of the self? (p. 279)

   _____

   _____

3. Describe two ways in which self-awareness is associated with early emotional and social development. (p. 279)

   A. _____

   _____

   B. _____

   _____

Categorizing the Self

1. Describe categorizations of the self that appear in toddlerhood, and cite an example of how children use this knowledge to organize their behavior. (pp. 279–280)

   _____

   _____

   _____

   _____

Emergence of Self-Control

1. Define *self-control*, and list three developmental milestones that are essential for the development of this capacity. (p. 280)

   Definition: _____

   _____

Milestones:

A. _____

B. _____

C. _____

2. True or False: Among toddlers who experience warm, sensitive caregiving, compliance is more common than opposition. (p. 280)

3. List several ways of helping toddlers develop compliance and self-control. (p. 280)

_____

_____

_____

_____

ASK YOURSELF . . .

For *Ask Yourself* questions for this chapter, please log on to the Companion Website at *www.ablongman.com/berk*.

SUGGESTED STUDENT READINGS

Brandstaetter, H., & Elias, A. (Eds.). (2001). *Persons, situations, and emotions: An ecological approach.* New York: Oxford University Press. An edited book highlighting the dynamic interaction between temperament and personality traits and their contribution to social and emotional development.

Holinger, P. C., & Doner, K. (2003). *What babies can say before they can talk.* New York: Simon & Schuster. Using research on basic and self-conscious emotions, the author examines the meanings of infant signals. Because babies' understanding of the world reflects experiences with parents and caregivers, understanding and responding to infant cues is essential for healthy development.

Wilkoff, W. G. (2003). *How to say no to your toddler: Creating a safe, rational, and effective program for your 9-month-old to 3-year-old.* New York: Broadway Books. Based on up-to-date child development literature, this book examines milestones of infant and toddler development, including ways to handle challenging behavior. In addition, the author strives to help parents and caregivers align their expectations with the young child's developing competencies.

PUZZLE 7.1 TERM REVIEW

Across

1. Social _____: relying on a trusted person's emotional reaction to decide how to respond in an uncertain situation
3. Interactional _____: a sensitively-tuned emotional dance, in which the caregiver responds to infant signals in a well-timed, appropriate fashion, and both partners match emotional states
4. Attachment style characterizing infants who respond in a confused, contradictory fashion when reunited with the parent
7. Attachment style characterizing infants who remain close to the parent prior to separation but display angry behavior upon reunion
8. Positive outcome of Erikson's psychological conflict of toddlerhood
9. Infants use the caregiver as a secure _____ from which to explore, returning for emotional support.
13. The _____ theory of attachment views the infant's emotional tie to the caregiver as an evolved response that promotes survival.
14. Negative outcome of Erikson's psychological conflict of infancy
15. Attachment style characterizing infants who are distressed at parental separation and are easily comforted upon parental return
16. _____ Situation: procedure involving brief separations from and reunions with the parent that assesses the quality of the attachment bond

Down

2. Model of attachment which states that an effective match between child-rearing practices and a child's temperament leads to favorable adjustment (3 words, hyph.)
5. _____ caregiving involves prompt, consistent, and appropriate responses to infant signals.
6. _____ working model: set of expectations derived from early caregiving experiences; guides all future close relationships
8. Attachment style characterizing infants who are unresponsive to the parent when she is present, not distressed when she leaves, and slow to greet her upon reunion
10. The strong, affectional tie that humans feel toward special people in their lives
11. Attachment _____: method for assessing the quality of the attachment bond in which a parent sorts a set of descriptors of attachment-related behaviors on the basis of how well they describe the child
12. The _____ smile is evoked by the stimulus of the human face.

PUZZLE 7.2 TERM REVIEW

Across

3. Stable individual differences in quality and intensity of emotional reaction, activity level, attention, and emotional self-regulation
4. Temperament style characterized by irregular daily routines, slow acceptance of new experiences, and negative, intense reactions
5. A child who reacts positively to and approaches novel stimuli
6. _____ anxiety: infant's distressed reaction to the departure of a familiar caregiver
9. Voluntary obedience to adult requests and commands
10. The capacity to understand another's emotional state and to feel with that person
11. Temperament style characterized by inactivity, mild, low-key reactions to environmental stimuli, negative mood, and slow adjustment to new experiences
14. _____ emotions can be directly inferred from facial expressions.
15. Sense of self as agent who is separate from but attends to and acts on objects and other people (2 words, hyph.)
16. Temperament style characterized by establishment of regular routines in infancy, general cheerfulness, and easy adaptation to new experiences

Down

1. Self-_____: capacity to resist an impulse to engage in socially disapproved behavior
2. Emotions involving injury or enhancement to the sense of self
7. Emotional self-_____: strategies for adjusting one's emotional state to a comfortable level of intensity
8. A child who reacts negatively to and withdraws from novel stimuli
12. Stranger _____: an infant's expression of fear in response to unfamiliar adults
13. Sense of self as an object of knowledge and evaluation (2 words, hyph.)

PRACTICE TEST #1

1. Basic emotions (p. 252)
   a. emerge during the first few months of life.
   b. have a long evolutionary history of promoting survival.
   c. can be directly inferred from vocalizations.
   d. exist only in humans.

2. The emergence of the social smile in infancy parallels the development of (p. 254)
   a. a "clear-cut" attachment to a primary caregiver.
   b. the me-self.
   c. self-conscious emotions.
   d. babies' sensitivity to the human face.

3. Which of the children below is likely to display the most intense anger reaction? (p. 254)
   a. a newborn with a dirty diaper
   b. an overstimulated 6-month-old
   c. a 12-month-old who has just had a toy taken away by a playmate
   d. an 18-month-old who has been put down for an unwanted nap by her mother

4. The most frequent expression of fear during infancy is in response to (p. 254)
   a. very active stimuli.
   b. heights.
   c. unfamiliar adults.
   d. loud noises.

5. When baby Max wandered over to a stranger in a doctor's waiting room, he looked at his mother's expression and then immediately crawled away. This example demonstrates the concept of (p. 255)
   a. avoidant attachment.
   b. social referencing.
   c. emotional self-regulation.
   d. interactional synchrony.

6. Self-conscious emotions (p. 256)
   a. involve injury or enhancement of our sense of self.
   b. emerge by the end of the first year.
   c. are universally felt in the same sorts of situations.
   d. are used to adjust our emotional state to a comfortable level of intensity.

7. Which of the following strategies can most newborns use to regulate emotion to a comfortable level of intensity? (p. 256)
   a. crawling
   b. shifting attention
   c. crying
   d. sucking

8. In Thomas and Chess's model of temperament, (p. 258)
   a. slow-to-warm up infants are slow to accept new experiences and tend to react negatively and intensely.
   b. difficult infants show low-key reactions and are negative in mood.
   c. easy infants quickly establish regular routines and easily adapt to new experiences.
   d. the majority of infants are classified as either difficult or slow-to-warm up.

9. Which of the following is supported by research on temperament? (p. 262)
   a. Temperament is relatively stable throughout infancy and childhood.
   b. Most irritable and active babies become difficult children.
   c. Children rarely change from one temperamental extreme to another.
   d. Temperament is rarely modifiable by experience.

10. The _____ describes the relationship between a child's temperament and child-rearing practices. (p. 261)
    a. ethological theory of attachment
    b. goodness-of-fit model
    c. concept of interactional synchrony
    d. internal working model

11. The psychoanalytic theory argues that infants develop attachments to their caregivers (p. 265)
    a. because the caregivers provide them with food.
    b. as the result of an automatic process that evolved over millions of years.
    c. because of built-in behaviors that keep the caregivers nearby.
    d. as the result of the contact comfort provided by the caregivers.

12. Baby Mary gets upset every morning when her mother leaves for work. This demonstrates the concept of (pp. 265–266)
    a. avoidant attachment.
    b. interactional synchrony.
    c. separation anxiety.
    d. social referencing.

13. As baby Jon explores the living room at his grandparents' house, he frequently returns to his father for emotional support. Jon's behavior demonstrates the concept of (p. 266)
    a. goodness-of-fit.
    b. a secure base.
    c. a slow-to-warm-up child.
    d. an inhibited child.

14. A parent leaves the room during the Strange Situation in order to observe _____, and returns again in order to obtain information on _____. (p. 267)
    a. the stability of a secure base; separation anxiety
    b. separation anxiety; infant memory of separation
    c. separation anxiety; reaction to a reunion
    d. reaction to a reunion; separation anxiety

15. During the Strange Situation, baby Ethan seems unresponsive to his mother and is not upset when she leaves the room. When reunited with his mother, Ethan does not seek contact with her. Ethan is exhibiting behaviors characteristic of (p. 267)
    a. an avoidant attachment.
    b. a resistant attachment.
    c. a secure attachment.
    d. a disorganized/disoriented attachment.

16. Research on the stability of attachment demonstrates that (p. 268)
    a. securely attached babies are more likely than insecurely attached babies to maintain their attachment status.
    b. only babies with stable family lives demonstrate secure attachment behaviors.
    c. cultural differences rarely affect infant-caregiver attachment status.
    d. SES usually does not affect attachment quality.

17. A sensitively tuned "emotional dance" in which the mother responds to the baby's signals in a well-timed and appropriate manner, and both partners match their emotional states, is called (p. 269)

a. sensitive caregiving.
b. interactional synchrony.
c. goodness of fit.
d. secure attachment.

18. _____ babies tend to receive _____ care from their mothers. (p. 270)
    a. Resistant; inconsistent
    b. Disorganized/disoriented; overstimulating
    c. Resistant; intrusive
    d. Avoidant; contradictory

19. Which attachment pattern is especially high among maltreated infants and infants of depressed mothers? (p. 270)
    a. disorganized / disoriented
    b. avoidant
    c. resistant
    d. secure

20. A toddler who gives a crying playmate a toy is demonstrating an early sign of (p. 279)
    a. social referencing.
    b. self-control.
    c. compliance.
    d. empathy.

PRACTICE TEST #2

1. According to Erikson, during the second year of life, toddlers must resolve the psychological conflict of (p. 251)
   a. intimacy versus isolation.
   b. basic trust versus mistrust.
   c. identity versus role confusion.
   d. autonomy versus shame and doubt.

2. Which of the following would MOST likely evoke a smile in a 1-week-old infant? (p. 253)
   a. sleep
   b. a game of peek-a-boo
   c. a raspberry kiss on her tummy
   d. a bright red circle that jumps suddenly across her field of vision

3. Which of the following are characterized as self-conscious emotions? (p. 254)
   a. shame and embarrassment
   b. fear and anger
   c. interest and surprise
   d. happiness and sadness

4. Research shows that Efe infants raised in Zaire (p. 255)
   a. display far greater stranger anxiety than do their city-reared counterparts as a result of widespread violence.
   b. display wariness of strangers among adults, a consequence of frequent terrorist attacks.
   c. show little stranger anxiety because they are carried around in cloth sacks harnessed to their mothers.
   d. show little stranger anxiety because of a collective caregiving system in which babies are passed from one adult to another.

5. While visiting at his grandparents' home for the first time, 1-year-old Sidney crawled towards an unfamiliar toy and glanced back at his mother. Sidney saw his mother smiling, so he began to play with the toy. In deciding whether to play with the toy, Sidney engaged in (p. 255)
   a. recursive thought.
   b. social referencing.
   c. social comparisons.
   d. emotional self-regulation.

6. Baby Jason's mother is shaking a brightly colored rattle in front of his face. Overwhelmed by the rattle, Jason turns his head away. By turning his head away from the unpleasant stimulation, Jason is demonstrating (p. 256)
   a. emotional self-regulation.
   b. social problem solving.
   c. self-conscious emotions.
   d. social referencing.

7. _____ and _____ are essential ingredients in the emergence of self-conscious emotions at the end of the second year. (p. 256)
   a. Self-awareness; adult instruction in when to feel self-conscious emotions
   b. Self-esteem; recursive thought
   c. Emotional self-regulation; advanced perspective-taking skills
   d. Self-concept; identity achievement

8. Infants who more readily turn away from unpleasant stimuli (p. 257)
   a. are less prone to distress.
   b. experience greater distress than other babies.
   c. tend to have an anxious, reactive temperament.
   d. often have parents who fail to regulate stressful experiences.

9. When Samantha was a baby, she was quick to establish a regular sleep-wake-feeding cycle. As a preschooler, she is generally cheerful and adapts easily to unfamiliar experiences. In Thomas and Chess's research, Samantha would most likely be classified as (p. 258)
    a. easy.
    b. popular.
    c. uninhibited.
    d. securely attached.

10. Which of the following is more likely to be found in shy, inhibited children than in highly sociable, uninhibited children? (p. 260)
    a. a higher heart rate in the first few weeks of life
    b. lower levels of amygdala activity in response to novel stimuli
    c. a drop in blood pressure in response to novelty
    d. lower concentration of cortisol in saliva

11. Research shows that children with difficult temperaments are at risk for later adjustment problems because they are far less likely than children with easy temperaments to receive sensitive caregiving. This finding supports the notion of (p. 263)
    a. interactional synchrony.
    b. authoritative parenting.
    c. internal working model.
    d. goodness-of-fit.

12. Research with rhesus monkeys reared with terry-cloth and wire-mesh "surrogate mothers" indicated that (p. 265)
    a. baby monkeys reared with wire-mesh "mothers" developed strong emotional ties to cuddly objects, such as blankets and teddy bears.
    b. the behaviorist explanation of attachment, which assumes that the mother–infant relationship is built on emotional rewards, is correct.
    c. baby monkeys preferred to cling to a wire-mesh "mother" that held a bottle instead of a terry-cloth "mother."
    d. the drive-reduction explanation of attachment is incorrect.

13. According to Bowlby, infants in the phase of "clearcut" attachment (p. 266)
    a. are easily comforted when picked up, rocked, or talked to softly by any adult.
    b. no longer display separation anxiety when the familiar caregiver leaves.
    c. use the familiar caregiver as a secure base from which to explore.
    d. no longer exhibit stranger anxiety in response to unfamiliar adults.

14. Studies of institutionalized infants indicate that (p. 267)
    a. infants fail to form close emotional bonds with caregivers when adopted after the first year of life.
    b. institutionalized infants experience fully normal development, even in the absence of close attachment relationships.
    c. when infants are adopted in early childhood, they easily formed strong attachments to caregivers and cease to exhibit further social and emotional problems.
    d. children adopted as late as 4 to 6 years of age are able to form a first attachment bond, although they continue to display emotional and social problems.

15. Insecurely attached infants who become adults with insecure internal working models often report (p. 272)
    a. having lives fraught with family crises.
    b. low levels of life satisfaction.
    c. having little social supports.
    d. career difficulties.

16. Research on attachment shows that a special form of communication called _____ distinguishes the experiences of secure and insecure babies. (p. 269)
    a. goodness-of-fit
    b. social referencing
    c. child-directed speech
    d. interactional synchrony

17. Research on child care and attachment security indicates that (p. 272)
    a. most infants of employed mothers are insecurely attached.
    b. early, extensive child care has a far stronger impact on preschoolers' problem behavior than does parenting.
    c. in some cases, the avoidant attachment pattern may represent healthy autonomy rather than insecurity.
    d. child care, over and above the effects of sensitivity of caregiving at home, predicts attachment insecurity during infancy.

18. Research on attachment and later development found that children who were avoidantly attached as infants were rated by their preschool teachers as (p. 277)
    a. isolated and disconnected.
    b. disruptive and difficult.
    c. resourceful and ambitious.
    d. inattentive and impulsive.

19. Two-year-old Isabella has a red dot on her nose. When she looks into a mirror she tries to rub the dot off of her own nose. This behavior indicates that she has developed a(n) (p. 278)
    a. me-self.
    b. inner-self.
    c. categorical-self.
    d. remembered-self.

20. The capacity to resist the momentary impulse to engage in a socially disapproved behavior is known as (p. 280)
    a. self-awareness.
    b. self-esteem.
    c. self-control.
    d. self-regulation.

CHAPTER 8
PHYSICAL DEVELOPMENT
IN EARLY CHILDHOOD

BRIEF CHAPTER SUMMARY

Compared to infancy, body size increases more slowly during early childhood, and the child's shape becomes more streamlined. The brain continues to grow faster than other parts of the body. The cortex, especially, shows gains in myelinization and formation of synapses, followed by synaptic pruning. Hand preference strengthens, a sign of greater brain lateralization. In addition, connections between different parts of the brain increase. These changes support improvements in a wide variety of physical and cognitive skills.

Factors affecting physical growth and health in infancy and toddlerhood continue to be influential in early childhood. Heredity affects physical growth by regulating the production of hormones. Extreme emotional deprivation can interfere with the production of growth hormone, thereby stunting children's growth. Sleep difficulties, in the form of night waking and nightmares, are common during the preschool years. Appetite declines due to a slower rate of physical growth. Since caloric intake is reduced, preschoolers need a high-quality diet. Disease can lead to malnutrition, seriously undermining children's growth, an effect that is especially common in developing countries. Unintentional injuries are the leading cause of childhood death. Efforts at several levels, including laws that promote safety, improvement of community environments, and efforts to change parents' and children's behavior, are necessary.

An explosion of new motor skills takes place in early childhood. Gross motor skills such as running, jumping, throwing, and catching appear and become better coordinated. Gains in fine motor development can be seen in preschoolers' ability to dress themselves, draw representational pictures, and print letters of the alphabet. As in other areas, heredity and environment combine to influence early childhood motor development.

LEARNING OBJECTIVES

After reading this chapter, you should be able to:

8.1 Describe changes in body size, body proportions, and skeletal maturity during early childhood, and discuss asynchronies in physical growth. (pp. 288–290)

8.2 Discuss brain development in early childhood, including synaptic growth and pruning, lateralization and handedness, and other advances in brain development that help to establish links between parts of the brain. (pp. 290–293)

8.3 Describe the factors affecting physical growth and health during early childhood, noting the impact of heredity and hormones, emotional well-being, sleep habits and problems, nutrition, infectious disease, and childhood injury. (pp. 293–302)

8.4 Summarize individual, family, community, and societal factors related to childhood injuries, and describe ways to prevent them. (pp. 302–303)

8.5 Cite major milestones of gross and fine motor development in early childhood. (pp. 304–309)

8.6 Discuss individual differences in early childhood motor skills, and cite ways to enhance early motor development. (pp. 309–310)

STUDY QUESTIONS

Body Growth

1. True or False: In contrast to the rapid increases in body size seen during infancy, early childhood is marked by a slower pattern of growth. (p. 288)

2. On average, children add _____ to _____ inches in height and about _____ pounds in weight each year. (p. 288)

3. True or False: Growth norms and trends in body size are cross-culturally consistent. (p. 288)

Skeletal Growth

1. Between ages 2 and 6, approximately 45 new _____, or growth centers in which cartilage hardens into bone, emerge in various parts of the skeleton. (p. 288)

2. Explain how both genetics and environment influence the age at which children lose their primary, or "baby," teeth. (pp. 288–289)

   Genetics: _____

   _____

   Environment: _____

   _____

Asynchronies in Physical Growth

1. Describe the *general growth curve,* which represents changes in body size from infancy to adolescence. (p. 290)

   _____

   _____

   _____

2. List two exceptions to the trend depicted by the general growth curve. (p. 290)

   A. _____

   B. _____

Brain Development

1. True or False: By 4 years of age, the child's brain has produced an overabundance of synaptic connections, contributing to the plasticity of the young brain. (pp. 290–291)

2. For most children, the (right / left) hemisphere is especially active between 3 and 6 years of age and then levels off. In contrast, activity in the (right / left) hemisphere increases steadily throughout early and middle childhood. This helps to explain the pattern of development for which two skills? (p. 291)

   A. _____   B. _____

   _____   _____

Handedness

1. By age 5, _____ percent of children prefer one hand over the other. (p. 292)

2. A strong hand preference reflects the greater capacity of one side of the brain, or the _____ *cerebral hemisphere,* to carry out skilled motor action. (p. 292)

3. True or False: The ambidextrous abilities displayed by many left-handers suggest that their brains tend to be more strongly lateralized than those of right-handers. (p. 292)

4. List three theories regarding the origins of handedness. (p. 292)

   A. _____

   _____

   B. _____

   _____

   C. _____

   _____

Other Advances in Brain Development

1. For each of the following brain structures, describe developmental changes in early childhood, and indicate their impact on children's physical and cognitive skills: (p. 293)

   Cerebellum

   Changes: _____

   _____

   Impact: _____

   _____

   Reticular Formation

   Changes: _____

   _____

   Impact: _____

   _____

   Corpus Callosum

   Changes: _____

   _____

   Impact: _____

   _____

Factors Affecting Physical Growth and Health

Heredity and Hormones

1. The _____ *gland,* located near the base of the brain, releases hormones affecting physical growth. (p. 294)

2. Describe the impact of growth hormone (GH) and thyroid stimulating hormone (TSH) on body growth, and indicate what happens when there are deficiencies of these hormones. (p. 294)

GH: _____

_____

_____

TSH: _____

_____

_____

Emotional Well-Being

1. Describe the cause and characteristics of *psychosocial dwarfism*. (p. 294)

Cause: _____

_____

Characteristics: _____

_____

_____

2. True or False: Even when children with psychosocial dwarfism are removed from their emotionally inadequate environments at an early age, they display lifelong growth hormone deficiencies and fail to grow appropriately. (p. 294)

Sleep Habits and Problems

1. Total sleep time (increases / decreases) in early childhood. (p. 295)

2. Provide three recommendations that parents can follow to help young children get a good night's sleep. (p. 295)

A. _____

B. _____

C. _____

3. Describe three sleep problems of early childhood. (pp. 295–296)

A. _____

_____

B. _____

_____

C. _____

_____

Nutrition

1. True or False: It is normal for children's appetite to decline in early childhood. (p. 296)

2. Explain how the social and emotional climate influence young children's food preferences and eating habits. (pp. 296–297)

Social: _____

_____

_____

Emotional: _____

_____

_____

3. Describe three ways to encourage healthy, varied eating in young children. (pp. 297–298)

A. _____

_____

B. _____

_____

C. _____

_____

Infectious Disease

1. Describe the bi-directional relationship between infectious disease and malnutrition. (p. 298)

_____

_____

_____

2. Most growth retardation and deaths due to diarrhea can be prevented with a nearly cost-free _____
_____, a glucose, salt, and water solution that quickly replaces fluids the body loses. (p. 298)

3. True or False: Nearly one-quarter of American preschoolers lack essential immunizations. (p. 298)

4. What are some causes of inadequate immunization in the United States? (p. 298)

_____

_____

5. Childhood illness (rises / remains the same) with child-care attendance. (p. 300)

Childhood Injuries

1. True or False: Unintentional injuries are the leading cause of childhood mortality in industrialized countries. (p. 300)

2. List the three most common causes of injury during the early childhood years. (p. 300)

A. _____

B. _____

C. _____

3. Summarize individual, family, community, and societal factors linked to childhood injury. (pp. 300–301)

Individual: _____

_____

Family: _____

_____

Community: _____

_____

Societal: _____

_____

4. Why are injury rates in the United States and Canada higher than in other developed nations? (p. 302)

_____

_____

_____

5. List at least four ways to reduce unintentional injuries in early childhood. (pp. 302–303)

A. _____

B. _____

C. _____

D. _____

Cultural Influences:
Child Health Care in the United States and Other Western Nations

1. Describe the relationship between socioeconomic status and health care coverage in the United States, noting how this impacts child development. (p. 299)

Relationship: _____

_____

_____

Impact: _____

_____

_____

2. Describe child health care initiatives in the Netherlands and Norway, two countries whose services stand in sharp contrast to those available in the United States. (p. 299)

Netherlands: _____

_____

_____

Norway: _____

_____

_____

3. Describe the State Children's Health Insurance Program (SCHIP), and note some of the problems with this health initiative. (p. 299)

Program: _____

_____

_____

Problems: _____

_____

_____

Social Issues: Health:
Otitis Media and Development

1. Discuss the impact of otitis media on language development and academic functioning. (p. 301)

_____

_____

_____

_____

2. List three factors linked to increased rates of otitis media. (p. 301)

A. _____

B. _____

C. _____

3. Describe four ways of preventing otitis media. (p. 301)

A. _____

_____

B. _____

_____

C. _____

_____

D. _____

_____

Motor Development

1. Which principle that governed motor development in the first 2 years continues to operate in early childhood? (p. 304)

   _____

Gross Motor Development

1. As children's bodies become more streamlined and their center of gravity shifts downward, _____ improves greatly, paving the way for new motor skills involving large muscles of the body. (p. 304)

2. Match the following sets of gross motor developments with the ages at which they are typically acquired. (p. 305)

   _____ Walks up stairs with alternating feet; flexes upper body when jumping and hopping; throws with slight involvement of upper body, still catches against chest; pedals and steers tricycle

   _____ Walks down stairs with alternating feet; gallops; throws ball with transfer of weight on feet; catches with hands; rides tricycle rapidly, steers smoothly

   _____ Hurried walk changes to true run; jumps, hops, throws, and catches with rigid upper body; little steering

   _____ Engages in true skipping; displays mature throwing and catching style; rides bicycle with training wheels

   1. 2 to 3 years
   2. 3 to 4 years
   3. 4 to 5 years
   4. 5 to 6 years

Fine Motor Development

1. To parents, fine motor development is most evident in which two areas? (p. 306)

   A. _____   B. _____

2. Match the following sets of fine motor developments with the ages at which they are typically acquired. (pp. 306–309)

   _____ Draws first tadpole image of a person; copies vertical line and circle; uses scissors; fastens and unfastens large buttons

   _____ Draws a person with six parts; copies some numbers and words; ties shoes; uses knife

   _____ Copies triangle, cross, and some letters; cuts along line with scissors; uses fork effectively

   _____ Scribbles gradually become pictures; puts on and removes simple items of clothing; zips large zippers; uses spoon effectively

   1. 2 to 3 years
   2. 3 to 4 years
   3. 4 to 5 years
   4. 5 to 6 years

3. List and briefly describe the three-stage sequence in which drawing skills develop during early childhood. (p. 306)

   A. _____

   B. _____

   C. _____

4. Describe evidence indicating that culture has a significant impact on the development of drawing skills. (p. 308)

   _____

   _____

   _____

160

5. At approximately what age do children realize that writing stands for language? (p. 308)

_____

Individual Differences in Motor Skills

1. Discuss sex differences in motor development during early childhood. (pp. 309–310)

_____

_____

_____

_____

2. Provide an example of how social pressures might exaggerate small, genetically-based sex differences in motor skills. (p. 310)

_____

_____

Enhancing Early Childhood Motor Development

1. True or False: Preschoolers exposed to formal lessons in motor skills are generally more advanced in their motor development than same-age peers who do not take such lessons. (p. 310)

2. List three ways to foster young children's motor development. (p. 311)

A. _____

B. _____

C. _____

ASK YOURSELF . . .

For *Ask Yourself* questions for this chapter, please log on to the Companion Website at *www.ablongman.com/berk*.

SUGGESTED STUDENT READINGS

Beaty, J. J. (2003). *Safety in preschool programs.* Upper Saddle River, NJ: Prentice Hall. Presents strategies for creating safe environments for preschoolers. Topics include: how to make young children feel safe in preschool programs, common childhood fears and ways to alleviate those fears, and how to prepare children for emergencies. This book is an excellent resource for anyone interested in early childhood education, health education, psychology, or related fields.

Endres, J., Mense, C. G., & Rockwell, R. (2003). *Food, nutrition, and the young child.* Upper Saddle River, NJ: Prentice Hall. Based on up-to-date research on child development, this book examines topics surrounding food and nutrition in children from birth through age 8. The authors address common food and nutrition problems in young children, ways to foster healthy eating habits, and the importance of parent and educator involvement in child health and nutrition.

Stores, G. (2001). *Clinical guide to sleep disorders in children and adolescents.* New York: Cambridge University Press. A comprehensive source of information about sleep disorders that cause great distress to children and their families. Discusses causes and health consequences of sleep problems and early identification and treatment.

PUZZLE 8.1 TERM REVIEW

Across

5. The _____ gland, located near the base of the brain, releases hormones affecting physical growth.
6. Corpus _____: large bundle of fibers that connects the two hemispheres of the brain
7. A pituitary hormone that stimulates the thyroid gland to release thyroxine, which is necessary for normal brain development and body growth (abbr.)
8. The _____ growth curve represents overall changes in body size: rapid growth during infancy, slow gains in early and middle childhood, and rapid growth once again during adolescence

Down

1. A brain structure that aids in balance and control of body movements
2. The _____ cerebral hemisphere of the brain is responsible for skilled motor action.
3. _____ formation: brain structure that maintains alertness and consciousness
4. _____ dwarfism is a growth disorder caused by extreme emotional deprivation.
8. A pituitary hormone that affects the development of all body tissues except the central nervous system and the genitals (abbr.)

162

PRACTICE TEST #1

1. During early childhood, most children add _____ in height and _____ in weight each year. (p. 288)
   a. 1 to 2 inches; 10 pounds
   b. 2 to 3 inches; 5 pounds
   c. 3 to 4 inches; 10 pounds
   d. 1 to 2 inches; 5 pounds

2. Because different body systems have their own unique, carefully timed patterns of maturation, physical development is (p. 289)
   a. an asynchronous process.
   b. a synchronous process.
   c. governed by genetic factors.
   d. governed by environmental factors.

3. During infancy and childhood, (p. 290)
   a. all internal organs follow the general growth curve.
   b. the heart grows more rapidly than any other part of the body.
   c. physical growth is rarely asynchronous.
   d. the lymph glands grow more rapidly than most other parts of the body.

4. Research on brain development demonstrates _____ during 3 to 6 years of age. (p. 291)
   a. that the left hemisphere is relatively inactive
   b. especially rapid growth in the frontal lobe
   c. a burst in activity in the right hemisphere
   d. a rapid change in density in the parietal lobe

5. Research on handedness indicates (p. 292)
   a. ordinary siblings are more likely than twins to differ in handedness.
   b. most preschoolers are ambidextrous.
   c. environmental experiences have little effect on hand preference.
   d. the brains of left-handers tend to be less strongly lateralized than those of right-handers.

6. The _____ is involved in balance and control of body movement. (p. 293)
   a. frontal lobe
   b. reticular formation
   c. cerebellum
   d. corpus callosum

7. When short, normal-GH children are given injections of synthetic GH (p. 294)
   a. their final height is increased only slightly.
   b. there is no effect on their final height.
   c. their final height is increased substantially.
   d. they show greater self-esteem and other aspects of psychological adjustment.

8. Psychosocial dwarfism is caused by (p. 294)
   a. a lack of thyroid-stimulating hormone.
   b. a deficiency in the pituitary gland.
   c. a lack of growth hormone.
   d. extreme emotional deprivation.

9. Difficulty falling asleep during early childhood is often associated with (p. 295)
   a. parent-child cosleeping.
   b. nightmares.
   c. parental problems in setting limits.
   d. neurological difficulties.

10. During the preschool years, (p. 296)
    a. there is no harm in eating a diet high in fats and salts.
    b. foods high in sugar have no affect on children's appetite for healthy foods.
    c. children require different foods than adults for a healthy diet.
    d. it is common for children's appetite to decline.

11. Children who drink little milk (p. 297)
    a. usually get enough calcium from other foods.
    b. are shorter in stature than their milk-drinking agemates.
    c. have the same risk of bone fractures as milk-drinking children.
    d. also tend to drink little juice or soda.

12. Tom's mother often tells him, "Finish your vegetables and you can have a cookie." This practice often (p. 297)
    a. makes children prefer vegetables over cookies.
    b. has no effect on children's vegetable-eating behavior.
    c. instigates children to eat their vegetables with little fuss.
    d. causes children to like the healthy food less and the treat more.

13. Worldwide, the leading cause of childhood death is (p. 298)
    a. infectious disease.
    b. chronic disease.
    c. unintentional injuries.
    d. malnutrition.

14. Oral rehydration therapy (p. 298)
    a. is expensive to administer.
    b. must be administered by trained medical personnel.
    c. saves the lives of more than 1 million children every year.
    d. is less effective than immunization in preventing childhood deaths due to diarrhea.

15. Which of the following is true concerning childhood immunizations? (pp. 299–300)
    a. All medically uninsured American children are guaranteed free immunizations.
    b. Childhood immunization rates in the United States are comparable to those in other industrialized countries.
    c. The measles-mumps-rubella vaccine has contributed to a rise in the number of children with autism.
    d. Only a minute proportion of preschoolers are not age-appropriately immunized.

16. By age 3, most children can (p. 305)
    a. dress and undress independently.
    b. use a knife to cut soft foods.
    c. take care of toileting needs by themselves.
    d. tie their shoes.

17. Children first represent objects and events on paper by (p. 306)
    a. drawing only the boundaries of objects.
    b. a "tadpole person" drawing.
    c. making gestures that leave marks.
    d. drawing stick figures.

18. Three-year-old Donovan prints the letter D in his name backwards and seems quite satisfied with his erroneous creations. Which of the following statements is most likely concerning Donovan? (p. 308)
    a. Compared to children who do not reverse letters in their printing, Donovan is more likely to become left-handed or ambidextrous.
    b. Donovan's brain is less strongly lateralized than those of children who do not reverse letters in their printing.
    c. Compared to children who do not reverse letters in their printing, Donovan is more likely to develop dyslexia.
    d. Donovan is developing normally, as many children reverse some letters in their printing well into the early elementary school years.

19. Which of the following is supported by research on the development of motor skills in early childhood? (pp. 309–310)
    a. Boys have better balance than girls.
    b. Girls can jump farther than boys.
    c. Boys can hop and skip better than girls.
    d. Girls are ahead of boys in drawing skill.

20. Which of the following is MOST likely to promote the development of fine motor skills in early childhood? (p. 310)
    a. engaging children in daily routines, such as pouring juice and dressing
    b. enrolling children in gymnastics, tumbling, and other physical exercise lessons
    c. providing play space appropriate for games like tag and hide-and-go-seek
    d. making jungle gyms, ladders, and horizontal bars available

PRACTICE TEST #2

1. Which of the following best reflects the pattern of growth during early childhood? (p. 288)
   a. Girls tend to be slightly larger than boys.
   b. Growth occurs more slowly than in infancy and toddlerhood.
   c. Body fat increases compared to infancy and toddlerhood.
   d. Individual differences in body size become less apparent than in infancy and toddlerhood.

2. X-rays of _____ permit doctors to estimate children's progress toward physical maturity. (p. 288)
   a. epiphyses
   b. growth cells
   c. fontanels
   d. cartilage cells

3. _____ does not follow the general growth curve. Rather, it grows at an astounding pace in infancy and childhood but declines in adolescence. (p. 290)
   a. The respiratory system
   b. The lymph tissue
   c. The skeletal system
   d. The central nervous system

4. _____ reduces the plasticity of the brain during childhood. (pp. 290–291)
   a. Myelination of the cerebellum
   b. Cerebral compression
   c. Synaptic pruning
   d. Lateralization of the corpus callosum

5. The more rapid growth of the left cerebral hemisphere between 3 and 6 years of age supports young children's rapidly developing _____ skills. (p. 291)
   a. spatial
   b. gross motor
   c. language
   d. fine motor

6. Which of the following is true about left-handed people? (p. 292)
   a. For left-handed people, language is housed in the right hemisphere.
   b. The brains of left-handers tend to be more strongly lateralized than those of right-handers.
   c. Language is often shared between the hemispheres in left-handed people.
   d. Singletons are more likely than twins to be left-handed.

7. During early childhood, fibers linking the cerebellum to the cerebral cortex myelinate, enhancing _____. (p. 293)
   a. balance and motor control
   b. language skills
   c. memory abilities
   d. emotional self-regulation

8. The pituitary gland plays a critical role in growth by releasing which two hormones? (p. 294)
   a. estrogen and testosterone
   b. progesterone and thyroxine
   c. oxytocin and corticotropin-releasing hormone
   d. growth hormone and thyroid-stimulating hormone

9. A decline in appetite during the preschool years (p. 296)
   a. indicates a deficiency of thyroxine.
   b. suggests a pituitary hormone disorder.
   c. is an early sign of deprivation dwarfism.
   d. occurs because growth has slowed.

10. On the average, 2- and 3- year olds need _____ hours of sleep and 4- to 6-year-olds need _____ hours. (p. 295)
    a. 14 to 15; 8 to 9
    b. 12 to 13; 10 to 11
    c. 10 to 11; 8 to 9
    d. 14 to 15; 10 to 11

11. Three-year-old Allison won't eat yogurt—a food that she has never eaten before. What should Allison's parents do to increase her willingness to eat the yogurt? (p. 297)
    a. They should add some sugar to the yogurt at first, and then take away the sugar once Allison has accepted the yogurt.
    b. They should reward her with a food that she does like, such as a cookie, if she agrees to eat the yogurt.
    c. They should forbid access to all other foods until she gets hungry enough to eat the yogurt.
    d. They should repeatedly expose Allison to the yogurt without any direct pressure to eat it.

12. The leading cause of deaths in children under age 5 in developing countries is (p. 298)
    a. infectious diseases.
    b. unintentional injuries.
    c. birth defects.
    d. cancer.

13. Compared to other industrialized countries, such as Canada, Denmark, and Sweden, the rate of childhood immunization is low in the United States because (p. 298)
    a. medically uninsured American children do not receive free immunizations.
    b. of the relatively higher rate of unemployment of American parents.
    c. government-sponsored health services are not offered to all children.
    d. of the relatively higher rate of poverty-stricken American children.

14. Fifty percent of early childhood drownings take place in (p. 302)
    a. public swimming pools.
    b. lakes.
    c. backyard swimming pools.
    d. the ocean.

15. Frequent episodes of otitis media hinder academic progress by (p. 301)
    a. interfering with myelination of neural fibers.
    b. impeding the ability to recognize letters.
    c. causing sleep difficulties.
    d. causing difficulties in hearing speech sounds.

16. Between the ages of 2 and 3, most children learn how to (p. 305)
    a. jump several inches off the floor with both feet.
    b. pedal and steer a tricycle.
    c. walk up stairs with alternating feet.
    d. catch a ball with their hands.

17. Around age 3 or 4, children use a tadpole form to draw their first picture of a person. This universal form mainly is due to the limits of the preschooler's (p. 306)
    a. representational thought.
    b. preoperational egocentrism.
    c. spatial understanding.
    d. fine motor skills.

18. Gross motor development involves improvement in the child's ability to (p. 307)
    a. put puzzles together.
    b. throw and catch a ball.
    c. build with small blocks.
    d. cut and paste.

19. Gains in fine motor development are due to increased control of the (pp. 309–310)
    a. arms and legs.
    b. hands and fingers.
    c. legs and feet.
    d. torso.

20. Direct instruction in which of the following activities is MOST likely to accelerate motor development in early childhood? (p. 310)
    a. throwing
    b. jumping
    c. running
    d. climbing

CHAPTER 9
COGNITIVE DEVELOPMENT
IN EARLY CHILDHOOD

BRIEF CHAPTER SUMMARY

Early childhood brings dramatic advances in mental representation. Aside from the development of language and make-believe play, Piaget's description of the preoperational stage emphasizes young children's cognitive limitations. Newer research reveals that preschoolers show the beginnings of logical, reflective thought when tasks are simplified and made relevant to their everyday experiences. Piaget's theory has had a powerful influence on education, promoting child-oriented approaches to teaching and learning.

Whereas Piaget believed that language is of little importance in cognitive development, Vygotsky regarded it as the foundation for all higher cognitive processes. As adults and more skilled peers provide children with verbal guidance on challenging tasks, children incorporate these dialogues into their self-directed speech and use them to regulate their own behavior. A Vygotskian classroom emphasizes assisted discovery, including verbal support from teachers and peer collaboration.

A variety of information-processing skills improve during early childhood. With age, preschoolers sustain attention for longer periods of time, and their recognition memory becomes highly accurate. Recall develops more slowly because preschoolers are not yet effective users of memory strategies. Like adults, young children remember everyday events in a logical, well-organized fashion, and their memory for special, one-time events improves. Preschoolers also make great strides in problem-solving skills, generating a variety of strategies for finding solutions. Around the same time, children begin to construct a set of beliefs about mental activities. Through informal experiences, preschoolers also develop a basic understanding of written symbols and mathematical concepts.

A stimulating home environment, warm parenting, and reasonable demands for mature behavior continue to predict mental development in early childhood. Formal academic training in early childhood undermines motivation and other aspects of emotional well-being. Although test score gains resulting from early intervention such as Head Start eventually decline, at-risk children show long-term benefits in school adjustment. High-quality child care can serve as effective intervention, whereas poor-quality child care undermines children's development regardless of SES background. Language development proceeds at a rapid pace during early childhood. By the end of the preschool years, children have an extensive vocabulary, use most of the grammatical constructions of their language competently, and are effective conversationalists. Opportunities for conversational give-and-take with adults enhance these skills.

LEARNING OBJECTIVES

After reading this chapter, you should be able to:

9.1 Describe advances in mental representation during the preschool years, including changes in make-believe play. (pp. 316–318)

9.2 Describe what Piaget believed to be the deficiencies of preoperational thought. (pp. 319–321)

9.3 Discuss recent research on preoperational thought and note the implications of such findings for the accuracy of Piaget's preoperational stage. (pp. 321–326)

9.4 Describe three educational principles derived from Piaget's theory. (pp. 327–328)

9.5 Contrast Piaget's view of children's private speech with that of Vygotsky. (p. 329)

9.6 Describe features of social interaction that foster cognitive development. (pp. 329–331)

9.7 Discuss how Vygotsky's ideas have been applied in educational settings. (p. 331)

9.8 Summarize recent challenges to Vygotsky's theory. (p. 331)

9.9 Describe the development of attention, memory, and problem solving during early childhood. (pp. 333–336)

9.10 Discuss preschoolers' understanding of mental activities, noting factors that contribute to early metacognition, as well as limitations of the young child's theory of mind. (pp. 336–338)

9.11 Describe early literacy and mathematical development during the preschool years, and discuss appropriate ways to enhance children's development in those areas. (pp. 338–342)

9.12 Describe the nature of early childhood intelligence tests, and explain the impact of home environment, preschool and child care, and educational television on mental development. (pp. 343–348)

9.13 Trace the development of vocabulary, grammar, and conversational skills in preschool children, and cite factors that support language development in early childhood. (pp. 348–353)

STUDY QUESTIONS

Piaget's Theory: The Preoperational Stage

1. As children move from the sensorimotor to the preoperational stage, the most obvious change is an extraordinary increase in _____. (p. 316)

Advances in Mental Representation

1. True or False: Piaget believed that language plays a major role in cognitive development. (p. 316)

Make-Believe Play

1. List three important changes in make-believe play during early childhood, and give an example of each. (p. 317)

   A. _____

   _____

   Example: _____

   B. _____

   _____

   Example: _____

   C. _____

   _____

   Example: _____

2. What is *sociodramatic play*? (p. 317)

   _____

   _____

3. Summarize contributions of make-believe play to children's cognitive and social development. (pp. 317–318)

Cognitive: _____

_____

_____

Social: _____

_____

_____

4. True or False: Recent research indicates that the creation of imaginary companions is a sign of maladjustment. (p. 318)

5. Describe three ways to enhance preschoolers' make-believe play. (p. 318)

A. _____

_____

B. _____

_____

C. _____

_____

Symbol–Real World Relations

1. _____ refers to the ability to view a symbolic object as both an object in its own right and a symbol. Provide an example, and note the age at which children typically acquire this understanding. (p. 319)

Example: _____

_____

Age: _____

2. How do children learn to understand the concept of dual representation? (p. 319)

_____

_____

Limitations of Preoperational Thought

1. Piaget described preschoolers in terms of what they (can / cannot) understand. (p. 319)

2. According to Piaget, young children are not capable of _____ , or mental actions that obey logical rules. (p. 319)

3. Piaget believed that _____, the inability to distinguish the symbolic viewpoints of others from one's own, is the most serious deficiency of preoperational thought. (p. 319)

4. The preoperational belief that inanimate objects have lifelike qualities, such as thoughts, wishes, and intentions, is called _____. (p. 320)

5. What is *conservation*? (p. 320)

_____

_____

6. Briefly describe three aspects of preoperational children's thought which are highlighted by their inability to conserve. (p. 321)

A. _____

_____

B. _____

_____

C. _____

_____

7. The most illogical feature of preoperational thought is _____, an inability to mentally go through a series of steps in a problem and then reverse direction, returning to the starting point. (p. 321)

8. What is *hierarchical classification*? (p. 321)

_____

_____

Follow-Up Research on Preoperational Thought

1. True or False: Current research supports Piaget's account of a cognitively deficient preschooler. (p. 321)

2. Cite two examples of nonegocentric responses in preschoolers' everyday interactions. (p. 321)

A. _____

B. _____

3. Describe the circumstances in which children are likely to make errors on problems that tap animistic thinking. (p. 322)

_____

_____

4. Between 4 and 8 years of age, as familiarity with physical events and principles increases, children's magical beliefs (increase / decline). (p. 322)

5. True or False: When preschoolers are given tasks that are simplified and made relevant to their everyday lives, they show less evidence of illogical thought than Piaget suggested. (p. 322)

6. Explain the sequence of children's categorical understanding across the early childhood years. (pp. 323–325)

_____

_____

_____

_____

7. What factor largely accounts for young children's difficulty on appearance–reality problems? (p. 326)

_____

Evaluation of the Preoperational Stage

1. The finding that logical operations develop gradually across the preschool years (supports / challenges) Piaget's stage concept. (p. 326)

2. Some neo-Piagetian theorists combine Piaget's stage concept with the information-processing emphasis on task-specific change. Briefly describe this viewpoint. (p. 327)

_____

_____

_____

Piaget and Early Childhood Education

1. List and describe three educational principles derived from Piaget's theory. (pp. 327–328)

   A. _____

   _____

   B. _____

   _____

   C. _____

   _____

Social Issues: Education: Young Children's Understanding of Death

1. Name and describe the three components of the death concept, listing them in the order in which they develop. (p. 324)

   A. _____

   _____

   B. _____

   _____

   C. _____

   _____

2. Most children grasp the three components of the death concept by age _____. (p. 324)

3. Describe two aspects of culture which influence children's understanding of death. (p. 324)

   A. _____

   _____

   B. _____

   _____

4. Explain how adults can help children develop an accurate understanding of death. (p. 324)

_____

_____

_____

Vygotsky's Sociocultural Theory

1. True or False: Vygotsky placed a greater emphasis than did Piaget on the role of language in cognitive development. (p. 328)

Children's Private Speech

1. Contrast Piaget's view of children's private speech with that of Vygotsky. (p. 329)

Piaget: _____

_____

Vygotsky: _____

_____

2. Most research findings have supported (Piaget's / Vygotsky's) view of children's private speech. (p. 329)

3. Under what circumstances are children likely to use private speech? (p. 329)

_____

_____

Social Origins of Early Childhood Cognition

1. Vygotsky believed that children's learning takes place within a *zone of proximal development.* Explain what this means. (p. 329)

_____

_____

2. Explain how two features of social interaction, *intersubjectivity* and *scaffolding,* facilitate children's cognitive development. (p. 330)

Intersubjectivity: _____

_____

Scaffolding: _____

_____

3. Define the term *guided participation*, noting how it differs from scaffolding. (p. 330)

_____

_____

_____

4. State the features of effective adult scaffolding which foster children's private speech and task success. (p. 330)

_____

_____

_____

Vygotsky and Early Childhood Education

1. What features do Piagetian and Vygotskian classrooms have in common? On which features do they differ? (p. 331)

   A. _____

   _____

   B. _____

   _____

2. Vygotsky saw _____ as the ideal social context for fostering cognitive development in early childhood. (p. 331)

Evaluation of Vygotsky's Theory

1. Discuss two contributions and two criticisms of Vygotsky's theory of cognitive development. (p. 331)

   Contributions:

   A. _____

   _____

   B. _____

   _____

   Criticisms:

   A. _____

   _____

   B. _____

   _____

Cultural Influences:
Children in Village and Tribal Cultures Observe and Participate in Adult Work

1. Summarize cultural differences in children's access to and participation in adult work, providing examples from American, Efe, and Mayan cultures. (p. 332)

   American: _____

   _____

   _____

   Efe: _____

   _____

   _____

Mayan: _____

_____

_____

2. Explain how cultural differences in young children's daily participation in adult work affects their competencies and behavior. (p. 332)

_____

_____

_____

_____

Information Processing

Attention

1. At what age do children display a sharp increase in sustained attention, and what factors are responsible for this change? (p. 333)

    Age: _____

    Factors: _____

    _____

2. Describe preschoolers' ability to plan, including what they are likely to plan well, as well as limitations in their planning. (p. 333)

    Planning abilities:

    _____

    _____

    Limitations:

    _____

    _____

Memory

1. Preschoolers' recall memory is much (better / worse) than their recognition memory. Why is this the case? (p. 334)

    _____

    _____

    _____

2. Explain why preschoolers are ineffective at using memory strategies. (p. 334)

    _____

    _____

3. What is *episodic memory*? (p. 334)

_____

_____

4. Like adults, preschoolers remember familiar experiences in terms of _____, general descriptions of what occurs and when it occurs in a particular situation. What are two benefits of using this strategy to aid memory and recall? (pp. 334–335)

   A. _____

   B. _____

5. Explain the two styles, elaborative and repetitive, which are used by adults to elicit children's autobiographical narratives, and note which style leads to better memory of events over time. (p. 335)

   Elaborative: _____

   _____

   Repetitive: _____

   _____

Problem Solving

1. Describe Siegler's *overlapping-waves theory* of problem solving. (p. 335)

   _____

   _____

   _____

2. List several factors that facilitate children's movement from less to more efficient problem-solving strategies. (pp. 335–336)

   A. _____

   B. _____

   C. _____

The Young Child's Theory of Mind

1. A theory of mind, also called _____, is a coherent set of ideas about mental activities. (p. 336)

2. Trace changes in children's awareness of mental life from the toddler years through the preschool years. (pp. 336–337)

   _____

   _____

   _____

3.   Describe three factors that contribute to preschoolers' theory of mind. (pp. 337–338)

A. _____

_____

B. _____

_____

C. _____

_____

4.   Cite two ways in which preschoolers' awareness of inner cognitive activities is incomplete. What can we conclude about the difference between the young child's theory of mind and that of the older child? (p. 338)

A. _____

B. _____

Conclusion: _____

_____

_____

Early Literacy and Mathematical Development

1.   True or False: Preschoolers cannot understand written language until they learn to read and write. (p. 338)

2.   Explain how preschoolers' ideas about written language differ from those of adults. (p. 340)

_____

_____

_____

_____

3.   _____ refers to the ability to reflect on and manipulate the sound structure of spoken language. (p. 340)

4.   List four ways in which adults can foster literacy development in young children. (p. 340)

A. _____

B. _____

C. _____

D. _____

5.   Discuss SES differences in language and literacy learning opportunities. (pp. 340–341)

_____

_____

_____

6. List four steps in the development of preschoolers' mathematical reasoning that correspond with the following general age ranges: (pp. 341–342)

14 to 16 months:

_____

_____

2 to 3 years:

_____

_____

3 to 4 years:

_____

_____

4 to 5 years:

_____

_____

7. True or False: Basic arithmetic knowledge emerges in a universal sequence around the world. (p. 342)

Biology and Environment: Mindblindness and Autism

1. Describe three core areas of functioning in which children with autism display deficits. (p. 339)

A. _____

_____

B. _____

_____

C. _____

_____

2. Summarize theory of mind and executive processing theories of autism. (p. 339)

Theory of mind:

_____

_____

Executive processing:

_____

_____

Early Childhood Intelligence Tests

1. What types of tasks are commonly included on early childhood intelligence tests? (p. 343)

    _____

2. Why do minorities and children from low-SES homes sometimes do poorly on intelligence tests? What steps can be taken to help improve their performance? (p. 343)

    A. _____

    _____

    B. _____

    _____

3. Intelligence tests (do / do not) sample all human abilities, and performance (is / is not) affected by cultural and situational factors. (p. 343)

4. True or False: By age 6 or 7, scores on early childhood intelligence tests are good predictors of later IQ and academic achievement. (p. 343)

Home Environment and Mental Development

1. Describe the characteristics of homes that foster young children's intellectual growth. (p. 343)

    _____

    _____

    _____

2. Research suggests that the home environment (does / does not) play a major role in the generally poorer intellectual performance of low-SES children in comparison to their higher-SES peers. Briefly elaborate on your response. (pp. 343–344)

    _____

    _____

Preschool, Kindergarten, and Child Care

1. Currently, _____ percent of American and _____ percent of Canadian preschool-age children have mothers who are employed. (p. 344)

2. A _____ is a program with planned educational experiences aimed at enhancing the development of 2- to 5-year-olds. In contrast, _____ identifies a variety of arrangements for supervising children of employed parents. (p. 344)

3. Describe the difference between child-centered preschools and academic preschools. (p. 345)

    Child-centered:

    _____

    _____

Academic:

_____

_____

4. True or False: Children in academic preschools demonstrate higher levels of achievement than those in child-centered preschools, including greater mastery of motor, academic, language, and social skills. (p. 345)

5. Summarize the goal and program components of *Project Head Start* and Canada's *Aboriginal Head Start.* (p. 345)

   Goal: _____

   Components of the program:

   _____

   _____

   _____

6. Describe the long-term impact of preschool intervention on low-SES children's development, comparing outcomes of university-based programs with those of Head Start programs. (pp. 345–346)

   _____

   _____

   _____

   _____

7. True or False: Research suggests that gains in IQ and achievement scores following attendance at Head Start and other early intervention programs are maintained across the school years. (p. 346)

8. Explain the *two-generation approach* to early intervention. (p. 346)

   _____

   _____

   _____

9. True or False: Preschoolers exposed to poor-quality child care, regardless of family SES level, score lower on measures of cognitive and social skills. (p. 346)

10. List four characteristics of high quality child care. (p. 346)

    A. _____

    B. _____

    C. _____

    D. _____

Educational Media

1. The average 2- to 6-year-old watches TV for _____ hours a day. (p. 347)

2. Describe the benefits of watching educational programs, such as *Sesame Street.* (p. 347)

   _____

   _____

   _____

3. Summarize the benefits children receive from using high quality educational computer programs. (p. 348)

_____

_____

_____

4. What does research reveal about the effects of heavy TV viewing on children's cognitive development? (p. 348)

_____

_____

Language Development

Vocabulary

1. True or False: Preschoolers learn an average of 5 new words each day, increasing their vocabulary from 200 words at age two to 10,000 words at age six. (p. 348)

2. Explain how children build their vocabularies so quickly over the preschool years. (p. 349)

_____

_____

_____

3. The principle of _____ refers to an assumption made by children in the early stages of vocabulary growth that words refer to entirely separate (nonoverlapping) categories. (p. 349)

4. When children figure out the meaning of a word by observing how it is used in the structure of a sentence, they are using _____ *bootstrapping.* (p. 349)

5. Preschool children (are / are not) able to effectively use social cues to identify word meanings. (p. 349)

Grammar

1. True or False: English-speaking children show wide variability in the sequence in which they master grammatical markers. (p. 350)

2. When children overextend grammatical rules to words that are exceptions—for example, saying "I runned fast" instead of "I ran fast"—they are making an error called _____. (p. 350)

3. True or False: By the end of the preschool years, children have mastered most of the grammatical constructions of their language. (pp. 350–351)

4. Describe at least two differing perspectives in the debate over how children acquire grammar. (p. 351)

   A. _____

   _____

   B. _____

   _____

Conversation

1. The practical, social side of language that is concerned with how to engage in effective and appropriate communication with others is known as _____. (p. 351)

2. Preschoolers (are / are not) capable of effective communication, such as initiating conversation, responding appropriately to another's comments, and conversational turn-taking. (p. 351)

3. True or False: Having an older sibling facilitates the acquisition of pragmatic language. (p. 351)

4. Preschoolers (do / do not) adjust their speech to fit the age, sex, and social status of their listeners. (p. 352)

5. Explain the conditions in which preschoolers are likely to experience a break down of conversational skills. (p. 352)

_____

_____

_____

Supporting Language Learning in Early Childhood

1. Explain how adults can use *expansions* and *recasts* to promote preschoolers' language development. (p. 352)

Expansions: _____

_____

Recasts: _____

_____

ASK YOURSELF . . .

For *Ask Yourself* questions for this chapter, please log on to the Companion Website at *www.ablongman.com/berk*.

SUGGESTED STUDENT READINGS

Berk, L. E. (2001). *Awakening children's minds: How parents and teachers can make a difference.* New York: Oxford University Press. Written for parents and teachers of young children, this book provides an overview of current theories of child development, straightforward advice for child rearing, and suggestions for concrete practice. Moreover, the author stresses the importance of parents and teachers in the development of competent, caring, and well-adjusted children.

Neuman, S. B., Copple, C., & Bredekamp, S. (2001). *Learning to read and write: Developmentally appropriate practice for young children.* Washington, DC: National Association of Young Children. Firmly grounded in empirical research, this book presents developmentally appropriate practice for fostering early literacy development in young children. Also included are guidelines and suggestions for ensuring that all children learn to read and write by the end of the third grade.

Roskos, K. A., & Christie, J. F. (Eds.). (2000). *Play and literacy in early childhood: Research for multiple perspectives.* Mahwah, NJ: Lawrence Erlbaum Associates. Explores the relationship between play and literacy by drawing on research from cognitive, ecological, and cultural perspectives. Also accompanying each chapter is a critical review of research by leading scholars in the field of child development.

PUZZLE 9.1 TERM REVIEW

Across

1. A changing quality of support over the course of a teaching session in which the adult adjusts the assistance provided to fit the child's current level of performance
5. Mental representations of actions that obey logical rules
6. Memory for everyday experiences
9. Tendency to focus on one aspect of a situation and neglect other important features
11. _____ participation calls attention to adult and child contributions to cooperative dialogue without specifying the precise features of communication.
13. Mutual _____ bias: assumption that words refer to entirely separate categories
14. Understanding that certain physical features of an object remain the same, even when their outward appearance changes
17. _____ classification: organization of objects into classes and subclasses based on similarities and differences
18. Process whereby two participants who begin a task with different understandings arrive at a shared understanding
19. Thinking out a sequence of acts ahead of time and allocating attention accordingly to reach a goal

Down

2. _____ thinking: the belief that inanimate objects have lifelike qualities
3. The inability to mentally go through a series of steps and then reverse direction, returning to the starting point
4. Make-believe play with others
7. Piaget's second stage; marked by rapid growth in representation
8. Thinking about thought
10. The inability to distinguish the symbolic viewpoints of others from one's own
12. Memory _____: deliberate mental activities that improve our chances of remembering
15. _____ representation: representations of a symbolic object as both an object in its own right and a symbol
16. General descriptions of what occurs and when it occurs in a particular situation

184

PUZZLE 9.2 TERM REVIEW

Across

1. Principle specifying order relationships between quantities
2. The practical, social side of language that is concerned with how to engage in effective and appropriate communication with others
3. Adult responses that elaborate on a child's utterance, increasing its complexity
5. Fast _____: connecting a new word with an underlying concept after only a brief encounter
7. _____ awareness: ability to reflect on and manipulate the sound structure of spoken language
8. Preschools in which the teacher structures the children's learning and teaches through formal lessons
9. _____-waves theory: children generate a variety of strategies on challenging problems and gradually select those that result in rapid, accurate solutions
11. Principle stating that the last number in a counting sequence indicates the quantity of items in the set
14. Preschools in which the teacher provides a variety of activities from which children select; most of the day is devoted to free play

Down

1. Application of regular grammatical rules to words that are exceptions
4. _____ bootstrapping: figuring out word meanings by observing how words are used in the structure of sentences
6. _____ speech: self-directed speech that children use to plan and guide their behavior
10. Adult responses that restructure children's incorrect speech into a more appropriate form
12. _____ literacy refers to young children's active efforts to construct literacy knowledge through informal experiences
13. _____ bootstrapping: figuring out grammatical rules by relying on word meanings
15. Project _____ _____ is a federal program that provides low-SES children with a year or two of preschool, along with nutritional and medical services.

185

PRACTICE TEST #1

1. Research on the development of play indicates that (p. 317)
   a. make-believe play becomes increasingly self-centered with age.
   b. children younger than 2 years tend to pretend with objects that bear little resemblance to the objects for which they stand.
   c. sociodramatic play decreases during the preschool years.
   d. preschoolers are aware that make-believe play is a representational activity.

2. In one study, 2 1/2-year-olds were unable to use a scale model of a room to find a toy hidden in the room that the model represented. This is because young preschoolers have difficulty with (p. 319)
   a. deferred imitation.
   b. analogical problem solving.
   c. transitive inference.
   d. dual representation.

3. According to Piaget, young children's thinking often is illogical because they are not capable of (p. 319)
   a. mental representations.
   b. animistic thinking.
   c. operations.
   d. accommodation.

4. In Piaget's theory, operations are mental representations of actions that (p. 319)
   a. are stored with the benefit of language.
   b. are not open to distortion from external influences.
   c. obey logical rules.
   d. focus on the perspectives of others.

5. Three-year-old Noah thinks that planes and helicopters are alive. This is an example of (p. 320)
   a. animistic thinking.
   b. dual representation.
   c. irreversibility.
   d. centration.

6. In Piaget's theory, centration refers to preoperational children's (p. 321)
   a. tendency to focus on one aspect of a situation while neglecting other important features.
   b. inability to mentally go through a series of steps in a problem and then reverse direction.
   c. idea that certain physical characteristics of objects remain the same, even when their outward appearance changes.
   d. belief that inanimate objects have lifelike qualities.

7. According to Piaget, the most serious deficiency of preoperational thought is (p. 321)
   a. animistic thinking.
   b. egocentrism.
   c. intersubjectivity.
   d. centration.

8. Which of the following suggests that Piaget may have overestimated preschoolers' egocentrism? (p. 321)
   a. Preschoolers often attribute lifelike qualities to inanimate objects.
   b. Preschoolers are capable of forming mental representations of their experiences.
   c. Preschoolers fail to distinguish the symbolic viewpoints of others from their own.
   d. Preschoolers use simpler, shorter expressions when talking with younger children than when talking with older children or adults.

9. Follow-up research on preoperational thought suggests that preschoolers are most likely to display illogical reasoning when tasks are (p. 322)
   a. based on appearances.
   b. made relevant to their everyday lives.
   c. unfamiliar.
   d. simplified.

10. After putting on a Halloween mask and looking at their reflection in a mirror, young preschoolers often are wary. This is because they do not yet fully grasp (p. 326)
   a. hierarchical categorization.
   b. cardinality.
   c. centration.
   d. the appearance-reality distinction.

11. In Anh's preschool, she can choose freely between a number of activities where she can interact spontaneously with a wide variety of materials and play areas. This preschool emphasizes the Piagetian principle of (p. 327)
   a. scaffolding.
   b. cooperative learning.
   c. discovery learning.
   d. intersubjectivity.

12. Most research indicates that young children use private speech (p. 329)
   a. because they are egocentric.
   b. when they are engaged in cooperative dialogues.
   c. during challenging activities.
   d. when they cannot find a conversational partner.

13. According to Vygotsky's theory, two important features of social interaction are (p. 330)
   a. intersubjectivity and scaffolding.
   b. recasts and expansions.
   c. pragmatics and fast mapping.
   d. egocentrism and private speech.

14. In Vygotsky's theory, _____ refers to adjusting the support offered during a teaching session to fit the child's current level of performance. (p. 330)
   a. intersubjectivity
   b. guided participation
   c. the zone of proximal development
   d. scaffolding

15. Memory for _____ is an example of an episodic memory. (p. 334)
   a. a visit to the zoo
   b. a classmate's face
   c. a set of words
   d. the hiding place of a favorite toy

16. Children whose parents use an elaborative style to talk about the past _____ than children whose parents use a repetitive style. (p. 335)
   a. produce more detailed autobiographical narratives
   b. are better at planning
   c. have better recognition memory
   d. are more skilled in memory strategy use

17. The term metacognition means thinking about (p. 336)
    a. memory.
    b. thought.
    c. attention.
    d. strategies.

18. Emergent literacy refers to (p. 338)
    a. the automatic retrieval of word meanings in long-term memory during reading and writing tasks.
    b. a method of reading instruction that parallels children's natural language learning and keeps reading materials whole.
    c. young children's active efforts to construct literacy knowledge through information experiences.
    d. an approach to beginning reading instruction that emphasizes phonics.

19. The principle of cardinality refers to the understanding that (p. 342)
    a. reducing the value of a column by one unit and increasing the value of the column immediately to its right by ten units leaves unchanged the value of the original number.
    b. the last word in a counting sequence indicates the quantity of items in a set.
    c. adding and subtracting the same number leaves the original quantity unchanged.
    d. the most efficient addition strategy is to start with the highest digit and count on.

20. According to the syntactic bootstrapping hypothesis, children (p. 349)
    a. discover many word meanings by observing how they are used in sentences.
    b. assume that words refer to entirely separate categories.
    c. overextend many grammatical rules to words that are exceptions.
    d. rely on word meanings to figure out grammatical rules.

PRACTICE TEST #2

1. Which of the following children is likely to be older? (p. 317)
   a. Tiffany, who pretends to make a doll comb its own hair
   b. Miguel, who pretends to comb his own hair
   c. Alicia, who pretends to comb her father's hair
   d. Brady, who pretends to comb his doll's hair

2. Preschoolers who spend more time in sociodramatic play are rated by their teachers as more _____ than their peers. (p. 317)
   a. socially isolated
   b. easily distracted
   c. socially skilled
   d. at risk for developmental problems

3. At what age do children begin to realize that drawings are symbols, and to produce their first recognizable drawings? (p. 319)
   a. 2
   b. 3
   c. 4
   d. 5

4. Which of the following is 3-year-old María Luisa likely to believe is alive? (p. 320)
   a. her house
   b. a rock in the garden
   c. an airplane
   d. a magic marker

5. In the three-mountains problem, preoperational children demonstrate less egocentrism when (p. 321)
   a. familiar objects and methods are used.
   b. they are tested in a new, interesting location.
   c. the method involves picture selection.
   d. the problem is presented as a "game."

6. According to Vygotsky, children's private speech is (p. 329)
   a. not useful.
   b. egocentric.
   c. nonsocial.
   d. used for self guidance.

7. Evidence of children's capacity for intersubjectivity (p. 330)
   a. is found in nonverbal, but not verbal, communication.
   b. increases as conversational skills improve.
   c. is not apparent before the age of 3.
   d. decreases throughout the preschool years.

8. Young children in the Yucatec Mayan culture (p. 332)
   a. demonstrate elaborate make-believe play.
   b. are constantly "on call" to support adult work.
   c. are expected to be dependent on adults for making basic decisions until they start school.
   d. are raised in ways very similar to Western parenting practices.

9. A researcher placed either an M&M or a wooden peg in each of 12 containers, and handed them to a preschooler one by one. The child was asked to remember where the candy was hidden. By age 4, children (p. 334)
   a. tried to memorize which containers held M&Ms and which held pegs.
   b. used the strategy of rehearsal for this task.
   c. put the candy containers in one place and the peg containers in another place on the table.
   d. were unable to demonstrate any strategy for remembering.

10. Which of the following is an example of a young child's script for going to bed? (p. 334)
    a. "Last night there was a monster in my closet."
    b. "I want to read a story tonight before I go to bed."
    c. "Can I stay up late?"
    d. "I brush my teeth, read my story, and go to sleep."

11. Jonathan is beginning to understand that his mother's beliefs about his innocence or guilt will influence her decision to punish him or not. He is most likely between the ages (p. (p. 336)
    a. 1 and 2
    b. 2 and 3
    c. 3 and 4
    d. 4 and 5

12. Which is the correct order in which children gain mathematical reasoning? (pp. 341–342)
    a. ordinality, cardinality, counting, one-to-one correspondence
    b. ordinality, counting, one-to-one correspondence, cardinality
    c. counting, one-to-one correspondence, ordinality, cardinality
    d. counting, one-to-one correspondence, cardinality, ordinality

13. A hotly debated topic in the area of early childhood intelligence tests is the issue of (p. 343)
    a. cultural bias.
    b. children's attention spans during testing.
    c. their use for screening of developmental problems.
    d. predictive validity.

14. Mandy and Michael attend a child-centered preschool. Which of the following best describes their classroom? (p. 345)
    a. Children select from a wide variety of activities and materials during long periods of free play.
    b. Children are supervised in someone's home during the day.
    c. Children are taught letters, numbers, colors, and shapes through structured activities.
    d. Children with specific problems in pre-reading and writing skills receive one-on-one tutoring.

15. Which of the following is true of Head Start? (pp. 345–346)
    a. Children in Head Start have not been shown to make IQ gains.
    b. Any preschool-age child qualifies for Head Start.
    c. Head Start emphasizes parent involvement in the classroom.
    d. Children in Head Start are more likely to receive special education in elementary school.

16. Jeremy is 6 years old. He has acquired approximately _____ vocabulary words. (p. 348)
    a. 1,000
    b. 5,000
    c. 7,500
    d. 10,000

17. Three-year-old Layla's teacher shows her a red ball, saying, "This is a bootron one." Layla understands the unfamiliar word as an adjective that describes some property of the ball. This is known as (p. 349)
   a. overregularizing.
   b. overlapping waves theory.
   c. fast mapping.
   d. syntactic bootstrapping.

18. Five-year-old Kari is playing with a hand puppet, pretending to be a doctor. When speaking for the puppet, she is likely to use many (p. 352)
   a. commands.
   b. indirect requests.
   c. polite terms.
   d. tag questions.

19. When asked to tell a listener how to solve a simple puzzle over the phone, preschoolers (p. 352)
   a. did not understand that the listener could not see them.
   b. gave more specific directions over the phone than in person.
   c. did not give the directions, but initiated friendly conversations with the listeners.
   d. gave general directions that could not be followed.

20. Collin says, "I see truck!" His grandmother responds, "Yes, you see a big, red fire truck!" His grandmother's response would be classified as a(n) (p. 352)
   a. overregularization.
   b. script.
   c. expansion.
   d. semantic bootstrap.

CHAPTER 10
EMOTIONAL AND SOCIAL DEVELOPMENT
IN EARLY CHILDHOOD

BRIEF CHAPTER SUMMARY

Erikson's stage of initiative versus guilt offers an overview of the personality changes of early childhood. During the preschool years, children's self-concepts begin to take shape. Their self-esteem is high, which supports their enthusiasm for mastering new skills. Preschoolers' understanding of emotion, emotional self-regulation, capacity to experience self-conscious emotions, and capacity for empathy and sympathy improve. Cognition, language, and warm, sensitive parenting support these developments.

During the preschool years, peer interaction increases, cooperative play becomes common, and children form first friendships. Preschoolers learn to resolve conflicts with new social problem-solving skills. Peer relations are influenced by parental encouragement and the quality of sibling ties. Peers provide an important context for the development of a wide range of social skills.

Three approaches to understanding early childhood morality—psychoanalytic, behaviorist and social learning, and cognitive-developmental—emphasize different aspects of moral functioning. While most researchers now disagree with Freud's account of conscience development, the power of inductive discipline is recognized. Social learning theorists believe that children learn to act morally through modeling. A third voice, the cognitive-developmental perspective, regards children as active thinkers about social rules. Hostile family atmospheres, poor parenting practices, and heavy viewing of violent television promote childhood aggression, which can spiral into serious antisocial activity.

Gender typing develops rapidly over the preschool years. Heredity contributes to several aspects of gender-typed behavior, but environmental forces—parents, siblings, teachers, peers, television, and the broader social environment—play powerful roles. Neither cognitive-developmental theory nor social learning theory provides a complete account of the development of gender identity. Gender schema theory is an information-processing approach that shows how environmental pressures and children's cognition combine to affect gender-role development.

Compared to children of authoritarian and permissive parents, children whose parents use an authoritative style are especially well adjusted and socially mature. Warmth, explanations, and reasonable demands for mature behavior account for the effectiveness of the authoritative style. Ethnic groups often have distinct child-rearing beliefs and practices that are adaptive when viewed in light of cultural values and the circumstances in which parents and children live.

Child maltreatment is the combined result of factors within the family, community, and larger culture. Interventions at all of these levels are essential for preventing it.

LEARNING OBJECTIVES

After reading this chapter, you should be able to:

10.1 Describe Erikson's initiative versus guilt stage, noting how this psychological conflict impacts children's emotional and social development. (p. 358)

10.2 Discuss preschool children's self-development, including characteristics of self-concept, ability to understand intentions, and emergence of self-esteem. (pp. 359–361)

10.3 Describe changes in the understanding of emotion during early childhood, noting achievements and limitations. (pp. 361–363)

10.4   Explain how language and temperament contribute to the development of emotional self-regulation during the preschool years, and discuss ways in which adults can help young children manage common fears of early childhood. (p. 363)

10.5   Discuss the development of self-conscious emotions, empathy, and sympathy during early childhood, noting how various parenting styles affect emotional development in these areas. (pp. 363–365)

10.6   Describe advances in peer sociability over the preschool years, with particular attention to the types of play outlined by Mildred Parten, and discuss cultural variations in peer sociability. (pp. 366–367)

10.7   Describe the quality of preschoolers' first friendships, noting how parents and siblings influence early peer relations, and discuss the emergence of social problem solving during early childhood. (pp. 368–370)

10.8   Compare psychoanalytic, behaviorist and social learning, and cognitive-developmental perspectives of moral development (pp. 371–375)

10.9   Trace milestones in preschoolers' understanding of morality, and discuss the importance of social experience in the development of moral understanding. (p. 375–376)

10.10   Describe the development of aggression in early childhood, noting the influences of family and television, and cite ways to control aggressive behavior. (pp. 377–380)

10.11   Describe preschoolers' gender-stereotyped beliefs and behaviors, and discuss genetic and environmental influences on gender-role development. (pp. 381–383)

10.12   Describe and evaluate the major theories of gender identity development, and cite ways to reduce gender stereotyping in young children. (pp. 385–387)

10.13   Describe the three features that distinguish major styles of child rearing. Compare each style, indicating which is most effective, and discuss cultural variations in child-rearing beliefs and practices. (pp. 388–390)

10.14   Describe the five forms of child maltreatment, and discuss factors associated with child maltreatment, consequences of child maltreatment, and strategies for the prevention of child maltreatment. (pp. 390–395)

STUDY QUESTIONS

Erikson's Theory: Initiative versus Guilt

1.   Define *initiative,* and describe how it is exhibited in preschoolers. (p. 358)

_____

_____

_____

_____

2.   Erikson regarded play as the central means through which children find out about themselves and their social world. Explain why this is the case. (p. 358)

_____

_____

_____

_____

3. Compare Erikson's theory of development during the preschool years with that of Freud. (p. 358)

_____

_____

_____

_____

_____

4. According to Erikson, what leads to a negative resolution of the initiative versus guilt stage? (p. 358)

_____

_____

_____

_____

Self-Understanding

1. Define *self-concept*. (p. 359)

_____

_____

_____

Foundations of Self-Concept

1. Describe the quality of preschoolers' self-descriptions. (p. 359)

_____

_____

_____

_____

2. Explain the link between preschoolers' self-development and their possessiveness of objects. Given this, how can adults promote friendly peer interaction? (p. 359)

_____

_____

_____

_____

_____

Emergence of Self-Esteem

1. Define *self-esteem*. (p. 360)

_____

_____

2. True or False: When making self-evaluations, preschoolers tend to rate their own ability as extremely low and often overestimate task difficulty. (p. 360)

3. List several things that adults can do to promote children's self-esteem. (p. 361)

_____

_____

_____

_____

Cultural Influences: Cultural Variations in Personal Storytelling: Implications for Early Self-Concept

1. Discuss differences in storytelling practices between Chinese and Irish-American parents, and explain the influence on children's self-image. (p. 360)

_____

_____

_____

_____

_____

Emotional Development

Understanding Emotion

1. By age _____ to _____, children can correctly judge the causes of many basic emotions. (p. 362)

2. Preschoolers (do / do not) realize that thoughts and feelings are interconnected. (p. 362)

3. True or False: In situations with conflicting cues about how a person is feeling, preschoolers can easily reconcile this differing information. (p. 362)

4. Explain how parent-child discussions can facilitate children's understanding of emotions. (p. 362)

_____

_____

_____

_____

Emotional Self-Regulation

1. Summarize how each of the following factors affect the development of emotional self-regulation during the preschool years: (p. 363)

Language:

_____

_____

Temperament:

_____

_____

_____

_____

Conversations with adults:

_____

_____

_____

_____

Self-Conscious Emotions

1. Preschoolers experience self-conscious emotions (more / less) often than do toddlers. Briefly explain your response. (p. 364)

_____

_____

2. Beginning in early childhood, (guilt / shame) is associated with feelings of personal inadequacy and is linked with maladjustment. In contrast, (guilt / shame), as long as it occurs in appropriate circumstances, is related to positive adjustment, perhaps because it helps children resist harmful impulses. (p. 364)

Empathy and Sympathy

1. Distinguish between *empathy* and *sympathy*. (pp. 364–365)

   Empathy:

   _____

   _____

   Sympathy:

   _____

   _____

2. Empathy serves as an important motivator of _____ behavior, or actions that benefit another person without any expected reward for the self. (p. 365)

3. True or False: In some children, empathizing with an upset peer or adult escalates into personal distress. (p. 365)

4. Discuss the impact of parenting on children's development of empathy and sympathy. (p. 365)

_____

_____

_____

_____

_____

Peer Relations

Advances in Peer Sociability

1. Describe Parten's three-step sequence of social development. (p. 366)

   A. _____

   _____

   B. _____

   _____

   C. 1. _____

   _____

   C. 2. _____

   _____

2. True or False: Longitudinal research shows that Parten's play types emerge in a developmental sequence, with later-appearing ones replacing earlier ones. (p. 366)

3. True or False: It is the *type*, rather than the *amount*, of solitary and parallel play that changes during early childhood. (p. 366)

4. True or False: High rates of any type of nonsocial activity during the preschool years is a sign of maladjustment. (pp. 366–367)

5. True or False: Peer sociability takes essentially the same form in collectivist and individualistic cultures. (p. 367)

6. Provide an example of how cultural beliefs about the importance of play affect early peer associations. (p. 367)

   _____

   _____

   _____

   _____

First Friendships

1. Summarize children's understanding of friendship in early childhood. (p. 368)

   _____

   _____

   _____

2. Summarize the unique quality of preschoolers' interactions with friends. (p. 368)

   _____

   _____

   _____

Social Problem Solving

1. Explain the importance of peer conflicts during early childhood. (p. 368)

   _____
   _____
   _____
   _____

2. List the six steps in Crick and Dodge's social problem-solving model. (p. 369)

   A. _____
   B. _____
   C. _____
   D. _____
   E. _____
   F. _____

3. Discuss how social problem solving affects peer relations. (p. 369)

   _____
   _____
   _____
   _____

4. Summarize improvements in social problem solving during the preschool and early school years. (p. 369)

   _____
   _____
   _____

5. Cite the benefits that children derive from training in social problem solving. (pp. 369–370)

   _____
   _____
   _____
   _____
   _____

Parental Influences on Early Peer Relations

1. List two ways that parents directly influence their children's social relationships. (p. 370)

   A. _____
   B. _____

2. Explain how parent–child attachment and parent–child play can promote children's peer interaction skills. (p. 370)
   Attachment:

   _____
   _____

Play:

_____

_____

Foundations of Morality

1. State two points on which most theories of moral development are in agreement. (p. 371)

   A. _____

   B. _____

2. Match each of the following major theories of moral development with the aspect of moral functioning that it emphasizes: (pp. 371–376)

   ____ Emotional side of conscience
   ____ Ability to reason about justice and fairness
   ____ Moral behavior

   1. Social learning theory
   2. Psychoanalytic theory
   3 Cognitive-developmental theory

The Psychoanalytic Perspective

1. Summarize Freud's psychoanalytic theory of morality development. (pp. 371–372)

   _____

   _____

   _____

   _____

2. True or False: Most researchers agree with Freud's assertion that fear of punishment and loss of parental love motivate children to behave morally. (p. 372)

3. A special type of discipline called _____ supports conscience development by pointing out the effects of the child's misbehavior on others. Cite three ways in which it does so. (p. 372)

   A. _____

   _____

   B. _____

   _____

   C. _____

   _____

4. Describe how the goodness-of-fit model is influential in conscience development. (pp. 372–373)

   _____

   _____

   _____

   _____

5. Recent research shows that Freud was (correct / incorrect) in his assertion that guilt is an important motivator of moral action. Briefly elaborate on your response. (p. 373)

_____

_____

_____

Social Learning Theory

1. Explain why operant conditioning is insufficient for children to acquire moral responses. (p. 373)

_____

_____

_____

_____

2. Social learning theorists believe that children learn to behave morally largely through _____—observing and imitating adults who demonstrate appropriate behavior. (p. 373)

3. List three characteristics of models that affect children's willingness to imitate them. (p. 373)

   A. _____

   B. _____

   C. _____

4. True or False: Punishment promotes immediate compliance but does not produce long-lasting changes in children's behavior. (p. 374)

5. List three undesirable side effects of harsh punishment. (p. 374)

   A. _____

   B. _____

   C. _____

6. Describe two alternatives to harsh punishment. (p. 374)

   A. _____

   _____

   B. _____

   _____

7. Describe three ways that parents can increase the effectiveness of punishment when they do decide to use it. (p. 375)

   A. _____

   _____

   B. _____

   _____

   C. _____

   _____

8. Explain *positive discipline,* noting how it reduces the need for punishment. (p. 375)

_____

_____

_____

_____

The Cognitive-Developmental Perspective

1. In what major way does the cognitive-developmental perspective of morality differ from the psychoanalytic and social learning approaches? (p. 375)

_____

_____

2. Preschoolers are able to distinguish _____ *imperatives,* which protect people's rights and welfare, from two other forms of action: _____ *conventions,* or customs determined solely by consensus, such as table manners and dress style, and *matters of* _____, which do not violate rights or harm others, are not socially regulated, and therefore are up to the individual. (p. 375)

3. Explain how young children learn to make distinctions between moral and social-conventional transgressions. (p. 376)

_____

_____

_____

_____

4. List three features of parent communication that help children reason about morality. (p. 376)

    A. _____

    B. _____

    C. _____

The Other Side of Morality: Development of Aggression

1. By the end of the preschool years, two general types of aggression emerge. The most common is _____ aggression, aimed at obtaining an object, privilege, or space with no deliberate intent to harm. The other type is _____ aggression, which is intended to hurt another person. (p. 377)

2. Distinguish between *overt* and *relational aggression.* (p. 377)

    Overt: _____

    _____

    Relational: _____

    _____

3. Discuss developmental and sex differences in aggression throughout the preschool years. (p. 377)

Developmental:

_____

_____

_____

_____

Sex:

_____

_____

_____

_____

4. Explain how a hostile family atmosphere promotes and sustains high rates of childhood aggression. (pp. 377–378)

_____

_____

_____

_____

5. True or False: Girls are more likely than boys to be targets of harsh physical discipline and parental inconsistency. (p. 378)

6. True or False: Violent content in children's programming occurs at above average rates, and cartoons are the most violent. (p. 378)

7. Explain why young children are especially likely to be influenced by television. (p. 378)

_____

_____

_____

_____

8. Summarize the long-term effects of TV violence on children's behavior. (pp. 378–379)

_____

_____

_____

_____

9. True or False: TV violence hardens children to aggression, making them more willing to tolerate it in others. (p. 379)

10. What is the V-Chip, and why is it an incomplete solution for regulating children's TV? (p. 379)

_____

_____

_____

_____

11. List several strategies parents can use to regulate children's TV viewing and computer use. (p. 380)

A. _____

_____

B. _____

_____

C. _____

_____

12. List several ways to help parents and children break the cycle of hostilities between family members. (pp. 379–380)

Parents:

A. _____

_____

B. _____

_____

C. _____

_____

Children:

A. _____

_____

B. _____

_____

Gender Typing

1. Define *gender typing.* (p. 381)

_____

_____

_____

Gender-Stereotyped Beliefs and Behaviors

1. Preschoolers' gender stereotypes are (flexible / rigid). Elaborate on your response. (p. 381)

    _____

    _____

    _____

2. True or False: Most preschoolers believe that the characteristics associated with each sex (for example, clothes, hairstyles, and occupation) determine whether a person is male or female. (p. 381)

Biological Influences on Gender Typing

1. Discuss Eleanor Maccoby's argument that hormonal differences between males and females have important consequences for gender typing, including play styles evidenced in early childhood. (p. 382)

    _____

    _____

    _____

    _____

    _____

2. Girls exposed to high levels of androgens prenatally display (more / less) "masculine" behavior. (p. 382)

Environmental Influences on Gender Typing

1. Describe ways in which parents encourage gender-stereotyped beliefs and behavior in their children. (pp. 382, 384)

    _____

    _____

    _____

    _____

    _____

2. True or False: Fathers are more likely to engage in differential treatment of boys and girls than are mothers. (p. 384)

3. Of the two sexes, (girls / boys) are clearly more gender-stereotyped. Why might this be the case? (p. 384)

    _____

    _____

    _____

    _____

4. Discuss gender typing in the classroom setting, noting its impact on social behaviors. (p. 384)

    _____

    _____

    _____

    _____

5. Peer rejection is greater for (girls / boys) who frequently engage in "cross-gender" behavior. (p. 384)

6. Discuss the different styles of social influence promoted within gender-segregated peer groups. (p. 384)

Boys: _____

_____

Girls: _____

_____

7. Describe the link between TV viewing and children's endorsement of gender stereotypes. (p. 385)

_____

_____

_____

_____

Gender Identity

1. Define *gender identity,* and indicate how it is measured. (p. 385)

_____

_____

_____

_____

2. _____ refers to a type of gender identity in which the person scores highly on both typically masculine and typically feminine personality characteristics. (p. 385)

3. How is gender identity related to psychological adjustment? (p. 385)

_____

_____

_____

4. Contrast social learning and cognitive-developmental accounts of the emergence of gender identity. (p. 385)

Social Learning:

_____

_____

_____

_____

Cognitive-Developmental:

_____

_____

_____

_____

5. *Gender* _____ refers to the understanding that sex is biologically-based and remains the same even if clothing, hairstyles, and play activities change. (p. 385)

6. Cite evidence supporting the notion that cognitive immaturity, not social experience, is largely responsible for preschoolers' difficulty grasping the permanence of sex. (p. 386)

_____

_____

_____

_____

7. Is gender constancy responsible for children's gender-typed behavior? Why or why not? (p. 386)

_____

_____

_____

8. Explain *gender schema theory.* (p. 386)

_____

_____

_____

9. What are *gender schemas*? (p. 386)

_____

_____

10. Explain how gender schemas influence gender-typed preferences and behavior. (pp. 386–387)

_____

_____

_____

_____

Reducing Gender Stereotyping in Young Children

1. Cite several ways that parents can reduce gender stereotyping in young children. (p. 387)

_____

_____

_____

_____

_____

1. Explain how David Reimer's personal experience confirms the impact of genetic sex and prenatal hormones on a person's sense of self as male or female, as well as highlighting the importance of social experience. (p. 383)

Genetic sex and prenatal hormones:

_____

_____

_____

_____

Social experience:

_____

_____

_____

_____

Child Rearing and Emotional and Social Development

Styles of Child Rearing

1. Based on the research findings of Baumrind and others, cite three features that consistently differentiate between more and less effective parenting styles. (p. 388)

A. _____

_____

B. _____

_____

C. _____

_____

2. Describe the four styles of child rearing, noting where each stands in relation to the characteristics listed above. (p. 388 (chart on bottom) or pp. 388–389)

Authoritative: _____

_____

Authoritarian: _____

_____

Permissive: _____

_____

Uninvolved: _____

_____

3. Summarize child outcomes associated with each of the following styles of parenting: (pp. 388–389)

Authoritative: _____

_____

Authoritarian: _____

_____

Permissive: _____

_____

Uninvolved: _____

_____

4. Which child-rearing approach is the most successful? (p. 388)

_____

_____

5. At its extreme, uninvolved parenting is a form of child maltreatment called _____.
(p. 389)

6. Cite four reasons that authoritative parenting is especially effective. (pp. 389–390)

A. _____

_____

B. _____

_____

C. _____

_____

D. _____

_____

Cultural Variations

1. Describe how the parenting practices of the following cultural groups often differ from those of Caucasian Americans: (p. 390)

Chinese: _____

_____

Hispanic and Asian Pacific Island: _____

_____

African-American: _____

_____

Child Maltreatment

1. List and describe four forms of child maltreatment. (p. 391)

   A. _____

   _____

   B. _____

   _____

   C. _____

   _____

   D. _____

   _____

2. True or False: Researchers have identified a single "abusive" personality type. (p. 391)

3. List parent, child, and family environment characteristics associated with an increased likelihood of abuse. (p. 391 (chart) or p. 392)

   Parent: _____

   _____

   Child: _____

   _____

   Family Environment: _____

   _____

4. Cite two reasons that most abusive parents are isolated from supportive ties to their communities. (p. 392)

   A. _____

   _____

   B. _____

   _____

5. Societies that view violence as an appropriate way to solve problems set the stage for child abuse. These conditions (do / do not) exist in the United States and Canada. Elaborate on your response. (p. 392)

   _____

   _____

   _____

   _____

6. Summarize the consequences of child maltreatment for abused children. (pp. 392–393)

   _____

   _____

   _____

   _____

7. Describe the pathways through which the damaging consequences of child maltreatment occur. (p. 393)

_____

_____

_____

_____

8. Discuss strategies for preventing child maltreatment at the family, community, and societal levels. (p. 393)

Family: _____

_____

Community: _____

_____

Societal: _____

_____

Social Issues: Health:
Healthy Start: Preventing Child Maltreatment Through Home Visitation

1. Explain how families at risk for child maltreatment are identified for participation in Hawaii's Healthy Start program, and describe the services offered through this program. (p. 394)

Identification:

_____

Services:

_____

2. Summarize outcomes of the Healthy Start program identified through a 3-year follow-up investigation. (p. 394)

_____

_____

_____

3. Describe the cognitive component sometimes combined with home visitation, noting the impact of this enhanced feature. (p. 394)

_____

_____

_____

_____

ASK YOURSELF . . .

For *Ask Yourself* questions for this chapter, please log on to the Companion Website at *www.ablongman.com/berk.*

SUGGESTED STUDENT READINGS

Colapinto, J. (2001). *As nature made him: The boy who was raised as a girl.* New York: Perennial. Based on a true story, this book examines the life of a man who experienced a sex change in infancy, which was followed by radical attempts to "feminize" him.

Gibbs, J. C. (2003). *Moral development and reality: Beyond the theories of Kohlberg and Hoffman.* Thousand Oaks, CA: Sage. Provides an extensive overview of moral development in childhood. The author also describes his EQUIP program, which was designed to teach antisocial children moral and prosocial behavior.

Straus, M. A. (2001). *Beating the devil out of them: Corporal punishment in American families and its effects on children.* Somerset, NJ: Transaction Publishers. Written primarily for parents, teachers, social workers, and others working with children and adolescents, this book presents the negative effects of physical punishment on child development.

Winn, M. (2002). *The plug-in drug: Television, computers, and family life.* New York: Penguin. Examines the negative impact televisions and computers can have on child development and school achievement. According to the author, extensive television viewing deprives children of valuable developmental experiences, such as playing. Other topics include: computers in the classroom, computer and video games, TV programming for babies, and the relationship between television viewing and physical health.

PUZZLE 10.1 TERM REVIEW

Across

2. Gender identity in which the person scores high on both masculine and feminine personality traits
4. Feelings of concern or sorrow for another's plight
5. Erikson regarded _____ *versus guilt* as the critical psychological conflict of the preschool years.
6. Set of attributes, abilities, attitudes, and values that individuals believe define who they are (2 words, hyph.)
7. A form of hostile aggression that harms another through physical injury or the threat of such injury
8. A form of hostile aggression that does damage to another's peer relationships
11. Play with others that is directed toward a common goal
13. Play that involves separate activities but exchange of toys and comments
14. _____ problem solving: resolving conflicts in ways that are both acceptable to others and beneficial to the self

Down

1. Actions that benefit another person without any expected reward for the self are known as _____, or altruistic, behaviors.
3. Judgments we make about our own self-worth and the feelings associated with those judgments
5. Aggression aimed at obtaining an object, privilege, or space with no intent to harm
9. Activity involving unoccupied, onlooker behavior and solitary play
10. Aggression intended to harm another person
12. Play that occurs near other children, with similar materials, but involves no interaction

PUZZLE 10.2 TERM REVIEW

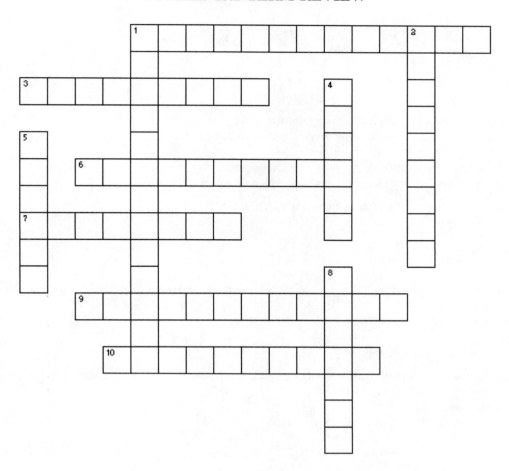

Across

1. Style of child rearing that involves high acceptance and involvement, adaptive control techniques, and appropriate autonomy granting
3. Gender _____: understanding that sex remains the same even if outward appearance changes
6. Child-rearing style that is high in acceptance but overindulging and inattentive, low in control, and lax rather than appropriate in autonomy granting
7. Gender _____: image of oneself as relatively masculine or feminine in characteristics
9. ___-___ styles: combinations of parenting behaviors that occur over a wide range of situations (2 words, hyph.)
10. Style of child rearing that combines low acceptance and involvement, little control, and indifference to autonomy granting

Down

1. Style of child rearing that is low in acceptance and involvement, high in coercive control, and low in autonomy granting
2. Type of discipline that involves communicating the effects of the child's misbehavior on others
4. Gender _____ theory: approach to gender typing that combines social learning and cognitive-developmental features
5. Gender _____: the process of developing gender roles
8. Mild punishment involving removal of the child from the immediate setting until he/she is ready to behave appropriately (2 words)

PRACTICE TEST #1

1. When preschoolers describe themselves they usually mention (p. 359)
   a. special competencies.
   b. observable characteristics.
   c. social virtues.
   d. personality traits.

2. Research on the development of self-esteem demonstrates that preschoolers (p. 360)
   a. have difficulty distinguishing between desired and actual competencies.
   b. usually evaluate their own abilities as low.
   c. do not yet have separate self-esteems for various activities.
   d. usually give up easily when faced with tasks on which they have failed earlier.

3. Preschoolers' explanations of emotions tend to emphasize (p. 362)
   a. negative feelings.
   b. beliefs.
   c. external factors.
   d. desires.

4. Children's increasing facility with _____ leads to fewer temper tantrums over the preschool years. (p. 363)
   a. prosocial behavior
   b. parallel play
   c. their imagination
   d. emotional self-regulation strategies

5. Research on self-conscious emotions suggests that parents who repeatedly give feedback about the worth of the child and her performance have children who (p. 364)
   a. rarely experience guilt.
   b. induce moderate levels of shame and pride.
   c. exhibit symptoms of withdrawal and depression.
   d. experience self-conscious emotions intensely.

6. When 4-year-old Rob began to cry when his mother dropped him off at school, Martine gave Rob a hug and shared his toy plane. Martine's behavior is an example of (p. 364)
   a. prosocial behavior.
   b. nonsocial activity.
   c. emotional self-regulation.
   d. social problem solving.

7. _____ is a form of play in which children engage in separate activities but exchange toys and talk with one another. (p. 366)
   a. Cooperative play
   b. Parallel play
   c. Nonsocial activity
   d. Associative play

8. Research demonstrates that preschoolers who spend large amounts of time playing alone (p. 366)
   a. are likely to develop normally.
   b. are cause for concern only if they engage in play involving immature, repetitive motor action.
   c. are socially fearful.
   d. have parents who criticize their social awkwardness.

9. Which of the following is supported by research on first friendships? (p. 368)
   a. Preschoolers' best friends tend to be children who share similar beliefs and attitudes.
   b. Most friendships during the preschool years have a long-term, enduring quality.
   c. Friends are more emotionally expressive than nonfriends.
   d. Preschoolers' friendships are based on mutual trust.

10. Research suggests that a special type of discipline known as _____ supports conscience development. (p. 368)
    a. social problem solving
    b. induction
    c. time out
    d. prosocial behavior

11. Research supports Freud's ideas that _____ is an important motivator of moral behavior. (p. 372)
    a. empathy
    b. punishment
    c. sympathy
    d. guilt

12. Which of the following is supported by research on morality? (p. 373)
    a. Young children are more willing to copy the prosocial behaviors of same age peers than those of older children and adults.
    b. Reinforcement is generally not effective at increasing the frequency of previously modeled prosocial behavior.
    c. Children tend to behave prosocially only when a model is present.
    d. When parents say one thing but do another, children are most likely to model the most lenient standard of behavior that adults demonstrate.

13. Which of the following is supported by research on punishment? (p. 374)
    a. Children who are repeatedly punished are especially passive and withdrawn outside the home.
    b. Punishment stops children's misbehavior only temporarily; it does not produce lasting behavioral changes.
    c. Children who are repeatedly punished quickly learn not to display the unacceptable behavior again.
    d. Children who are repeatedly punished often seek increasing interaction with the punishing adult.

14. Research on time out suggests that (p. 374)
    a. use of time out is closely linked to physical abuse.
    b. time out is useful when the child is out of control.
    c. harsh punishment is more effective than time out.
    d. time out is rarely successful in altering behavior.

15. Which of the following is an example of positive discipline? (p. 375)
    a. encouragement of good conduct
    b. time out
    c. withdrawal of privileges
    d. corporal punishment

16. Between 2 and 6 years of age, (p. 377)
    a. physical aggression is replaced by verbal aggression.
    b. instrumental aggression increases.
    c. relational aggression is replaced by overt aggression.
    d. hostile aggression decreases.

17. Which of the following is supported by research on gender typing? (p. 381)
    a. Children's gender-stereotyped beliefs become less strong over the preschool years.
    b. Most preschoolers realize that characteristics associated with one's sex, such as hairstyle and clothing, do not determine whether a person is male or female.
    c. Hormones have little, if any, effect on gender-stereotyped behaviors.
    d. As early as 18 months of age, boys prefer toy cars and girls prefer dolls.

18. Research on gender typing demonstrates that (pp. 382, 384)
    a. mothers are more likely than fathers to encourage "gender-appropriate" behavior in their children.
    b. parents more often explain emotions when talking to their daughters and label emotions when talking to their sons.
    c. parents actively reinforce independence in boys and dependence in girls.
    d. parents place more pressure on daughters than sons to achieve.

19. Androgynous children (p. 384)
    a. have higher self-esteem than feminine children.
    b. score high on masculine and low on feminine personality characteristics.
    c. often think poorly of themselves.
    d. are less adaptable than children with masculine or feminine gender identities.

20. Parents who use a(n) _____ parenting style are low in acceptance and involvement, high in coercive control, and low in autonomy granting. (p. 389)
    a. authoritative
    b. permissive
    c. authoritarian
    d. uninvolved

PRACTICE TEST #2

1. Freud believed that children develop a conscience through (p. 358)
   a. play activities.
   b. punishment of hostility toward their opposite-sex parent.
   c. identifying with their same-sex parent.
   d. rejecting the morals and standards of society, and developing their own.

2. One day in preschool, Jerilyn becomes very angry. When asked what Jerilyn might do, her classmate Adam (p. 362)
   a. cannot yet predict what Jerilyn will do.
   b. predicts that Jerilyn will yell at someone.
   c. expects Jerilyn to start laughing.
   d. thinks Jerilyn is experiencing mixed emotions of sadness and anger.

3. Compared to nonabused peers, preschoolers who have been abused (p. 365)
   a. demonstrate more empathy toward children in distress.
   b. are less angry and aggressive.
   c. exhibit more altruistic behavior.
   d. rarely show signs of empathy.

4. Cultural research on play indicates that (p. 367)
   a. Korean-American children spend less time in joint make-believe play than their Caucasian-American peers.
   b. Indian children's play involves very few games that require cooperation in large groups.
   c. Yucatec Mayan children spend the majority of their time in sociodramatic play activities.
   d. children's play is very similar, no matter the culture.

5. All theories agree that moral development begins to take shape during (p. 371)
   a. infancy.
   b. toddlerhood.
   c. the preschool years.
   d. first grade.

6. Parents who use inductive discipline (p. 372)
   a. talk to their children about the effects of misbehavior.
   b. reward children for good behavior, and ignore misbehavior.
   c. put children in time out to consider why they misbehaved.
   d. avoid making children feel guilty for their misdeeds.

7. The cognitive-developmental approach to morality suggests that children (p. 375)
   a. are sponges that "soak in" the morality of society.
   b. behave in ways that allow them to avoid guilty thoughts during early childhood.
   c. cannot translate moral thought into behavior until after the preschool years.
   d. actively think about social rules.

8. Erin shoves David in order to get him away from a tricycle she wants. Erin is exhibiting _____ aggression. (p. 377)
   a. relational
   b. instrumental
   c. hostile
   d. passive

9. Recent research on peer interaction indicates that (p. 377)
   a. it is the *type,* rather than the *amount,* of play that changes during early childhood.
   b. Parten's play types emerge in a developmental sequence, with later appearing ones replacing earlier ones.
   c. nonsocial activity among preschoolers is a sign of maladjustment.
   d. sociodramatic play declines during the preschool years.

10. Children who are raised in families with harsh and inconsistent discipline are more likely to interpret others' actions as (p. 377)
    a. unintentional.
    b. hostile.
    c. unaggressive.
    d. sympathetic.

11. Which theory emphasizes the role of modeling and reinforcement on gender typing? (p. 381)
    a. psychoanalytic theory
    b. social learning theory
    c. informational-processing theory
    d. cognitive-developmental theory

12. Ricky wants to paint his fingernails. His ___ is most likely to discourage this behavior. (p. 381)
    a. sister
    b. teacher
    c. father
    d. mother

13. When 5-year-old Esther is asked, "Can you be a daddy when you grow up?" Esther will respond that she (p. 381)
    a. can be a daddy when she grows up.
    b. can only be a mommy.
    c. won't know until she grows up.
    d. doesn't understand the question.

14. Amanda's preschool teacher tells a story about a boy who took an airplane ride. The pilot of the plane was Mary. When Amanda tells her father the story after school, she will likely say that Mary was (p. 384)
    a. the pilot.
    b. a man.
    c. a flight attendant.
    d. a mean lady.

15. Individuals who are androgynous (p. 385)
    a. display highly gender-stereotyped behavior.
    b. demonstrate mostly cross-gender behaviors.
    c. score highly on both masculine and feminine personality characteristics.
    d. have a poorly developed gender identity.

16. Riley's parents require him to behave appropriately. They also provide him with a warm, loving environment. They respond to his emotions with sensitivity, and maintain open communication in the family. Riley's parents can be classified as (pp. 388–389)
    a. authoritative.
    b. authoritarian.
    c. uninvolved.
    d. permissive.

17. Lora's parents neglected her throughout her childhood. In light of Baumrind's research, you might expect her to display _____ as an adolescent. (p. 389)
    a. high academic ambitions
    b. strong emotional control
    c. dependency
    d. delinquent behavior

18. Cultural variations in child-rearing practices reveal that (p. 390)
    a. Chinese parents are less demanding than Caucasian parents.
    b. Hispanic and Pacific Island families do not insist on respect for the father as much as Caucasian families do.
    c. low-SES ethnic minority parents who use more controlling strategies have children who are more cognitively and socially competent.
    d. single African-American women tend not to demand immediate obedience.

19. Of the following, who is most likely to abuse his child? (p. 391)
    a. John Paul, who didn't have children until he and his wife were in their late 30s
    b. Joel, whose baby is passive and quiet
    c. Emilio, who is a graduate student and works part time
    d. Ted, who is unemployed

20. Which form of abuse is likely to be the most common, since it also accompanies most other types? (p. 391)
    a. physical abuse
    b. psychological abuse
    c. emotional neglect
    d. physical neglect

CHAPTER 11
PHYSICAL DEVELOPMENT
IN MIDDLE CHILDHOOD

BRIEF CHAPTER SUMMARY

The slow gains in body growth that took place during the preschool years continue in middle childhood. Large individual differences in body size that are the combined result of heredity and environment remain apparent. Bones of the body lengthen and broaden, and primary teeth are replaced with permanent ones. Because of better nutrition and health care, children in industrialized nations are growing larger and reaching physical maturity earlier than they did in previous generations.

Although many children are at their healthiest in middle childhood, health problems do occur. Vision and hearing difficulties, malnutrition, obesity, nighttime bedwetting, asthma, and unintentional injuries are among the most frequent health concerns of the school years. School-age children can learn a wide range of health information, but it has little impact on their everyday behavior. Interventions must also provide them with healthier environments and consistently reward good health practices.

Growth in body size and muscle strength supports the refinement of many gross motor capacities in middle childhood. Gains in flexibility, balance, agility, force, and reaction time underlie improvements in children's gross motor skills. Fine motor coordination also increases. Children's writing becomes more legible, and their drawings show greater organization, more detail, and the addition of the depth dimension.

The physical activities of school-age children reflect advances in the quality of their play. Child-organized games with rules become common. These games support emotional and social development. Increasingly, children are participating in adult-oriented youth sports. Some researchers are concerned that this trend may have an adverse effect on development. Rough-and-tumble play and dominance hierarchies are features of children's interaction that reflect our evolutionary past. Wide individual differences in athletic performance exist that are influenced by both genetic and environmental factors. Physical education classes help ensure that all children have access to the benefits of regular exercise and play.

LEARNING OBJECTIVES

After reading this chapter, you should be able to:

11.1 Describe changes in body size, body proportions, and skeletal maturity during middle childhood, noting secular trends in physical growth. (pp. 402–404)

11.2 Describe brain development in middle childhood, including the influence of neurotransmitters and hormones. (p. 404)

11.3 Identify common health problems in middle childhood, discuss their causes and consequences, and cite ways to alleviate them. (pp. 405–414)

11.4 Summarize findings on school-age children's concepts of health and illness, and indicate ways that parents and teachers can foster healthy lifestyles in school-age children. (pp. 414–416)

11.5 Cite major milestones of gross and fine motor development during middle childhood. (pp. 417–418)

11.6 Describe individual and group differences in motor performance during middle childhood. (pp. 418–419)

11.7 Describe qualities of children's play during middle childhood, including participation in adult-organized youth sports and engagement in rough-and-tumble play. (pp. 420–422)

11.8 Describe the state of physical education programs in most American schools, and discuss the importance of high-quality physical education during the school years. (pp. 422–423)

STUDY QUESTIONS

Body Growth

1. During middle childhood, children continue to add _____ inches in height and _____ pounds in weight each year. (p. 402)

2. Describe sex differences in body growth and proportions during middle childhood. (p. 402)

_____

_____

_____

_____

Worldwide Variations in Body Size

1. True or False: Growth norms in countries throughout the world reveal few individual differences in body growth. (pp. 402–403)

2. Discuss both hereditary and environmental factors that account for differences in physical size among children around the world. (p. 403)

Hereditary: _____

_____

Environmental: _____

_____

Secular Trends in Physical Growth

1. What are *secular trends in physical growth*? (p. 403)

_____

2. Summarize the factors responsible for current secular growth patterns. (p. 403)

_____

_____

_____

Skeletal Growth

1. True or False: Over 50 percent of North American children have some tooth decay. (p. 404)

2. One-third of school-age children suffer from _____, a condition in which the upper and lower teeth do not meet properly. (p. 404)

3. List two causes of malocclusion. (p. 404)

   A. _____

   B. _____

Brain Development

1. List four advances in brain development that occur in middle childhood. (p. 404)

   A. _____

   B. _____

   C. _____

   D. _____

2. Summarize changes in neurotransmitters and hormones during middle childhood, noting their effects on brain functioning. (p. 404)

   Neurotransmitters: _____

   _____

   _____

   _____

   Hormones: _____

   _____

   _____

   _____

Common Health Problems

Vision and Hearing

1. The most common vision problem of middle childhood is _____, or nearsightedness. (p. 405)

2. Cite evidence indicating that both heredity and environment contribute to myopia. (pp. 405–406)

   Heredity: _____

   _____

   _____

   _____

   Environment: _____

   _____

   _____

   _____

3. True or False: Repeated ear infections put children at risk for hearing loss. (p. 406)

Malnutrition

1. Cite the benefits of family dinnertimes. (p. 406)

    _____

    _____

2. True or False: The nutritional deficiencies that result from children's busy daily schedules usually have a long-term negative impact on development. (p. 406)

3. Summarize the effects of prolonged malnutrition that become apparent by middle childhood. (p. 406)

    _____

    _____

    _____

    _____

Obesity

1. *Obesity* is a greater-than-_____-percent increase over average body weight based on an individual's age, sex, and physical build. (p. 407)

2. About _____ percent of Canadian children and _____ percent of American children are obese. (p. 407)

3. About _____ percent of obese children retain their overweight status into adulthood. (p. 407)

4. Summarize the lifelong health problems for which obese children are at risk. (p. 407)

    _____

    _____

    _____

    _____

5. True or False: Heredity is the single most important contributing factor to childhood obesity. (p. 407)

6. (Low-SES / Middle-SES) children are more likely to be overweight. Cite three factors that contribute to this trend. (pp. 407–408)

    A. _____

    B. _____

    C. _____

7. Describe parenting practices that contribute to obesity, along with their consequences for children's eating habits. (p. 408)

    _____

    _____

    _____

8. Describe evidence of the relationship between TV viewing and obesity. (p. 408)

    _____

    _____

    _____

9. Summarize the emotional and social consequences of childhood obesity. (p. 409)

_____

_____

_____

10. List characteristics of effective interventions for treating obesity. (p. 409)

_____

_____

_____

11. What can schools do to help reduce childhood obesity? (p. 409)

_____

_____

Bedwetting

1. Ten percent of American school-age children suffer from _____, or bedwetting during the night. (p. 412)

2. In the majority of cases, nocturnal enuresis is caused by (biological / environmental) factors. (p. 412)

3. Describe the most effective treatment for enuresis. (p. 412)

_____

_____

_____

Illnesses

1. What accounts for the somewhat higher rate of illness during the first two years of elementary school? (p. 412)

_____

2. The most common chronic illness, representing the most frequent cause of school absence and childhood hospitalization, is _____. (p. 412)

3. Describe the characteristics of children who are at greatest risk for asthma. (p. 412)

_____

_____

_____

4. List six interventions for chronically ill children and their families that foster improvements in family interactions and child adjustment. (p. 413)

   A. _____

   B. _____

   C. _____

   D. _____

E. _____

F. _____

Unintentional Injuries

1. What is the leading cause of injury during the school years? (p. 413)

   _____

2. Cite three characteristics of effective safety education programs. (p. 413)

   A. _____

   B. _____

   C. _____

3. Describe characteristics of children who are most at risk for injury in middle childhood. (p. 414)

   _____

   _____

   _____

Social Issues: Health: The Obesity Epidemic: How Americans Became the Heaviest People in the World

1. What percent of American children and adults are overweight or obese? (p. 410)

   Children and adolescents: _____   Adults: _____

2. Summarize four societal factors that have contributed to the widespread, rapid weight gain among Americans. (p. 410)

   A. _____

   _____

   B. _____

   _____

   C. _____

   _____

   D. _____

   _____

3. Cite three suggestions for combating obesity at the societal level. (p. 410)

   A. _____

   B. _____

   C. _____

Health Education

1. Why is the school-age period especially important for fostering healthy lifestyles? (p. 414)

   _____

   _____

   _____

2. List three reasons why efforts to impart health concepts to school-age children often have little impact on their behavior. (p. 414)

   A. _____

   B. _____

   C. _____

3. Discuss at least four strategies for fostering healthy lifestyles in school-age children. (p. 416)

   A. _____

   _____

   B. _____

   _____

   C. _____

   _____

   D. _____

   _____

Social Issues: Education:
Children's Understanding of Health and Illness

1. Trace changes in children's understanding of health and illness from preschool into adolescence. (p. 415)

   Preschool and early school-age (4- to 8-year-olds): _____

   _____

   Older school-age (9- to 10-year-olds): _____

   _____

   Early adolescence: _____

   _____

2. Describe factors that affect children's understanding of health and illness. (p. 415)

   _____

   _____

   _____

Gross Motor Development

1. Describe gains in four basic motor capacities that support improvements in gross motor skills during middle childhood. (pp. 417–418)

   A. _____

   _____

   B. _____

   _____

   C. _____

   _____

   D. _____

   _____

2. Explain how more efficient information processing contributes to the improved motor performance of school-age children. (p. 418)

   _____

   _____

Fine Motor Development

1. Describe typical gains in writing and drawing during middle childhood. (p. 418)

   Writing: _____

   _____

   Drawing: _____

   _____

Individual Differences in Motor Skills

1. Discuss the influence of socioeconomic status on children's motor development. (p. 418)

   _____

   _____

   _____

2. Summarize sex differences in motor skills, and explain how environmental factors contribute to these differences. (p. 419)

   _____

   _____

   _____

   _____

3. List two extra measures that can help raise girls' participation, self-confidence, and sense of fair treatment in athletics. (p. 419)

   A. _____

   B. _____

Child-Organized Games

1. What cognitive capacity permits the transition to rule-oriented games during middle childhood? (p. 420)

   _____

2. Explain how child-invented games contribute to emotional and social development. (p. 420)

   _____

   _____

   _____

Adult-Organized Youth Sports

1. Participation on community athletic teams (is / is not) associated with greater social competence. (p. 420)

2. Summarize four criticisms of adult-organized youth sports. (p. 421)

   A. _____

   _____

   B. _____

   _____

   C. _____

   _____

   D. _____

   _____

3. Explain four ways to ensure that organized sports provide positive, developmentally appropriate experiences for children. (p. 421)

   A. _____

   _____

   B. _____

   _____

   C. _____

   _____

   D. _____

   _____

Shadows of Our Evolutionary Past

1. _____ *play* is a form of peer interaction involving friendly chasing and play-fighting. (p. 421)

2. Explain how rough-and-tumble play assists children in establishing a *dominance hierarchy,* and note how this is adaptive for peer relations. (p. 422)

_____

_____

_____

_____

Physical Education

1. True or False: Nearly 90 percent of North American school children receive at least one hour of physical education each week. (p. 422)

2. What kinds of activities should physical education classes emphasize to help the largest number of children develop active and healthy lifestyles? (p. 423)

_____

_____

3. List three benefits of being physically fit in childhood. (p. 423)

A. _____

B. _____

C. _____

ASK YOURSELF . . .

For *Ask Yourself* questions for this chapter, please log on to the Companion Website at *www.ablongman.com/berk.*

SUGGESTED STUDENT READINGS

Critser, G. (2003). *Fat land: How Americans became the fattest people in the world.* Boston: Houghton Mifflin. Explores how multiple aspects of American life—class, politics, culture, and economics—have contributed to the obesity epidemic. In addition, presents up-to-date research on childhood obesity, marketing tactics of fast-food chains, adult-onset diabetes resulting from poor eating habits, and suggestions for how to tackle this growing epidemic.

Tinsley, B. J. (2003). *How children learn to be healthy.* Cambridge, U.K.: Cambridge University Press. Examines children's understanding of health and ways parents, peers, schools, and neighborhoods influence children's attitudes, beliefs, and behaviors.

Woolf, A., Howard, S. C., Kenna, M. A., & Allison, K. C. (Eds.). (2002). *Children's Hospital guide to your child's health and development.* Boston: Perseus Publishing. Details physical development through the school years, common childhood illnesses, risk factors associated with obesity, and relevant health and safety information. Written for parents, teachers, and other professionals interested in working with children.

PUZZLE 11.1 TERM REVIEW

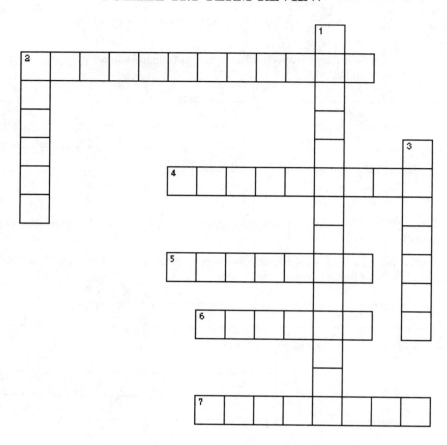

Across

2. Condition in which the upper and lower teeth do not meet properly
4. _____ hierarchy: stable ordering of group members that predicts who will win when conflict arises
5. A greater-than-20-percent increase over average body weight based on sex, age, and physical build
6. An illness in which highly sensitive bronchial tubes fill with mucus, leading to episodes of coughing, wheezing, and breathing difficulties
7. Nocturnal _____: repeated bedwetting during the night

Down

1. ___-__-___ play: a form of peer interaction involving friendly chasing and play-fighting (3 words, hyph.)
2. Nearsightedness
3. _____ trends in physical growth refer to changes in body size from one generation to the next.

PRACTICE TEST #1

1. Which of the following is supported by research on body growth during middle childhood? (p. 402)
   a. Girls have slightly more body fat than boys.
   b. Upper portions of the body grow fastest.
   c. Cultural differences in body size are largely genetic.
   d. Short physiques are typical in tropical regions, and tall physiques are common in Arctic regions.

2. Over the past 30 years, (p. 403)
   a. secular trends in physical growth have become more evident in low-income than high-income children.
   b. the average height of schoolchildren has risen nearly 1/3 inch per decade.
   c. the rate of physical growth during childhood has slowed due to increased exposure to environmental toxins.
   d. secular gains in height and weight have slowed.

3. Which of the following is true? (p. 404)
   a. Parents need not brush children's primary teeth because they are replaced by permanent ones during middle childhood.
   b. Only about 10 percent of North American school age children have some tooth decay.
   c. Boys lose their primary teeth slightly earlier than girls.
   d. Malocclusion can be caused by thumb and finger sucking.

4. During middle childhood and adolescence (p. 404)
   a. gray matter declines.
   b. the weight of the brain nearly doubles.
   c. lateralization of the cerebral hemispheres declines.
   d. the production of neurons rapidly increases.

5. During middle childhood, (p. 405)
   a. myopia is a common cause of blindness.
   b. low-income children are more likely to be myopic than high-income children.
   c. the more time children spend reading and writing, the more likely they are to be myopic.
   d. myopia progresses more rapidly during the summer months than during the school year.

6. _____ percent of American children are obese. (p. 407)
   a. Five
   b. Ten
   c. Fifteen
   d. Twenty-five

7. Obese children (p. 408)
   a. are not more likely than their normal-weight peers to become overweight adults.
   b. are more responsive to internal hunger cues than are normal-weight children.
   c. eat slower than normal-weight children.
   d. are more responsive to external stimuli associated with food than are normal-weight children.

8. Which of the following is supported by research on obesity? (p. 409)
   a. Children rate obese youngsters as lazy, sloppy, ugly, and stupid.
   b. Obese children rarely exhibit signs of depression that are characteristic of obese adults.
   c. Obese children tend to be jolly and good natured.
   d. Obese children usually reach puberty later than normal-weight children.

9. Most cases of bedwetting during the night, or nocturnal enuresis, (p. 412)
   a. are due to overeating.
   b. have biological roots.
   c. are caused by overly strict and demanding parents.
   d. can be treated successfully by gently punishing children for wetting.

10. During middle childhood, the most frequent cause of school absence and hospitalization is (p. 412)
   a. motor vehicle accidents.
   b. asthma.
   c. viral infections.
   d. bicycle accidents.

11. Which of the following is supported by research on asthma? (p. 412)
   a. The number of children with asthma has more than doubled in the past 30 years.
   b. Less than 5 percent of North American children have asthma.
   c. The number of childhood deaths due to asthma has substantially decreased in the past 30 years.
   d. Childhood asthma rates are essentially equivalent among various racial and economic groups in North America.

12. _____ are the leading cause of unintentional injury in middle childhood. (p. 413)
   a. Bicycle accidents
   b. Pool accidents
   c. Roller blading accidents
   d. Motor vehicle accidents

13. One reason that most efforts to impart health concepts to school-age children have little impact on behavior is because (p. 414)
   a. most environments in developed countries are relatively free of health risks.
   b. most parents tend to reinforce unhealthy rather than healthy behaviors.
   c. most children naturally engage in healthy behaviors.
   d. health is usually not an important goal for children because they feel good most of the time.

14. Younger children often have difficulty with dribbling and batting because (p. 418)
   a. they do not yet have the physical strength to perform these skills.
   b. they have poor balance.
   c. they are not yet physically pliable enough to perform these skills.
   d. they have difficulty with skills such as these that require immediate responding.

15. The fancy footwork of jump rope and dodging opponents in tag are characteristics of (p. 418)
   a. agility.
   b. flexibility.
   c. balance.
   d. force.

16. The writing of most 6-year-olds is large because (p. 418)
   a. they have difficulty seeing smaller letters.
   b. they use the entire arm to make strokes.
   c. they have trouble making horizontal and vertical motions.
   d. they rely on their wrist and fingers to make strokes.

17. During middle childhood, (p. 419)
   a. boys are more adept than girls at fine motor skills.
   b. girls outperform boys in batting and dribbling.
   c. girls are better than boys at skipping, jumping, and hopping.
   d. boys outperform girls in drawing and handwriting.

18. Gains in _____ permit the growth of games with rules during middle childhood. (p. 420)
    a. fine motor skills
    b. perspective taking
    c. emotional self-regulation
    d. metacognition

19. Which of the following is supported by research on adult-organized youth sports? (p. 421)
    a. For most children, participating in community athletic teams is associated with decreases in social competence.
    b. When coaches create a climate in which winning is paramount, children tend to become better competitors.
    c. Children who join teams that require skills beyond their capabilities usually maintain their interest in sports longer than other children.
    d. High parental pressure to win is associated with early athletic dropout.

20. During middle childhood, rough-and-tumble play (p. 421)
    a. is associated with an increase in injuries.
    b. is seen in boys but not girls.
    c. may assist children in establishing a dominance hierarchy.
    d. is viewed by most as harmful, aggressive fighting.

PRACTICE TEST #2

1. In longitudinal studies of children's growth, researchers observe that height between ages 3 and 10 increases (p. 402)
   a. slowly and steadily.
   b. at about 1 inch per year.
   c. in slight spurts and lulls.
   d. more for boys than girls.

2. Of the following, a child from _____ is likely to be tallest. (p. 403)
   a. the United States
   b. South America
   c. Ethiopia
   d. Thailand

3. Long, lean physiques are more common in regions of the world that are (p. 403)
   a. mild in climate.
   b. hot and tropical.
   c. cold.
   d. dry and windy.

4. What percentage of school-age children complain of evening "growing pains"? (p. 403)
   a. less than 20 percent
   b. 33 percent
   c. 50 percent
   d. more than 70 percent

5. Malocclusion can be caused by (p. 404)
   a. eating too many sweets.
   b. calcium deficits.
   c. eating hard, crunchy foods such as popcorn.
   d. thumb sucking after the appearance of permanent teeth.

6. Your friend is curious about the changes that will occur in his 5-year-old son's brain over the next few years. You inform him that (p. 404)
   a. growth in the frontal lobes and corpus callosum will slow and cease before age 7.
   b. the frontal lobes will double in surface area during the next two years due to new synaptic connections between neurons.
   c. the corpus callosum will thin out in a process called "pruning."
   d. the frontal lobes will show a slight increase in surface area, due to continued myelinization.

7. As Hong Kong changed from a largely illiterate society to one that is highly educated, children have developed higher levels of (p. 405)
   a. malocclusion.
   b. farsightedness.
   c. otitis media.
   d. myopia.

8. Highly active boys (p. 414)
   a. have as much safety knowledge as their peers, but do not implement it.
   b. do not know as much about safety as their peers.
   c. know much more than their peers about safety but do not implement it.
   d. are more likely to implement safety precautions than their peers.

9. Dale is obese. In other words, he is _____ percent over average body weight for his sex, age, and physical build. (p. 407)
   a. 10
   b. 20
   c. 25
   d. 30

10. One disadvantage of using antidepressants to treat nocturnal enuresis is that (p. 412)
    a. they are addictive.
    b. children start wetting again after they stop taking the medication.
    c. most children experience mood problems while taking them.
    d. they increase the amount of urine produced during the night.

11. Terrence is an African-American boy growing up in the inner city. Compared to Christopher, a Caucasian-American boy who is growing up in the suburbs, (p. 412)
    a. Terrence has a lower risk of developing asthma.
    b. Terrence has the same risk of developing asthma.
    c. Terrence has a higher risk of developing asthma.
    d. Because heredity causes asthma, information about the boys' family histories is necessary to make this prediction.

12. Short, growth-stunted children have been shown to be at a higher risk for _____ in several developing nations as well as in ethnic minority groups in the United States. (p. 408)
    a. body injuries
    b. myopia
    c. obesity
    d. malocclusion

13. A 12-year-old would view health (p. 414)
    a. as unimportant.
    b. in terms of people's behavior, such as washing their hands and eating fruits and vegetables.
    c. as a long-term condition that depends on the interaction of body, mind, and environment.
    d. as unrelated to biological processes.

14. During middle childhood, increasingly efficient information processing allows for steady improvement in _____. (p. 418)
    a. hand-eye coordination
    b. reaction time
    c. physical reasoning
    d. physical strength

15. Aidan has just learned to accurately copy a picture of a three-dimensional form. He is most likely _____ years old. (p. 418)
    a. 4
    b. 6
    c. 8
    d. 12

16. Kindergarteners through third graders view sports as (p. 419)
    a. more important for boys.
    b. more important for girls.
    c. equally important for boys and girls.
    d. unimportant for either boys or girls.

17. Which of the following statements is true? Adult-organized youth sports (p. 420)
    a. are losing popularity.
    b. lead to psychological damage for many children.
    c. are as beneficial to children as child-organized games.
    d. fill hours that children used to spend in spontaneous play.

18. Adrienne's parents pressure her to participate in gymnastics. They criticize her performance because they want her to be "the best." On several occasions, they have encouraged her to continue practicing when she had a mild injury. Adrienne will most likely (p. 421)
    a. believe that her parents are only doing what is best for her, and feel good about her participation and ability.
    b. put pressure on herself to practice until she becomes an elite athlete.
    c. drop out of gymnastics in the future.
    d. love gymnastics more than other children.

19. Rough-and-tumble play among girls is (p. 421)
    a. nonexistent.
    b. more likely to involve hitting.
    c. more likely to involve wrestling.
    d. more likely to involve chasing.

20. What percent of school-age children have a daily physical education class? (p. 422)
    a. 17 percent
    b. 27 percent
    c. 37 percent
    d. 47 percent

CHAPTER 12
COGNITIVE DEVELOPMENT
IN MIDDLE CHILDHOOD

BRIEF CHAPTER SUMMARY

During Piaget's concrete operational stage, thought becomes more logical, flexible, and organized. However, children cannot yet think abstractly. Cross-cultural findings raise questions about whether mastery of Piagetian tasks emerges spontaneously in all children. The gradual development of operational reasoning challenges Piaget's assumption of an abrupt, stagewise transition to logical thought.

Brain development leads to gains in information-processing capacity and cognitive inhibition, which facilitate diverse aspects of thinking. Information-processing research reveals that attention becomes more controlled, adaptable, and planful, and memory strategies become more effective. By the end of the school years, knowledge acquisition and use of memory strategies are intimately related and support one another. Metacognition moves from a passive to an active view of mental functioning. Still, school-age children have difficulty regulating their progress toward a goal and redirecting unsuccessful efforts. Academic instruction that combines an emphasis on meaning and understanding with training in basic skills may be most effective in reading and mathematics.

Intelligence tests for children measure overall IQ as well as a variety of separate intellectual factors. Sternberg's triarchic theory of intelligence extends our understanding of the determinants of IQ scores. Gardner's theory of multiple intelligences highlights several intelligences not measured by IQ scores. Heritability and adoption research shows that both genetic and environmental factors contribute to individual differences in intelligence. Because of different language customs and lack of familiarity with test content, IQ scores of low-SES, ethnic minority children often do not reflect their true abilities. Supplementing IQs with measures of adaptive behavior and adjusting testing procedures to take cultural differences into account are ways of reducing test bias.

Language development continues during the school years, although changes are less dramatic than they were during early childhood. Vocabulary increases rapidly, and pragmatic skills are refined. Bilingual children are advanced in cognitive development and metalinguistic awareness.

Schools are powerful forces in children's development. Class size, the school's educational philosophy, teacher–pupil interaction, grouping practices, and the way computers are integrated into classroom learning experiences affect motivation and achievement in middle childhood. Teachers face special challenges in meeting the needs of children who have learning difficulties or special intellectual strengths. American pupils have fared unevenly in recent international comparisons of academic achievement. Efforts are currently underway to upgrade the quality of American education.

LEARNING OBJECTIVES

After reading this chapter, you should be able to:

12.1   Describe the major characteristics of concrete operational thought, including limitations of cognition during this stage. (pp. 428–429)

12.2   Discuss recent research on concrete operational thought, noting the implications of recent findings for the accuracy of Piaget's concrete operational stage. (pp. 429–430)

12.3   Describe two basic changes in information processing which occur during middle childhood. (p. 432)

12.4   Describe changes in attention and memory during middle childhood, and discuss the role of knowledge in memory performance. (pp. 432–436)

12.5   Describe the school-age child's theory of mind and capacity to engage in cognitive self-regulation. (pp. 437–438)

12.6   Discuss the application of information-processing research to children's learning in the areas of reading and mathematics, noting current controversies as to how to teach children in these areas. (pp. 438–441)

12.7   Describe the Stanford-Binet Intelligence Scale and the Wechsler Intelligence Scale for Children-III, the two scales most commonly used to assess intelligence in school-age children. (pp. 442–443)

12.8   Discuss recent developments in defining intelligence, including Sternberg's triarchic theory of intelligence and Gardner's theory of multiple intelligences. (pp. 443–445)

12.9   Discuss evidence indicating that both heredity and environment contribute to intelligence. (p. 446)

12.10 Describe cultural influences on intelligence test performance, and discuss efforts to overcome cultural bias in intelligence testing. (pp. 446–450)

12.11 Describe changes in metalinguistic awareness, vocabulary, grammar, and pragmatics during middle childhood. (pp. 451–452)

12.12 Discuss the major issues surrounding bilingual development and bilingual education. (pp. 453–454)

12.13 Discuss the impact of class size, educational philosophy, teacher–student interaction, and grouping practices on student motivation and academic achievement. (pp. 454–459)

12.14 Describe learning advantages of and concerns about computers in classrooms. (pp. 459–460)

12.15 Explain issues surrounding the educational placement of students with learning disabilities, noting the effectiveness of mainstreaming and full inclusion. (pp. 460–461)

12.16 Describe the characteristics of gifted children, and discuss current efforts to meet their educational needs. (pp. 461–463)

12.17 Compare the American cultural climate for academic achievement with that of Asian nations. (pp. 463–465)

STUDY QUESTIONS

Piaget's Theory: The Concrete Operational Stage

Achievements of the Concrete Operational Stage

1.   Generally speaking, how does thought change as children enter the concrete operational stage? (p. 428)

_____

2.   Match the following terms with the appropriate descriptions and examples. (p. 428)

_____ The ability to order items along a quantitative dimension, such as length or weight

_____ The ability to focus on relations between a general category and two specific categories

_____ The ability to seriate mentally

_____ The ability to focus on several aspects of a problem and relate them rather than centering on just one aspect

_____ Thinking through a series of steps and then mentally reversing direction, returning to the starting point

1. Seriation
2. Decentration
3. Reversibility
4. Classification
5. Transitive inference

3. Advances in spatial reasoning are evidenced by children's understanding of maps and ability to give directions. Summarize changes in these two areas as children move from preoperational thought to concrete operational thought. (p. 429)

Maps: _____

_____

_____

Directions: _____

_____

_____

Limitations of Concrete Operational Thought

1. Describe the major limitation of concrete operational thought. (p. 429)

_____

_____

2. Explain what is meant by the term *horizontal décalage,* noting how it is related to concrete operational thought. (p. 429)

_____

_____

Follow-Up Research on Concrete Operational Thought

1. Cite two examples that illustrate how culture and schooling contribute to children's mastery of conservation and other Piagetian tasks. (p. 430)

A. _____

_____

B. _____

_____

2. True or False: The forms of logic required by Piagetian tasks appear to emerge spontaneously during childhood and are not heavily influenced by training, context, or cultural conditions. (p. 430)

3. Summarize Case's information-processing view of cognitive development. (p. 430)

_____

_____

_____

_____

4. What are *central conceptual structures*? (p. 430)

_____

_____

5. Based on Case's theory, cite two reasons why children show a horizontal décalage. (p. 431)

A. _____

_____

B. _____

_____

Evaluation of the Concrete Operational Stage

1. Many researchers believe that two types of change may be involved in the school-age child's approach to Piagetian problems. List these two changes. (p. 431)

A. _____

B. _____

Information Processing

1. Discuss two ways in which brain development contributes to changes in information processing. (p. 432)

A. _____

_____

B. _____

_____

Attention

1. Describe three ways in which attention changes during middle childhood. (pp. 432–433)

A. _____

_____

B. _____

_____

C. _____

_____

2. List and describe the four-step sequence of attentional strategy development. (p. 433)

A. _____

_____

B. _____

_____

C. _____

_____

D. _____

_____

3. Cite two ways in which school-age children's attentional strategies become more planful. (p. 433)

   A. _____

   _____

   B. _____

   _____

4. Explain how children typically learn planning skills, and discuss what parents can do to foster the development of planning in their children. (p. 433)

   _____

   _____

   _____

Memory Strategies

1. List and describe three memory strategies that emerge during middle childhood, noting the order in which they typically appear. (pp. 434–436)

   A. _____

   _____

   B. _____

   _____

   C. _____

   _____

2. Because the strategies of organization and elaboration combine items into _____, they permit children to hold on to much more information, thus expanding working memory. (p. 436)

The Knowledge Base and Memory Performance

1. Explain how extensive knowledge and use of memory strategies are closely related to and support one another. (p. 436)

   _____

   _____

   _____

2. Explain why knowledge is not the only important factor in children's memory processing. (p. 436)

   _____

   _____

Culture, Schooling, and Memory Strategies

1. True or False: People in non-Western cultures who have no formal schooling are likely to use and benefit from instruction in memory strategies. (p. 436)

2. Discuss how culture and schooling are related to the development of memory strategies. (p. 436)

_____

_____

_____

The School-Age Child's Theory of Mind

1. Describe how a school-age child's theory of mind differs from that of a preschooler. (p. 437)

_____

_____

_____

2. How does schooling contribute to the school-age child's theory of mind? (p. 437)

_____

_____

Cognitive Self-Regulation

1. What is *cognitive self-regulation*? (p. 438)

_____

_____

2. School-age children (are / are not) good at cognitive self-regulation. Cite evidence to support your response. (p. 438)

_____

_____

_____

3. Discuss ways that parents and teachers can foster self-regulation. (p. 438)

_____

_____

_____

Applications of Information Processing to Academic Learning

1. List the diverse information-processing skills that contribute to the process of reading. (p. 439)

_____

_____

2. Summarize the two sides of the debate over how to teach beginning reading. (p. 439)

    A. _____

    _____

    B. _____

    _____

3. Explain why combining phonics with whole language is often the best strategy for teaching children to read. (p. 439)

_____

_____

_____

4. Arguments about how to teach mathematics closely resemble those in reading. Summarize these arguments. (p. 440)

   A. _____

   _____

   B. _____

   _____

Biology and Environment: Children with Attention-Deficit Hyperactivity Disorder

1. Describe typical characteristics of children with attention-deficit hyperactivity disorder (ADHD). (p. 434)

   _____

   _____

   _____

2. True or False: Children with ADHD perform as well as other children on tests of intelligence. (p. 434)

3. Cite evidence that ADHD is influenced by both heredity and environment. (pp. 434–435)

   Heredity: _____

   _____

   _____

   Environment: _____

   _____

   _____

4. Discuss three ways to treat ADHD, noting which method is the most *common* and which method is the most *effective*. (p. 435)

   A. _____

   _____

   B. _____

   _____

   C. _____

   _____

5. True or False: ADHD is a lifelong disorder, with problems usually persisting into adulthood. (p. 435)

Defining and Measuring Intelligence

1. Describe the types of items commonly included on intelligence tests for children. (p. 442)

    _____

    _____

    _____

2. Distinguish between group- and individually-administered intelligence tests, and cite the advantages of each. (p. 442)

    Group administered: _____

    _____

    _____

    Individually administered: _____

    _____

    _____

3. Match the following intelligence tests with the appropriate descriptions. (pp. 442–443)

    ____ Appropriate for individuals age 6–16   1. Stanford-Binet Intelligence Scale
    ____ Appropriate for individuals between 2 years of age   2. Wechsler Intelligence Scale for Children-IV
         and adulthood
    ____ Assesses four broad intellectual factors: verbal reasoning,
         perceptual reasoning, working memory, and processing speed
    ____ Assesses four broad intellectual factors: verbal reasoning,
         quantitative reasoning, abstract / visual reasoning, and short-term memory
    ____ First test to be standardized on samples representing the total population
         of the United States, including ethnic minorities

Recent Efforts to Define Intelligence

1. What is a *componential analysis,* and why is it used? (p. 443)

    _____

    _____

    _____

2. What is the major shortcoming of the componential approach? (p. 443)

    _____

    _____

    _____

    _____

3. List and briefly describe the three broad intelligences outlined in Sternberg's *triarchic theory of intelligence.* (pp. 443–444)

    A. _____

    _____

B. _____

_____

C. _____

_____

4. Explain how Sternberg's theory is relevant to the controversy surrounding cultural bias in intelligence testing. (p. 444)

_____

_____

_____

5. State how Gardner defines intelligence, and list Gardner's eight intelligences. (pp. 444–445)

_____

_____

A. _____   B. _____
C. _____   D. _____
E. _____   F. _____
G. _____   H. _____

6. True or False: In Gardner's theory, intelligence has a purely biological basis and is not affected by cultural values or learning opportunities. (p. 444)

7. Gardner's theory (is / is not) firmly grounded in research. (p. 444)

8. Cite one contribution of Gardner's theory. (p. 445)

_____

_____

Explaining Individual and Group Differences in IQ

1. Summarize evidence related to ethnic and SES differences in IQ. (pp. 445–446)

Ethnic differences: _____

_____

_____

SES differences: _____

_____

_____

2. What do kinship studies reveal about the role of heredity in IQ? (p. 446)

_____

_____

_____

3. What do adoption studies suggest about the contribution of environmental factors in IQ? (p. 446)

_____

_____

_____

4. Explain how ethnic minority families foster unique communication skills that do not fit with the expectations of most classrooms and testing situations. (p. 448)

_____

_____

_____

_____

5. Describe the difference between collaborative and hierarchical styles of communication, noting how each is likely to affect performance in school and on IQ tests. (p. 448)

Collaborative: _____

_____

_____

Hierarchical: _____

_____

_____

6. True or False: Using nonverbal intelligence tests that tap spatial reasoning and performance skills considerably raises the scores of ethnic minority children. Why or why not? (p. 448)

_____

_____

7. Define *stereotype threat,* and explain how it is likely to influence low-SES minority children's performance on intelligence tests. (p. 449)

Definition: _____

_____

Impact: _____

_____

Reducing Cultural Bias in Intelligence Testing

1. Why is assessment of adaptive behavior especially important for minority children? (pp. 449–450)

_____

_____

2. Describe *dynamic assessment,* and discuss its effectiveness for reducing cultural bias in testing. (p. 450)

_____

_____

_____

_____

Cultural Influences: The Flynn Effect: The Massive Generational Gains in IQ

1. What is the *Flynn effect*? (p. 447)

_____

_____

_____

2. The Flynn effect is (biological / environmental). Briefly explain your response. (p. 447)

_____

_____

_____

3. Explain how the Flynn effect challenges genetic theories of the black-white IQ gap. (p. 447)

_____

_____

_____

Language Development

1. School-age children develop _____ *awareness,* the ability to think about language as a system. (p. 451)

Vocabulary

1. True or False: The rate of vocabulary growth during the school years exceeds that of early childhood. (p. 451)

2. Cite four strategies that assist school-age children in building their vocabularies. (p. 451)

A. _____

_____

B. _____

_____

C. _____

_____

D. _____

_____

3. List three changes in school-age children's vocabularies aside from knowledge of more word meanings. (pp. 451–452)

A. _____

_____

B. _____

_____

C. _____

_____

Grammar

1. Cite two grammatical achievements of middle childhood. (p. 452)

A. _____

_____

B. _____

_____

Pragmatics

1. Describe three advances in pragmatic speech that take place during middle childhood. (p. 452)

A. _____

_____

B. _____

_____

C. _____

_____

Learning Two Languages at a Time

1. Cite two ways in which children can become bilingual, and discuss children's development in each instance. (p. 453)

A. _____

_____

B. _____

_____

2. True or False: There is a sensitive period for second language development. (p. 453)

3. List the cognitive benefits of bilingualism. (p. 453)

_____

_____

_____

4. Briefly describe Canada's language immersion programs. (p. 453)

_____

_____

5. Summarize the current debate regarding how American ethnic minority children with limited English proficiency should be educated. (pp. 453–454)

_____

_____

_____

_____

6. Discuss the benefits of integrating children's native language into the classroom while at the same time fostering mastery of English. (p. 454)

_____

_____

_____

Children's Learning in School

1. Describe four characteristics of high-quality education in elementary school. (p. 455)

   A. _____

   _____

   B. _____

   _____

   C. _____

   _____

   D. _____

   _____

Class Size

1. Describe evidence that class size is influential in children's learning. (pp. 454–455)

   _____

   _____

   _____

2. List two reasons why small class size is beneficial. (p. 455)

   A. _____

   B. _____

Educational Philosophies

1. Explain how *traditional classrooms* differ from *constructivist classrooms,* and cite educational outcomes associated with each. (pp. 455–456)

   Traditional: _____

   _____

   Outcomes: _____

   _____

   Constructivist: _____

   _____

   Outcomes: _____

   _____

2. Describe the nature of *social-constructivist* classrooms. (p. 456)

   _____

   _____

3. List and describe three educational themes that were inspired by Vygotsky's emphasis on the social origins of learning. (p. 456)

   A. _____

   _____

   B. _____

   _____

   C. _____

   _____

4. _____ refers to a method of learning in which a teacher and 2 to 4 students form a cooperative group and take turns leading dialogues on the content of a text passage. Describe four cognitive strategies that group members apply during these dialogues. (pp. 456–457)

   A. _____

   B. _____

   C. _____

   D. _____

5. What are *communities of learners,* and what is the philosophy behind this educational approach? (p. 458)

   Description: _____

   _____

   Philosophy: _____

   _____

Teacher–Student Interaction

1. Describe how teachers interact differently with high-achieving, well-behaved students versus low-achieving, disruptive students. (p. 458)

   High-achieving, well-behaved students:

   _____

   _____

   Low-achieving, disruptive students:

   _____

   _____

2. What is an *educational self-fulfilling prophecy,* and how does it affect students' motivation and performance? (p. 458)

   Definition: _____

   _____

   Affect: _____

   _____

   _____

Grouping Practices

1. What are homogeneous groups, and how can they be a potential source of self-fulfilling prophecies? (p. 459)

   _____

   _____

   _____

2. Discuss the benefits of multigrade classrooms, noting how student training in *cooperative learning* impacts the success of such classrooms. (p. 459)

   Benefits: _____

   _____

   _____

   Impact of training in cooperative learning: _____

   _____

   _____

   _____

Computers and Academic Learning

1. Explain how the use of word processing programs can be beneficial to children as they learn to read and write. (p. 459)

   _____

   _____

   _____

2. Summarize the competencies gained by children who learn computer-programming skills. (pp. 459–460)

_____

_____

_____

3. By the end of elementary school, (girls / boys) spend more time using computers, thereby contributing to concerns of a "digital divide." (p. 460)

Teaching Children with Special Needs

1. Distinguish between *mainstreaming* and *full inclusion.* (p. 460)

   Mainstreaming: _____

   _____

   Full inclusion: _____

   _____

2. Describe the characteristics of a *learning disability.* (p. 460)

   _____

   _____

   _____

3. Discuss findings on the effectiveness of mainstreaming and full inclusion in relation to student academic experiences and integrated participation in classroom life. (pp. 460–461)

   _____

   _____

   _____

   _____

4. Special-needs children placed in regular classrooms often do best when they receive instruction in a resource room for part of the day and in the regular classroom for the remainder of the day. Describe this approach to instruction. (pp. 460–461)

   _____

   _____

   _____

5. Cite three ways in which teachers can promote peer acceptance of mainstreamed children. (p. 461)

   A. _____

   B. _____

   C. _____

6. Describe the characteristics of *gifted* children. (p. 461)

   _____

   _____

7. _____ refers to the ability to produce work that is original yet appropriate. (p. 461)

8. Distinguish between *convergent* and *divergent thinking*. (p. 461)

Convergent: _____

_____

Divergent: _____

_____

9. _____ refers to outstanding performance in a particular field. (p. 461)

10. Describe family characteristics that foster talent. (pp. 461–462)

_____

_____

_____

11. True or False: Gifted children report more emotional and social difficulties than do their ordinary agemates. (p. 462)

12. List three models for educating gifted children. (pp. 462–463)

A. _____

B. _____

C. _____

How Well Educated Are North American Children?

1. Explain how instructional practices and student study habits contribute to American children's lagging academic accomplishments. (p. 463)

Instructional practices: _____

_____

Student study habits: _____

_____

2. Describe four social forces that foster a stronger commitment to learning in Asian families and schools than in their North American counterparts. (pp. 463–464)

A. _____

_____

B. _____

_____

C. _____

_____

D. _____

_____

1. Delaying kindergarten entry (is / is not) beneficial for children whose birth dates are close to the cutoff for enrollment. Provide evidence to support your response. (p. 457)

   _____

   _____

   _____

   _____

2. True or False: Children retained in kindergarten or one of the primary grades show many learning benefits, as well as other positive consequences in motivation, self-esteem, and attitudes toward school. Explain your response. (p. 475)

   _____

   _____

   _____

3. _____ classes, or waystations between kindergarten and first grade, are a form of homogeneous grouping and have the same implications for teacher–student interactions as other "low-ability" groups. (p. 457)

ASK YOURSELF . . .

For *Ask Yourself* questions for this chapter, please log on to the Companion Website at *www.ablongman.com/berk*.

SUGGESTED STUDENT READINGS

Bray, M., Brown, A., & Green, T. D. (2004). *Technology and the diverse learner.* Thousand Oaks, CA: Sage. Supported by extensive research in education, this book explores the many ways technology can be used in the classroom. The authors place particular emphasis on topics related to children with special needs, gender, and culture.

Champion, T. B. (2003). *Understanding storytelling among African-American children: A journey from Africa to America.* Mahwah, NJ: Erlbaum. A useful resource for teachers, researchers, and professionals working with African-American children, this book explores the unique communication style of black children, including the structure of their storytelling and its impact on learning and achievement.

Jensen, P. S. (2004). *Making the system work for your child with ADHD.* New York: Guildford. Provides an extensive overview of ADHD, including diagnostic criteria, healthcare, resources, and problem-solving strategies to help parents effectively advocate for school services.

Rogoff, Barlett, L., & Turkanis (Eds.). (2002). *Learning together: Children and adults in a school community.* New York: Oxford University Press. This book highlights the many benefits of open classrooms, focusing on the importance of adult involvement in children's education.

PUZZLE 12.1 TERM REVIEW

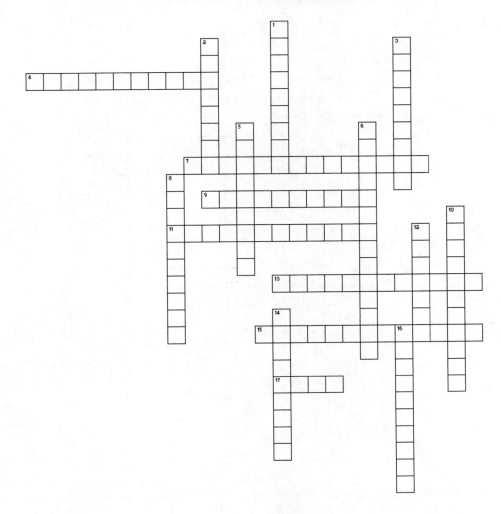

Across

4. _____ deficiency: inability to improve performance even with consistent use of a mental strategy

7. Cognitive __-____: process of continually monitoring progress toward a goal, checking outcomes, and redirecting unsuccessful efforts (2 words, hyph.)

9. ____ décalage: development within a Piagetian stage

11. The ability to focus on and relate several aspects of a problem at the same time

13. Memory strategy of grouping together related items

15. Ability to mentally go through a series of steps in a problem and then reverse direction, returning to the starting point

17. Disorder involving inattentiveness, impulsivity , and excessive motor activity that results in academic and social problems (abbr.)

Down

1. _____ strategy use: consistent use of a mental strategy that leads to improved performance

2. Piaget's ____ operational stage is marked by logical, flexible, and organized thought.

3. The ability to order items along a quantitative dimension

5. Transitive _____: ability to *mentally* order items along a quantitative dimension

6. The ability to think about language as a system is known as _____ awareness.

8. _____ deficiency: failure to produce a mental strategy when it could be helpful

10. Memory strategy of creating a relation between two or more items that are not members of the same category

12. _____ deficiency: inability to consistently execute a mental strategy

14. Memory strategy of repeating information

16. Cognitive _____: ability to resist interference from distracting stimuli

PUZZLE 12.2 TERM REVIEW

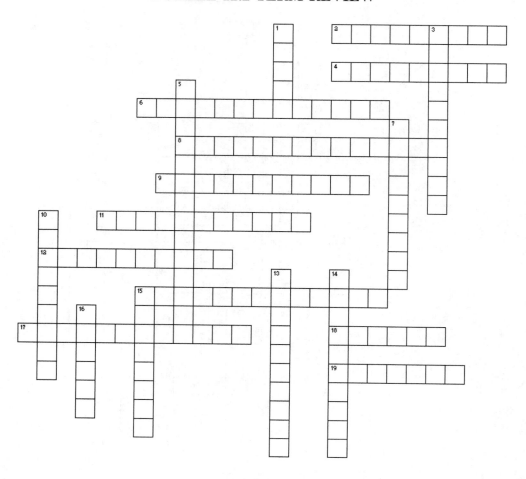

Across

2. Sternberg's _____ theory of intelligence states that information processing skills, ability to learn efficiently in novel situations, and contextual factors interact to determine intelligent behavior.

4. _____ of learners: teachers guide the overall learning process, but otherwise, no distinction is made between adult and child contributors

6. Approach to beginning reading that parallels children's natural language learning (2 words, hyph.)

8. Educational __-___ prophecy: children may adopt teachers' positive or negative attitudes toward them and start to live up to these expectations

9. In _____ classrooms, children are passive learners who acquire information presented by teachers.

11. Approach to beginning reading that emphasizes training in phonics and simplified reading materials (2 words, hyph.)

12. The ability to produce work that is original yet appropriate

15. Placement of pupils with learning difficulties in regular classrooms for part of the school day

17. Learning _____: specific learning disorders leading to poor academic achievement despite average or above-average IQ

18. Stereotype _____: fear of being judged on the basis of a negative stereotype

19. _____ assessment: individualized teaching is introduced into the testing situation to see what the child can attain with social support

Down

1. _____ effect: steady increase in IQ from one generation to the next

3. _____ thinking: generation of a single correct answer to a problem

5. In _____ classrooms, children construct their own knowledge and are viewed as active agents who reflect on and coordinate their own thoughts rather than absorbing those of others.

7. _____ thinking: generation of multiple and unusual possibilities when faced with a problem

10. Placement of pupils with learning difficulties in regular classrooms for the entire school day is known as full _____.

13. Vygotsky-inspired method of teaching in which a teacher and 2 to 4 students form a cooperative learning group

14. Exceptional intellectual strengths

15. Gardner's theory of _____ intelligences proposes at least eight independent intelligences.

16. Outstanding performance in a particular field

256

PRACTICE TEST #1

1. During a conservation-of-mass problem, Tom can mentally reverse the steps of the task in which the clay ball was smashed. This example demonstrates that Tom is capable of (p. 428)
   a. seriation.
   b. decentration.
   c. reversibility.
   d. hypothetico-deductive reasoning.

2. Most school-age children pass Piaget's class inclusion problem. This indicates that they (p. 428)
   a. can focus on several aspects of a problem rather than centering on just one.
   b. have the capacity to think through a series of steps and then mentally reverse them.
   c. can order items along a quantitative dimension.
   d. are aware of classification hierarchies.

3. Sabrina is able to mentally represent her school and describe the space to others. Her mental representation of her school is known as a (p. 429)
   a. cognitive map.
   b. transitive inference.
   c. script.
   d. memory strategy.

4. Nine-year-old Albert easily solves Piaget's transitive inference problem with sticks. However, Albert has difficulty solving the following problem: "Jim is taller than Frank, and Frank is taller than Joe. Who is the tallest?" Piaget would attribute Albert's failure on the latter task to (p. 429)
   a. egocentrism.
   b. centration.
   c. reversibility.
   d. horizontal décalage.

5. Follow-up research on concrete operational thought suggests that the forms of logic required by Piagetian tasks (p. 430)
   a. emerge spontaneously as children interact with the environment.
   b. are heavily influenced by cultural conditions.
   c. develop at the same rate all over the world.
   d. progress more quickly in non-Western societies.

6. According to Case's neo-Piagetian theory, as children get older (p. 430)
   a. cognitive schemes demand more attention.
   b. thought becomes increasingly concrete.
   c. cognitive schemes becomes increasingly deliberate.
   d. working memory space is freed up.

7. Dave's drawings show both the features of objects and the relationships among objects. According to Case, Dave's drawing demonstrates that (p. 431)
   a. he is in the formal operational stage.
   b. his central conceptual structures coordinated multiple dimensions.
   c. he understands transitive inference.
   d. he is capable of cognitive inhibition.

8. Cognitive inhibition refers to the (p. 432)
   a. failure to produce a mental strategy when it could be helpful.
   b. ability to think out a sequence of acts and allocate attention accordingly to reach a goal.
   c. process of continuously monitoring toward a goal, checking outcomes, and redirecting unsuccessful efforts.
   d. ability to control internal and external distracting stimuli.

9. A production deficiency refers to the (p. 433)
   a. failure to use an already learned mental strategy.
   b. inability to execute a mental strategy effectively.
   c. failure to benefit from using a mental strategy.
   d. use of an inappropriate mental strategy.

10. Which of the following is supported by research on memory strategies in middle childhood? (p. 435)
    a. Organization is usually an inefficient strategy.
    b. Rehearsal is the most effective and widely used memory strategy.
    c. Children rarely experiment with strategies when faced with a challenging problem.
    d. Elaboration is a late developing memory strategy.

11. Schneider and Bjorklund's study of child soccer experts versus soccer novices demonstrated that compared to novices, expert children are more likely to (p. 436)
    a. retrieve meaningful material from long-term memory.
    b. apply organizational strategies during retrieval.
    c. rehearse the test items during encoding.
    d. engage in reconstructive processing during storage.

12. Cross-cultural research demonstrates that (p. 436)
    a. nonschooled children benefit greatly from instruction in memory strategies.
    b. children from Western cultures always show better memory performance than those in non-Western cultures.
    c. Western children get so much practice with memory strategies that they do not refine other techniques that rely on cues readily available in everyday life.
    d. the more developed the memory strategies, the more competent the information-processing system.

13. Cognitive self-regulation is (p. 438)
    a. the process of monitoring progress toward a goal, checking outcomes, and redirecting unsuccessful efforts.
    b. deliberate mental activities that are used to store and retain information.
    c. the gradual mastery of logical concepts.
    d. the ability to resist interference from internal and external distracting stimuli.

14. Educators who advocate a whole-language approach argue that (p. 439)
    a. from the beginning, children should be exposed to text in its complete form.
    b. reading instruction should focus on coaching in phonics.
    c. children should learn the basic rules for translating written symbols into sounds before being given reading material.
    d. young children should be given simplified text materials to facilitate beginning reading.

15. Research on math instruction demonstrates that _____ is essential for mastering complex skills. (p. 440)
    a. drill in computational skills
    b. teaching by rote
    c. retrieving answers automatically
    d. experience with problem solving and evaluating solution techniques

16. In Sternberg's triarchic theory of intelligence, _____ refers to information-processing skills. (p. 443)
    a. practical intelligence
    b. creative intelligence
    c. analytical intelligence
    d. componential intelligence

17. Kinship studies (p. 446)
    a. underestimate genetic influences and overestimate environmental factors.
    b. do not reveal the processes through which genes and experiences influence intelligence as children develop.
    c. demonstrate convincingly that heredity is largely responsible for individual, ethnic, and SES variations in intelligence.
    d. reveal that the effects of poverty severely depress the intelligence of ethnic minority children.

18. Which of the following is believed to contribute to IQ test bias against certain ethnic minority groups? (p. 448)
    a. Compared to white children, ethnic minority children have less prior exposure to specific information resembling IQ test content.
    b. Ethnic minority children often grow up in "object-oriented" rather than "people-oriented" homes.
    c. Compared to white parents, ethnic minority parents do not foster in their children complex verbal skills such as storytelling.
    d. Ethnic minority children are less concerned with pleasing their teachers than are white children.

19. Dynamic assessment (p. 451)
    a. is more effective in predicting grades than are traditional IQ tests.
    b. often underestimates the IQs of ethnic minority children.
    c. presents challenges that are easier than those faced in traditional, static assessments.
    d. introduces purposeful teaching to ascertain what the child can accomplish with social support.

20. Children of bilingual parents who teach them both languages in infancy and early childhood (p. 453)
    a. attain language milestones at a slower rate than their monolingual agemates.
    b. often confuse the two language systems.
    c. usually attain proficiency in both languages.
    d. have trouble distinguishing the sounds of each language.

PRACTICE TEST #2

1. A teacher gives a group of 7-year-olds some sticks of varying lengths. At this age, the children will (p. 428)
   a. put them in order from shortest to longest, using an orderly plan.
   b. attempt to order them by height, but will make many mistakes and take a long time to correct them.
   c. put them in a completely random order and not attempt to correct mistakes.
   d. not understand the task.

2. Juley is standing with a piano on her right and a flag on her left. Seven-year-old Lin is facing Juley. When asked to name what is on Juley's left, Lin will say (p. 429)
   a. "the flag."
   b. "the piano."
   c. "both the flag and the piano are on the left."
   d. "I can't tell unless I stand where Juley is standing."

3. Conservation of _____ is usually mastered before conservation of _____. (p. 430)
   a. length; number
   b. weight; length
   c. mass; number
   d. number; weight

4. Research has demonstrated that the everyday activities found in a particular culture may promote the kind of logic required for Piagetian tasks. This idea is most similar to _____ theory. (p. 430)
   a. the information-processing
   b. Vygotsky's
   c. Erikson's
   d. dynamic systems

5. People from Korea, Canada, and the United States were given a variety of cognitive tasks. Researchers who measured their processing speed found rapid age-related declines in time needed to process information during (p. 432)
   a. early adulthood for Koreans only.
   b. early adulthood for all cultural groups.
   c. adolescence for those from the United States and Canada and during middle childhood for Koreans.
   d. middle childhood for all cultural groups.

6. Attention-deficit hyperactivity disorder (ADHD) affects _____ percent of school-age children. (p. 434)
   a. 1 to 2
   b. 2 to 3
   c. 3 to 5
   d. 5 to 8

7. Researchers showed video clips of people using different recall strategies. When they asked school-age children to identify which strategy would result in better memory, (p. 434)
   a. young elementary school children thought all of the strategies were equal.
   b. young elementary school children knew that rehearsing would work better than just looking or naming.
   c. older elementary school children thought rehearsing and organizing would be equally effective.
   d. they could not answer the question; children do not evaluate memory strategies until they are in junior high school.

8. Compared to children who are taught to read with the whole-language approach, children who are trained in phonics (p. 439)
   a. are better spellers by third grade.
   b. enjoy reading more.
   c. are more likely to comprehend what they read.
   d. have better metacognitive knowledge of effective reading strategies.

9. IQ becomes stable around age (p. 442)
    a.   4.
    b.   6.
    c.   8.
    d.   10.

10. The Stanford-Binet Intelligence Scale (p. 442)
    a.   yields verbal and performance factors.
    b.   is a group administered IQ test.
    c.   has not undergone factor analysis.
    d.   can be administered from age 2 through adult.

11. Sternberg's triarchic theory emphasizes (p. 444)
    a.   the importance of practical intelligence.
    b.   the need for IQ tests.
    c.   academic skills as central for life success.
    d.   linguistic and spatial intelligence.

12. Tom is highly insightful about his personal emotions and behavior. According to Gardner, Tom is high in _____ intelligence. (p. 445)
    a.   experiential
    b.   social
    c.   intrapersonal
    d.   interpersonal

13. According to Arthur Jensen, heredity accounts for (p. 446)
    a.   mathematical and logical intelligence, while verbal intelligence is influenced mostly by the child's environment.
    b.   at least eight independent areas of intelligence for each individual.
    c.   ethnic and SES variations in intelligence.
    d.   nothing when it comes to IQ; it is influenced primarily by environmental factors.

14. One-week-old Cassandra, whose biological mother had a low IQ, is being adopted by a high-SES family. You would expect Cassandra's IQ during the school years to be (p. 446)
    a.   higher than her biological mother's IQ.
    b.   the same as her biological mother's IQ.
    c.   the same as her adopted sibling's IQ.
    d.   lower than her biological sibling's IQ.

15. Which of the following phrases would be easier for a school-age child to understand than for a preschooler? (p. 452)
    a.   "The girl was kissed by the boy."
    b.   "The boy was licked by the dog."
    c.   "The dog was hit by the car."
    d.   "The car was liked by the girl."

16. Armando is semilingual. In other words (p. 453)
    a.   he speaks two languages but is not proficient in either one.
    b.   he speaks one language well and is just beginning to learn another.
    c.   he speaks two languages fluently.
    d.   he is proficient in more than two languages.

17. Reciprocal teaching is designed to help students improve their (p. 456)
    a.   reading comprehension.
    b.   peer relationships in school.
    c.   public speaking skills.
    d.   self-esteem.

18. Johanna's intelligence is average. However, her achievement is much lower than would be expected for a child with her IQ. Johanna (p. 460)
    a. is mildly mentally retarded.
    b. has a learning disability.
    c. is gifted.
    d. has adaptive skills deficits.

19. Jeri's IQ was assessed, and she has been labeled "gifted." In other words, her IQ is over (p. 461)
    a. 100.
    b. 110.
    c. 120.
    d. 130.

20. An American elementary school added 30 days to its school calendar. Students who attended for the extended school year _____ compared to students from schools with a traditional calendar. (p. 464)
    a. were more likely to drop out of school
    b. scored lower in math and science, and complained of "burn-out"
    c. scored higher in reading, general knowledge, and math
    d. scored higher in reading but lower in math and general knowledge

CHAPTER 13
EMOTIONAL AND SOCIAL DEVELOPMENT
IN MIDDLE CHILDHOOD

BRIEF CHAPTER SUMMARY

Erikson's stage of industry versus inferiority captures the school-age child's capacity for productive work and new feelings of competence and mastery. During middle childhood, psychological traits and social comparisons appear in children's self-concepts, and a hierarchically organized self-esteem emerges. Attribution research has identified adult communication styles that affect children's explanations for success and failure and, in turn, their academic self-esteem, motivation, and task performance. Self-conscious emotions become clearly governed by personal responsibility, and both emotional understanding and emotional self-regulation improve. Perspective taking undergoes major advances, and moral understanding expands.

By the end of middle childhood, children form peer groups. Friendships change, emphasizing mutual trust and assistance. Researchers have identified four categories of social acceptance: popular, rejected, controversial, and neglected children. Peer acceptance is a powerful predictor of current and future psychological adjustment. The antisocial behavior of rejected children leads to severe dislike by agemates. During the school years, boys' masculine gender identities strengthen, whereas girls' identities become more flexible. However, cultural values and practices can modify these trends.

In middle childhood, child rearing shifts toward coregulation. Parents exercise general oversight while granting children more decision-making power. Sibling rivalry tends to increase, and siblings often take steps to reduce it by striving to be different from one another. Only children are just as well developed as children with siblings, and they are advantaged in self-esteem and achievement motivation. Children of gay and lesbian parents are well adjusted, and the large majority are heterosexual. The situations of children in never-married, single-parent families can be improved through strengthening social support, education, and employment opportunities for parents.

Large numbers of American children experience the divorce and remarriage of their parents. Child, parent, and family characteristics influence how well they fare. Maternal employment can lead to many benefits for school-age children, although outcomes vary with the child's sex and SES, the demands of the mother's job, the father's participation in child rearing, and the availability of high quality after-school programs as an alternative to self-care.

Fears and anxieties change during middle childhood as children experience new demands in school and begin to understand the realities of the wider world. Child sexual abuse, a serious problem in the United States, has devastating consequences for children and is especially difficult to treat. Personal characteristics of children, a warm, well-organized home life, and social supports outside the family are related to children's ability to cope with stressful life conditions.

LEARNING OBJECTIVES

After reading this chapter, you should be able to:

13.1 Explain Erikson's stage of industry versus inferiority, noting major personality changes. (p. 470)

13.2 Describe school-age children's self-concept and self-esteem, as well as factors that affect their achievement-related attributions. (pp. 471–476)

13.3 Describe changes in self-conscious emotions, understanding of emotional states, and emotional self-regulation in middle childhood. (pp. 478–480)

13.4 Trace the development of perspective taking, and discuss the relationship between perspective taking and social skills. (pp. 480–481)

13.5 Describe changes in moral understanding during middle childhood, and discuss the debate over moral education in the schools, including Narvaez's four-component model of morality education. (p. 481)

13.6 Describe changes in peer relations during middle childhood, including characteristics of peer groups and friendships and the contributions of each to social development. (pp. 485–487)

13.7 Describe the four categories of peer acceptance, noting how each is related to social behavior, and discuss ways to help rejected children. (pp. 487–489)

13.8 Describe changes in gender-stereotyped beliefs and gender identity during middle childhood, noting sex differences and cultural influences. (pp. 490–491)

13.9 Discuss changes in the parent–child relationship during middle childhood, including new issues confronting parents and changes in parent–child communication. (p. 492)

13.10 Describe changes in sibling relationships during middle childhood, noting the impact of birth order on sibling experiences, and compare the experiences and developmental outcomes of only children with those of children with siblings. (p. 493)

13.11 Describe gay and lesbian families, and discuss the developmental outcomes of children raised in such families. (p. 494)

13.12 Describe the characteristics of never-married, single-parent families, and explain how living in a single-parent household affects children. (pp. 494–495)

13.13 Discuss children's adjustment to divorce and blended families, noting the influence of parent and child characteristics and social supports within the family and surrounding community. (pp. 495–499)

13.14 Discuss the impact of maternal employment and dual-earner families on school-age children's development, noting the influence of social supports within the family and surrounding community, and explain issues regarding child care for school-age children. (pp. 500–501)

13.15 Discuss common fears and anxieties in middle childhood, with particular attention to school phobia. (p. 502)

13.16 Discuss factors related to child sexual abuse, its consequences for children's development, and ways to prevent and treat it. (pp. 504–505)

13.17 Cite factors that foster resilience in middle childhood, and describe the RCCP program, a school-based program aimed at reducing violence and antisocial behavior. (pp. 505–508)

STUDY QUESTIONS

Erikson's Theory: Industry versus Inferiority

1. Erikson's theory of personality change during the school years builds upon Freud's _____ stage. (p. 470)

2. According to Erikson, what two factors set the stage for the psychological conflict of middle childhood, *industry versus inferiority*? (p. 470)

    A. _____

    B. _____

3. Discuss factors that lead to a positive resolution of the industry versus inferiority stage. (p. 470)

    _____

    _____

    _____

4. Explain how the beginning of formal schooling puts some children at risk for developing a sense of inferiority during middle childhood. (p. 470)

_____

_____

_____

Self-Understanding

Self-Concept

1. List three ways in which self-concept changes during middle childhood. (p. 471)

   A. _____

   B. _____

   C. _____

Cognitive, Social, and Cultural Influences on Self-Concept

1. Discuss the relationship between perspective-taking skills and self-concept development. (pp. 471–472)

   _____

   _____

   _____

   _____

2. True or False: The content of children's self-concept varies little from culture to culture. (p. 472)

Self-Esteem

1. List four self-esteems that children form by the age of 7 or 8. (p. 473)

   A. _____

   B. _____

   C. _____

   D. _____

2. True or False: Once children's self-esteem takes on a hierarchical structure, separate self-esteems contribute equally to general self-esteem. (p. 473)

3. Self-esteem (rises / drops) during the early elementary school years. Explain why this is the case. (p. 473)

   _____

   _____

   _____

Influences on Self-Esteem

1. Summarize sex and ethnic differences in children's self-esteem. (p. 473)

   Sex: _____

   _____

   _____

   Ethnic: _____

   _____

   _____

2. Differentiate parenting practices associated with high versus low self-esteem in middle childhood. (p. 474)

   High: _____

   _____

   Low: _____

   _____

3. _____ are our common, everyday explanations for the causes of behavior. (p. 474)

4. Distinguish between mastery-oriented attributions and learned helplessness. (p. 475)

   Mastery-oriented attributions: _____

   _____

   _____

   Learned helplessness: _____

   _____

   _____

5. Briefly explain how children's attributions impact their goals. (p. 475)

   _____

   _____

   _____

6. Summarize how communication from parents and teachers influences children's attributional style. (pp. 475–476)

   Parents: _____

   _____

   Teachers: _____

   _____

7. True or False: Girls and low-income ethnic minority children are especially vulnerable to learned helplessness. (p. 476)

8. _____ is an intervention that encourages learned-helpless children to believe that they can overcome failure by exerting more effort. Briefly describe this technique. (p. 476)

_____

_____

_____

9. Discuss four ways to foster a mastery-oriented approach to learning in middle childhood. (p. 477)

A. _____

_____

B. _____

_____

C. _____

_____

D. _____

_____

Emotional Development

Self-Conscious Emotions

1. Discuss changes in how children experience the self-conscious emotions of pride and guilt during middle childhood. (p. 478)

Pride: _____

_____

Guilt: _____

_____

Emotional Understanding

1. List three advances in school-age children's understanding of emotions. (p. 478)

A. _____

B. _____

C. _____

Emotional Self-Regulation

1. Differentiate between *problem-centered* and *emotion-centered* coping strategies, noting the circumstances in which children are likely to use one strategy versus the other. (p. 479)

Problem-centered: _____

_____

_____

Emotion-centered: _____

_____

_____

2. When the development of emotional self-regulation has gone well, young people acquire a sense of *emotional*
    _____—a feeling of being in control of their emotional experience. (p. 479)

3. Distinguish characteristics of emotionally well-regulated children versus children with poor emotional regulation.
    (pp. 479–480)

    Well-regulated: _____

    _____

    Poorly-regulated: _____

    _____

Understanding Others: Perspective Taking

1. Define *perspective taking.* (p. 480)

    _____

    _____

2. Match each of Selman's stages of perspective taking with the appropriate descriptions. (p. 480)

    _____ Understanding that third-party perspective taking can be influenced   1. Undifferentiated
          by larger societal values   2. Social-informational
    _____ Recognize that self and others can have different perspectives,   3. Self-reflective
          but confuse the two   4. Third-party
    _____ Understand that different perspectives may be due to access   5. Societal
          to different information
    _____ Can imagine how the self and others are viewed from the perspective
          of an impartial third person
    _____ Can view own thoughts, feelings, and behavior from others' perspectives

3. What factors contribute to individual differences in perspective-taking skill? (p. 480)

    _____

    _____

    _____

Moral Development

Learning About Justice Through Sharing

1. Define *distributive justice.* (p. 481)

    _____

    _____

2. Using Damon's three-step sequence, trace the development of children's conception of distributive justice during middle childhood. (p. 481)

A. _____

_____

B. _____

_____

C. _____

_____

3. True or False: Peer interaction is particularly important in the development of standards of justice. (p. 481)

Understanding Moral, Social-Conventional, and Personal Matters

1. Describe two changes in moral and social-conventional understanding that take place during middle childhood. (p. 482)

A. _____

_____

B. _____

_____

2. True or False: Children in Western and non-Western cultures use the same criteria to distinguish moral and social-conventional concerns. (p. 482)

Moral Education

1. Describe Narvaez's four-component model of morality education. (p. 484)

A. _____

_____

B. _____

_____

C. _____

_____

D. _____

_____

Cultural Influences: Children's Understanding of God

1. Trace children's understanding of God from preschool through adolescence. (p. 483)

Preschool and school-age children: _____

_____

_____

Adolescents: _____

_____

_____

2. Explain how the research strategies used to study children's understanding of God impact the types of responses they provide. (p. 483)

_____

_____

_____

3. Children's understanding of God (is / is not) limited to an anthropomorphic, "big person" image. (p. 483)

4. True or False: All children develop similar images of God regardless of their denominational affiliation. (p. 483)

Peer Relations

Peer Groups

1. Describe the characteristics of a *peer group*. (p. 485)

_____

_____

_____

2. Describe the functions of children's peer groups. (p. 485)

_____

_____

_____

_____

3. How do school-age boys and girls express hostility toward the "outgroup" differently? (pp. 485–486)

Boys: _____

_____

Girls: _____

_____

Friendships

1. Describe changes in children's conception of friendship during middle childhood. (p. 486)

_____

_____

_____

_____

2. True or False: New ideas about the meaning of friendship lead school-age children to be less selective in their choice of friends than they were at younger ages. (p. 486)

3. Friendships (do / do not) tend to remain stable over middle childhood. (p. 486)

4. Discuss the qualities of aggressive children's friendships. (p. 487)

Aggressive girls: _____

_____

Aggressive boys: _____

_____

Peer Acceptance

1. Define *peer acceptance*, noting how it is different than friendship. (p. 487)

_____

_____

_____

2. Explain how researchers commonly assess peer acceptance. (p. 487)

_____

_____

3. Name and describe four categories of peer acceptance. (p. 487)

A. _____

B. _____

C. _____

D. _____

4. True or False: All school-age children fit into one of the four categories of peer acceptance described above in Question 3. (p. 487)

5. Discuss emotional and social outcomes associated with peer rejection. (p. 487)

_____

_____

_____

6. Identify and describe two subtypes of popular children. (p. 487)

A. _____

_____

B. _____

_____

7. Describe the social behavior of *rejected-aggressive* and *rejected-withdrawn* children. (p. 488)

Aggressive: _____

_____

Withdrawn: _____

_____

8. True or False: Controversial children are hostile and disruptive but also engage in high rates of positive, prosocial acts. (p. 488)

9. True or False: Controversial children have as many friends as do popular children. (p. 488)

10. True or False: Neglected children are more poorly adjusted and display less socially competent behavior than do their "average" counterparts. (p. 488)

11. Describe three interventions designed to help rejected children. (p. 488–489)

A. _____

_____

B. _____

_____

C. _____

_____

Biology and Environment: Bullies and Their Victims

1. What is *peer victimization*? (p. 489)

_____

_____

2. Describe characteristics common to victimized children. (p. 489)

_____

_____

_____

3. True or False: Victims of peer victimization are rarely, if ever, aggressive. Elaborate on your response. (p. 489)

_____

_____

_____

4. Discuss individual and school-based interventions for peer victimization. (p. 489)

Individual: _____

_____

School-based: _____

_____

Gender Typing

Gender-Stereotyped Beliefs

1. Describe ways in which children extend their gender-stereotyped beliefs during middle childhood. (p. 490)

   _____

   _____

   _____

2. Differentiate academic subjects and skills that children regard as either masculine or feminine. (p. 490)

   Masculine: _____

   _____

   Feminine: _____

   _____

3. True or False: As school-age children extend their knowledge of gender stereotypes, they become more closed-minded about what males and females can do. (p. 490)

Gender Identity and Behavior

1. Contrast the gender identity development of girls and boys during middle childhood, and note implications for behavior. (pp. 490–491)

   Girls: _____

   _____

   Boys: _____

   _____

Cultural Influences on Gender Typing

1. Using cross-cultural evidence, describe how assignment of "cross-gender" tasks can influence gender-typed behavior. (p. 491)

   _____

   _____

   _____

2. True or False: Research overwhelmingly shows that all boys benefit from assignment of "cross-gender" tasks. (p. 491)

Family Influences

Parent–Child Relationships

1. True or False: In middle childhood, the amount of time that children spend with their parents declines dramatically. (p. 492)

2. During the school years, child rearing becomes easier for those parents who established a(n) _____ style during the early years. (p. 492)

3. What is *coregulation,* and how does it foster a cooperative relationship between parent and child? (p. 492)

_____

_____

_____

Siblings

1. During middle childhood, sibling rivalry tends to (increase / decrease). Why is this the case? (p. 493)

_____

_____

2. School-age siblings (do / do not) rely on each other for companionship and assistance. Elaborate on your response. (p. 493)

_____

_____

One-Child Families

1. True or False: Research indicates that sibling relationships are essential for healthy development. (p. 493)

2. True or False: Research supports the commonly held belief that only children are spoiled and selfish. (p. 493)

3. Discuss the adjustment of children in one-child families. (p. 493)

_____

_____

_____

Gay and Lesbian Families

1. True or False: Research shows that gay and lesbian parents are as committed to and effective at child-rearing as are heterosexual parents. Provide evidence to support your response. (p. 494)

_____

_____

_____

2. True or False: Children from homosexual families are as well-adjusted as other children. (p. 494)

Never-Married Single-Parent Families

1. What group constitutes the largest proportion of never-married parents, and what factors may contribute to this trend? (p. 494)

_____

_____

2. Cite outcomes associated with children raised in never-married, single-parent families. (p. 495)

_____

_____

_____

Divorce

1. True or False: The United States has the highest divorce rate in the world. (p. 495)

2. Of the 45 percent of American and 30 percent of Canadian marriages that end in divorce, _____ percent involve children. (p. 495)

3. Summarize ways in which divorce has an immediate impact on the home environment. (p. 496)

_____

_____

_____

_____

4. Discuss how children's ages affect their reactions to divorce, noting differences between younger and older children. (p. 496)

_____

_____

_____

_____

5. Summarize sex differences in children's reactions to divorce. (p. 496)

Boys: _____

_____

_____

Girls: _____

_____

6. (Boys / Girls) of divorcing parents receive less emotional support from mothers, teachers, and peers. (p. 497)

7. Most children show improved adjustment by _____ years after divorce. (p. 497)

8. Summarize the potential long-term negative consequences of parental divorce, noting who is most at risk for such adjustment difficulties. (p. 497)

_____

_____

_____

_____

9. What is the overriding factor in positive adjustment following divorce? (p. 497)

_____

10. Explain why a good father–child relationship is important for both boys and girls following divorce. (p. 497)

   Girls: _____

   _____

   Boys: _____

   _____

11. True or False: Making the transition to a low-conflict, single-parent household is better for children than staying in a high-conflict intact family. (p. 497)

12. Describe divorce mediation, and explain why it is likely to have benefits for children. (pp. 497–498)

   _____

   _____

   _____

   _____

13. In _____, the court grants the mother and father equal say in important decisions regarding the child's upbringing. Describe common living arrangements associated with this option, noting their impact on children's adjustment. (p. 498)

   Living arrangements: _____

   _____

   Impact: _____

   _____

14. Describe four ways to help children adjust to divorce. (p. 498)

   A. _____

   _____

   B. _____

   _____

   C. _____

   _____

   D. _____

   _____

Blended Families

1. What is a *blended*, or *reconstituted*, family? (p. 499)

   _____

   _____

2. List two reasons why blended families present adjustment difficulties for most children. (p. 499)

   A. _____

   _____

   B. _____

   _____

3. The most frequent form of blended family is a _____ arrangement. Contrast boys' and girls' adjustment in this family arrangement. (p. 499)

   Boys: _____

   _____

   Girls: _____

   _____

4. Explain why older children and adolescents of both sexes living in mother-stepfather families display more irresponsible, acting out, and antisocial behavior than do their agemates in nonstepfamilies. (p. 499)

   _____

   _____

   _____

5. Remarriage of noncustodial fathers often leads to (reduced / increased) contact with children. (p. 499)

6. Cite two reasons why children tend to react negatively to the remarriage of custodial fathers. (p. 499)

   A. _____

   B. _____

7. (Girls / Boys) have an especially hard time getting along with stepmothers. Briefly explain your response. (p. 499)

   _____

   _____

   _____

8. Explain how family life education and counseling can help parents and children in blended families adapt to the complexities of their new circumstances. (p. 500)

   _____

   _____

   _____

   _____

Maternal Employment and Dual-Earner Families

1. Approximately what percent of mothers of school-age children are employed? (p. 500) _____

2. Describe potential benefits of maternal employment for school-age children, and note the circumstances under which such outcomes are achieved. (p. 500)

_____

_____

_____

3. True or False: Maternal employment results in more time with fathers, who take on greater responsibility with child care. (p. 500)

4. List four supports which help parents juggle the demands of work and child rearing. (p. 500)

   A. _____

   B. _____

   C. _____

   D. _____

5. Differentiate self-care children who fare well from those who fare poorly. (p. 501)

   Children who fare well: _____

   _____

   _____

   Children who fare poorly: _____

   _____

   _____

6. Before age _____ or _____, children should not be left unsupervised because most are not yet competent to handle emergencies. (p. 501)

7. True or False: After-school enrichment programs are especially common in inner-city neighborhoods. (p. 501)

Some Common Problems of Development

Fears and Anxieties

1. Summarize new fears and anxieties that emerge in middle childhood. (p. 502)

_____

_____

_____

2. Explain how children's fears are shaped by their culture. (p. 502)

_____

_____

_____

3. An intense, unmanageable fear that leads to persistent avoidance of the feared situation is called a(n) _____. (p. 502)

4. Describe the symptoms associated with *school phobia.* (p. 502)

_____

_____

5. Distinguish common causes of school phobia in early childhood from those in later childhood and adolescence, noting implications for treatment. (p. 502)

Early childhood: _____

_____

_____

Later childhood and adolescence: _____

_____

_____

Child Sexual Abuse

1. Sexual abuse is committed against children of both sexes, but more often against (girls / boys). (p. 504)

2. Describe typical characteristics of sexual abusers. (p. 504)

_____

_____

_____

_____

3. Describe the characteristics of children who are more vulnerable to abuse. (p. 504)

_____

_____

_____

4. Discuss the adjustment problems of sexually abused children, noting differences between younger children and adolescents. (p. 505)

Younger children: _____

_____

Adolescents: _____

_____

5. Describe common behavioral characteristics of sexually abused children as they move into young adulthood. (p. 505)

_____

_____

_____

6. Why is it difficult to treat victims of child sexual abuse? (p. 505)

_____

_____

_____

7. Discuss the role of educational programs in preventing child sexual abuse. (p. 505)

_____

_____

_____

Fostering Resilience in Middle Childhood

1. Cite personal, family, school, and community resources that foster resilience in middle childhood. (p. 507)

Personal: _____

_____

Family: _____

_____

School: _____

_____

Community: _____

_____

2. Summarize components of the *Resolving Conflicts Creatively Program,* and note program outcomes for child behavior. (p. 508)

Components: _____

_____

_____

Outcomes: _____

_____

_____

Cultural Influences:
The Impact of Ethnic and Political Violence on Children

1. Discuss children's adjustment to war and social crises, noting differences between situations involving temporary crises and those involving chronic danger. (p. 503)

_____

_____

_____

_____

2. What is the best safeguard against lasting problems? (p. 503)

_____

3. Discuss some interventions used to help children from Public School 31 in Brooklyn, New York in the wake of the September 11 attack on the World Trade Center. (p. 503)

_____

_____

_____

Social Issues: Health: Children's Eyewitness Testimony

1. True or False: Children as young as age 3 are frequently asked to provide testimony in court cases involving child abuse and neglect. (p. 506)

2. Summarize age differences in children's ability to provide accurate testimony. (p. 506)

_____

_____

_____

_____

3. Identify several reasons why young children are more prone to memory problems. (p. 506)

_____

_____

_____

4. True or False: When adults lead children by suggesting incorrect information, they increase the likelihood of incorrect reporting among preschool and school-age children alike. (p. 506)

5. True or False: Special interviewing methods involving the use of anatomically correct dolls have been successful in prompting more accurate recall of sexual abuse experiences, particularly among preschoolers. (p. 506)

6. Summarize interventions that can be used to assist child witnesses. (p. 506)

_____

_____

_____

_____

ASK YOURSELF . . .

For *Ask Yourself* questions for this chapter, please log on to the Companion Website at *www.ablongman.com/berk*.

SUGGESTED STUDENT READINGS

Amato, P. R., & Booth, A. C. (2000). *Generation at risk: Growing up in an era of family upheaval.* Cambridge, MA: Harvard University Press. Based on fifteen years of research, this book examines how familial and historical contexts affect children and adolescents as they approach adulthood.

Freedman, J. S. (2002). *Easing the teasing: Helping your child cope with name-calling, ridicule, and bullying.* McGraw-Hill. Provides practical advice to parents and educators who want to equip children with the skills necessary to manage teasing and bullying. Additional topics include: reasons children tease, consequences of teasing and bullying, and strategies to promote empathy and respect in all children.

Hetherington, E. M., & Kelly, J. (2003). *For better or worse: Divorce reconsidered.* New York: Norton. A longitudinal approach to understanding the effects of divorce on children, this book presents the nature and consequences of divorce in American culture.

Kindlon, D. J. (2003). *Tough times, strong children: Lessons from the past for your child's future.* New York: Miramax. Examines the effects of terrorism, school violence, war, and ethnic violence on children, including factors related to resilience. The author argues that parents and community members must work together to promote the well-being of children during difficult times.

PUZZLE 13.1 TERM REVIEW

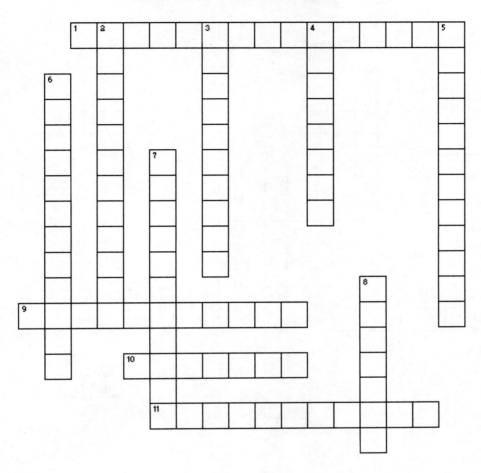

Across

1. _____-_____ attributions credit success to high ability and failure to insufficient effort.
9. _____ taking: the capacity to imagine what others may be thinking and feeling
10. _____-centered coping: appraising a situation as changeable, identifying the difficulty, and deciding what to do about it
11. Social _____: judgments of appearance, abilities, behavior, and other characteristics in relation to those of others

Down

2. Common, everyday explanations for the causes of behavior
3. Attribution _____ is an intervention aimed at modifying the attributions of learned-helpless children.
4. _____ versus inferiority: Erikson's psychological conflict of middle childhood
5. Beliefs about how to divide up material goods fairly is known as _____ justice.
6. Learned _____: attributions that credit success to luck and failure to low ability
7. _____ techniques: self-report measures that ask peers to evaluate one another's likability
8. _____-centered coping: internal, private, and aimed at controlling distress when little can be done about an outcome

PUZZLE 13.2 TERM REVIEW

Across

1. Rejected-_____ children are a subgroup of rejected children who are passive and socially awkward.

4. Children who are actively disliked and get many negative votes on sociometric measures of peer acceptance

6. Children who are seldom chosen, either positively or negatively, on sociometric measures of peer acceptance

8. ___-___ children look after themselves while their parents are at work. (2 words, hyph.)

10. An intense, unmanageable fear that leads to persistent avoidance of a feared situation

13. Children who get a large number of positive and negative votes on sociometric measures of peer acceptance

14. Rejected-_____ children are a subgroup of rejected children who engage in high rates of conflict, hostility, hyperactivity, inattention, and impulsivity.

16. Children who get many positive votes on sociometric measures of peer acceptance

17. _____ custody: arrangement following divorce in which both parents are granted equal say in important decisions regarding the child's upbringing

Down

2. Popular-_____ children: highly aggressive, yet viewed by peers as "cool"

3. Divorce _____ attempts to settle disputes of divorcing adults while avoiding legal battles that intensify family conflict.

5. Family structure resulting from cohabitation or remarriage that includes parent, child, and step-relatives

7. Peer _____: the extent to which a child is viewed by a group of agemates as a worthy social partner

9. Peer _____: certain children become frequent targets of verbal and physical attacks or other forms of abuse

11. Supervision in which parents exercise general oversight but permit children to manage moment-to-moment decisions

12. Popular-_____ children: good students who communicate with peers in sensitive, friendly, and cooperative ways

15. A peer _____ is a social unit with shared values and standards for behavior, as well as a social structure of leaders and followers.

PRACTICE TEST #1

1. In Erikson's theory, the psychological conflict of middle childhood is resolved positively when experiences lead children (p. 470)
   a. to develop a sense of competence at useful skills and tasks.
   b. to choose and make decisions for themselves.
   c. to gain a sense of trust or confidence that the world is good.
   d. to develop a sense of ambition and responsibility.

2. Beginning in middle childhood, children's self descriptions often mention their appearance, abilities, and behavior in relation to those of others. This is because children of this age (p. 471)
   a. become better at "reading" messages they receive from others and incorporating these into their self-descriptions.
   b. are typically very preoccupied with being liked and viewed positively by others.
   c. tend to describe themselves as a blend of what they imagine important people in their lives think of them.
   d. begin to make frequent social comparisons.

3. When children enter elementary school, their self-esteem typically (p. 472)
   a. raises to a more realistic level.
   b. raises to an unrealistically high level.
   c. drops to a more realistic level.
   d. drops to an unrealistically low level.

4. By middle childhood, children in Western cultures have formed at least these four self-esteems: (p. 472)
   a. inner self, categorical self, remembered self, and generalized other.
   b. academic competence, social competence, athletic competence, and physical appearance.
   c. familial, parental, peer, and teacher.
   d. foreclosure, diffusion, moratorium, and achievement.

5. Despite their higher academic achievement, Taiwanese and Japanese children score lower in self-esteem than do American children. Research suggests that this difference is in part due to (pp. 473–474)
   a. low achievement motivation among Asian children.
   b. conditional parental support among Asian children.
   c. a strong emphasis on social comparison among Asian children.
   d. a lack of feedback regarding school performance among Asian children.

6. Research on child rearing demonstrates that when parents _____, children suffer from low self-esteem. (p. 474)
   a. too often help to make decisions for their youngsters
   b. use an authoritarian child-rearing style
   c. are overly tolerant and indulgent
   d. make frequent social comparisons

7. Children who are high in academic self-esteem (p. 475)
   a. attribute their successes to external factors.
   b. hold a fixed view of ability.
   c. attribute their failures to a lack of ability.
   d. credit their successes to ability.

8. Which of the following is supported by research on children's achievement-related attributions? (p. 475)
   a. Children who develop learned-helplessness focus on performance goals.
   b. Children who hold a fixed view of ability attribute their failures to insufficient effort.
   c. Children who hold an incremental view of ability attribute their success to ability.
   d. Children who are low in academic self-esteem make mastery-oriented attributions.

9. Interventions aimed at fostering a mastery-oriented approach often emphasize (p. 476)
   a. performance goals rather than learning goals.
   b. giving feedback to low-effort children that helps them view failure as due to lack of ability.
   c. encouraging students to focus less on grades and more on mastering a task for its own sake.
   d. giving children only tasks in which they will succeed.

10. In contrast to preschoolers, school-age children (p. 478)
    a. are likely to explain emotion by referring to external events.
    b. report guilt for most mishaps, not just intentional wrongdoings.
    c. realize that they can experience more than one emotion at a time.
    d. need a teacher or other adult to be present to spark pride.

11. _____ is an internal strategy aimed at controlling distress when little can be done about an outcome. (p. 479)
    a. Problem-centered coping
    b. Attribution retraining
    c. Social comparison
    d. Emotion-centered coping

12. According to Selman's theory, children in the self-reflective perspective taking stage (p. 480)
    a. understand that different perspectives may result because people have access to different information.
    b. can step outside a two-person situation and imagine how the self and others are viewed from the point of view of a third party.
    c. understand that third-party perspective taking can be influenced by one or more systems of larger societal values.
    d. can "step into another person's shoes" and view their own thoughts, feelings, and behavior from the other person's perspective.

13. Sarah and two of her friends are watching a movie when her mother brings them a bowl of popcorn. Sarah is intent on making sure that she and her friends get an equal amount of popcorn to eat, even though her friend Dora has not yet had lunch. According to Damon's theory, Sarah thinks of fairness in terms of (p. 481)
    a. merit.
    b. equality.
    c. benevolence.
    d. reciprocity.

14. Which of the following is supported by research on peer relations during middle childhood? (p. 486)
    a. Most children believe that it is acceptable to exclude other children from their peer group.
    b. Relational aggression rises among girls.
    c. Children who have been ejected from one peer group easily establish themselves in other peer groups.
    d. Aggressive children are almost always excluded from peer groups made up of nonaggressive children.

15. During middle childhood, _____ become(s) a defining feature of one-to-one friendships. (p. 486)
    a. proximity
    b. trust
    c. shared interests
    d. availability to play

16. When Donovan's classmates were asked to rate each other's likeability, he received a large number of positive and negative votes. He would be classified as (p. 487)
    a. rejected.
    b. popular.
    c. neglected.
    d. controversial.

17. _____ children are often "tough" boys who are athletically skilled but poor students. (p. 487)
   a. Popular-prosocial
   b. Rejected-aggressive
   c. Popular-antisocial
   d. Controversial

18. During middle childhood, (p. 490)
   a. gender stereotyping decreases steadily with age.
   b. parents use more directive speech with boys than with girls.
   c. girls have higher grades but stronger doubts about their academic abilities than boys.
   d. children are very tolerant of "cross-gender" acts, such as boys playing with dolls.

19. Parents use coregulation as a form of supervision during middle childhood primarily because (p. 492)
   a. it is the result of a cycle of hostile, aggressive interactions.
   b. tight control over older children requires too much energy.
   c. child rearing is easier if the workload is spread over two parents.
   d. it supports a child who is not yet ready for total independence.

20. When both parents are employed, children (p. 500)
   a. devote more daily hours to doing homework under parental guidance.
   b. often suffer from low self-esteem and poor family relations.
   c. participate less in household chores.
   d. tend to do less well in school.

PRACTICE TEST #2

1. Erikson's industry versus inferiority stage corresponds with which of Freud's developmental stages? (p. 470)
   a. oral
   b. Oedipal complex
   c. latency
   d. phallic

2. The way children and adolescents perceive their _____ is more strongly related to their self-worth than any other self-esteem factor. (p. 472)
   a. physical appearance
   b. physical and athletic competence
   c. social competence
   d. academic competence

3. Carrie is in sixth grade. She is likely to feel especially good about her (p. 473)
   a. artwork.
   b. academic skills.
   c. peer relationships.
   d. physical attractiveness.

4. When Jordon performs poorly on a spelling test, he blames it on his failure to study hard enough. He is probably a _____ child. (p. 475)
   a. learned-helplessness
   b. mastery-oriented
   c. performance-oriented
   d. self-authoritative

5. Six- to 11-year-olds (p. 478)
   a. experience guilt only when adults are around.
   b. feel guilt for any wrongdoing, such as breaking a glass by accident.
   c. do not yet demonstrate a sense of personal responsibility.
   d. may experience pride when no one else is around.

6. Which of the following is true about 9-year-olds? (p. 478)
   a. They do not yet hide negative emotions out of concern for others.
   b. They hide their feelings to avoid being scolded.
   c. They do not yet understand self-conscious emotions.
   d. They understand that people can experience more than one emotion at once.

7. Which of the following is true with regard to emotional self-regulation during middle childhood? (p. 479)
   a. Most children this age cannot yet use problem-centered coping strategies effectively, and as a result they rely solely on emotion-centered coping techniques.
   b. While children of this age know a variety of coping strategies, cognitive inflexibility does not enable them to implement these strategies in an adaptive manner.
   c. Cultural differences exert a strong influence on children's emotional self-regulation.
   d. Children with poor emotion regulation skills are just as well adjusted as emotionally well-regulated children.

8. The capacity to imagine what other people are thinking and feeling is called (p. 480)
   a. social referencing.
   b. self-conceptualization.
   c. perspective taking.
   d. intermodal perception.

9. Vanessa thinks her father has a different perspective because he doesn't have access to the same information she has. According to Selman, Vanessa is probably (p. 480)
    a. 3 to 6 years old.
    b. 4 to 9 years old.
    c. 7 to 12 years old.
    d. 10 to 15 years old.

10. Children who are categorized as neglected on sociometric measures (p. 488)
    a. are usually well adjusted.
    b. report being unhappy.
    c. are less socially skilled than average children.
    d. usually require psychological treatment.

11. Rejected social status can be divided into the subtypes (p. 488)
    a. rejected-antisocial and rejected-victim.
    b. rejected-aggressive and rejected-withdrawn.
    c. rejected-passive and rejected-hostile.
    d. rejected-average and rejected-controversial.

12. In a study of over 2,000 students from diverse cultures, (p. 491)
    a. females were rated as "the smarter sex."
    b. boys had higher grades than girls.
    c. the United States was the only country in which children had stereotypical beliefs about gender and intelligence.
    d. girls were more likely than boys to discount their talent.

13. Boys whose fathers hold traditional gender-role beliefs _____ when they do "feminine" housework. (p. 491)
    a. experience stress relief
    b. judge themselves as more competent
    c. experience strain in their relationships with their fathers
    d. lead their fathers to feel proud

14. Cory's parents give him responsibility for making moment-by-moment decisions, while providing general supervision. This is known as (p. 492)
    a. self-care.
    b. coregulation.
    c. mastery orientation.
    d. induction.

15. Trevor's parents are gay. Research shows that he (p. 494)
    a. is likely to be gay when he grows up.
    b. is likely to be homophobic when he grows up.
    c. receives a great deal of support from his peers.
    d. is as well adjusted as other children.

16. The largest group of never-married parents are (p. 494)
    a. young African-American women.
    b. gay men.
    c. Hispanic men and women.
    d. middle-SES white teenage women.

17. Which of the following statements is true? (p. 495)
    a. At any given time, about one-fourth of American children live in single-parent households.
    b. The highest divorce rate in the world is found in Europe.
    c. Twenty-five percent of children in single-parent households live with their fathers.
    d. The average child spends one year living in a single-parent home.

18. Divorce mediation (p. 498)
    a. has been shown to be detrimental to the welfare of children because of the stress it puts on divorcing parents.
    b. increases the likelihood of a lengthy legal battle between divorcing parents.
    c. increases the feelings of well-being reported by divorcing parents.
    d. has the purpose of trying to help parents avoid divorce.

19. Which of the following family supports is mandated by U.S. law? (p. 500)
    a. paid leave for family emergencies
    b. job-sharing
    c. unpaid employment leave when a child is ill
    d. flexible schedules for new parents

20. A child who _____ is especially vulnerable to sexual abuse. (p. 504)
    a. appears physically healthy and strong
    b. is a bully
    c. is happy-go-lucky
    d. is emotionally deprived

CHAPTER 14
PHYSICAL DEVELOPMENT IN ADOLESCENCE

BRIEF CHAPTER SUMMARY

Adolescence is a time of dramatic physical change leading to an adult-sized body and sexual maturity. Although early biologically-oriented theories viewed puberty as a period of storm and stress, recent research shows that serious psychological disturbance is not a common feature of the teenage years. Adolescent development and adjustment are products of both biological and social forces.

The physical changes of puberty are regulated by growth and sex hormones. On the average, girls experience puberty 2 years earlier than do boys, although there are wide individual differences. Regional and SES differences also exist, along with a secular trend toward earlier maturation in industrialized nations. Most teenagers greet the beginning of menstruation and the first ejaculation of seminal fluid with mixed feelings. Puberty is related to increased moodiness and a mild rise in conflict between parents and children. Timing of pubertal maturation affects adolescent adjustment in an opposite way for girls than for boys, and the effects of maturational timing involve a complex blend of biological, social, and cultural factors. The arrival of puberty is accompanied by new health concerns. For some teenagers, the cultural ideal of thinness combines with family and psychological problems to produce the serious eating disorders of anorexia nervosa and bulimia nervosa. Unintentional injuries increase in adolescence, largely due to motor vehicle collisions—the leading killer of American teenagers. Firearm injuries and deaths are also high in the United States.

Teenage sexual activity in the United States has increased over several decades but recently declined slightly. Sexual orientation is affected strongly by heredity but also by a variety of biological and environmental combinations. Adolescents have the highest rate of sexually transmitted disease of any age group. Sexual activity is accompanied by high rates of adolescent pregnancy and parenthood. Although most teenagers engage in some experimentation with alcohol and drugs, a worrisome minority make the transition from use to abuse.

LEARNING OBJECTIVES

After reading this chapter, you should be able to:

14.1 Discuss changing conceptions of adolescence over the twentieth century, and identify the three phases of adolescence recognized in modern industrialized nations. (pp. 516–517)

14.2 Describe physical changes associated with puberty, including hormonal changes, changes in body size, body proportions, and muscle–fat makeup, and sexual maturation. (pp. 517–522)

14.3 Cite factors that influence the timing of puberty. (pp. 522–525)

14.4 Discuss adolescents' reactions to the physical changes of puberty, noting factors that influence their feelings and behavior. (pp. 525–529)

14.5 Discuss the impact of maturational timing on adolescent adjustment, noting sex differences, as well as immediate and long-term consequences. (pp. 529–530)

14.6 Describe the nutritional needs of adolescents. (pp. 531–532)

14.7 Describe the symptoms of anorexia nervosa and bulimia nervosa, and cite factors within the individual, the family, and the larger culture that contribute to these disorders. (pp. 532–533)

14.8 Cite common unintentional injuries in adolescence. (pp. 533–534)

14.9 Discuss personal, familial, and cultural influences on adolescent sexual attitudes and behavior. (pp. 534–537)

14.10 Discuss biological and environmental contributions to homosexuality. (pp. 538–540)

14.11 Discuss the risk of sexually transmitted diseases in adolescence, particularly AIDS, and cite strategies for STD prevention. (pp. 540–542)

14.12 Discuss factors related to adolescent pregnancy, consequences of early childbearing for adolescent parents and their children, and strategies for preventing adolescent pregnancy. (pp. 542–545)

14.13 Distinguish between substance use and abuse, describe personal and social factors related to each as well as consequences of substance abuse, and cite strategies for prevention and treatment. (pp. 545–547)

STUDY QUESTIONS

Conceptions of Adolescence

1. Contrast the biological and social perspectives of adolescence. What evidence suggests that adolescent development is a product of both biological and social forces? (pp. 516–517)

   Biological: _____

   _____

   Social: _____

   _____

   Evidence of dual influence: _____

   _____

2. True or False: Rates of psychological disturbance increase dramatically during adolescence, supporting the conclusion that it is a period of storm and stress. (p. 516)

3. True or False: Adolescence, as an intervening phase between childhood and full assumption of adult roles, can be found in almost all societies. (p. 517)

Puberty: The Physical Transition to Adulthood

Hormonal Changes

1. During sexual maturation, the boy's testes release large quantities of the androgen _____, which leads to muscle growth, body and facial hair, and other male sex characteristics, as well as contributing to gains in body size. (p. 518)

2. The release of _____ from the girl's ovaries causes the breasts, uterus, and vagina to mature, the body to take on feminine proportions, and fat to accumulate. (p. 518)

Body Growth

1. The first outward sign of puberty is the rapid gain in height and weight known as the _____. (p. 518)

2. On average, the adolescent growth spurt is underway for North American girls shortly after age _____ and for boys around age _____. (p. 518)

3. True or False: During puberty, the cephalocaudal trend reverses, with hands, legs, and feet growing first, followed by growth of the torso. (p. 519)

4. Describe sex differences in body proportions and muscle–fat makeup during adolescence. (pp. 519–520)

Boys: _____

_____

Girls: _____

_____

Motor Development and Physical Activity

1. Briefly summarize sex differences in gross motor development during adolescence. (p. 520)

Boys: _____

_____

Girls: _____

_____

2. True or False: Use of creatine and anabolic steroids improves teenagers' athletic performance while having no adverse side effects. (p. 520)

3. Among American and Canadian youths, rates of physical activity (rise / decline) during adolescence. (p. 520)

4. Cite the benefits of sports participation and exercise during adolescence. (pp. 520–521)

_____

_____

_____

Sexual Maturation

1. Distinguish between *primary* and *secondary sexual characteristics.* (p. 521)

Primary: _____

_____

Secondary: _____

_____

2. _____ is the scientific name for first menstruation. It typically happens around _____ years of age for North American girls. (p. 521)

3. List early signs of puberty in boys. (p. 522)

_____

_____

4. The growth spurt occurs much (earlier / later) in the sequence of pubertal events for boys than for girls. (p. 522)

5. Around age 13½, _____, or first ejaculation, occurs in boys. (p. 522)

Individual Differences in Pubertal Growth

1. Explain how heredity, nutrition, and exercise contribute to the timing of puberty. (pp. 522–523)

    Heredity: _____

    _____

    Nutrition: _____

    _____

    Exercise: _____

    _____

2. Describe how SES and ethnicity influence pubertal growth. (p. 523)

    _____

    _____

    _____

The Secular Trend

1. Describe the secular trend in pubertal timing in industrialized nations, noting factors believed to be responsible for it. (pp. 523–524)

    _____

    _____

    _____

Brain Development

1. Briefly summarize changes in synaptic pruning, myelination, and lateralization of the cerebral cortex during adolescence, noting the impact of such changes on adolescent cognitive functioning. (p. 524)

    _____

    _____

    _____

    _____

2. Describe changes in neurotransmitter activity during the teenage years, and explain how this impacts adolescent behavior. (p. 524)

    Changes: _____

    _____

    Impact: _____

    _____

Changing States of Arousal

1. On average, sleep (increases / declines) from middle childhood into adolescence. Explain why this is the case. (p. 524)

   _____

   _____

   _____

2. List the negative consequences of sleep deprivation. (p. 525)

   _____

   _____

The Psychological Impact of Pubertal Events

Reactions to Pubertal Changes

1. Discuss two factors that affect girls' reactions to menarche. (p. 525)

   A. _____

   _____

   B. _____

   _____

2. Overall, boys seem to get (more / less) social support for the physical changes of puberty than do girls. (p. 526)

3. Many tribal and village societies celebrate puberty with a _____ —
   a community-wide event that marks an important change in privilege and responsibility. Contrast this experience with that of adolescents in Western societies. (pp. 526–527)

   _____

   _____

   _____

   _____

Pubertal Change, Emotion, and Social Behavior

1. Research shows that adolescents report (more / less) favorable moods than school-age children and adults. (pp. 527–528)

2. Cite factors associated with high and low points in mood during adolescence. (p. 528)

   High points: _____

   _____

   Low points: _____

   _____

3. How might parent–child conflict during adolescence serve an adaptive function? (p. 529)

   _____

   _____

4.   Most disputes between parents and adolescents are (mild / severe). (p. 529)

Early versus Late Pubertal Timing

1.   Discuss research findings on the effects of maturational timing for the following groups of adolescents: (p. 529)

Early maturing boys: _____

_____

Early maturing girls: _____

_____

Late maturing boys: _____

_____

Late maturing girls: _____

_____

2.   List two factors that appear to account for trends in the effects of maturational timing. (p. 529)

A. _____

B. _____

3.   Discuss the impact of maturational timing on adolescents' body images. (p. 530)

_____

_____

_____

_____

4.   Early maturing adolescents of both sexes tend to seek (younger / older) companions. Describe the consequences of this trend in peer relations. (p. 530)

_____

_____

5.   Explain how school context can modify the effects of maturational timing. (p. 530)

_____

_____

_____

6.   Describe the long-term effects of maturational timing for early and late maturing individuals. (p. 530)

Early maturing: _____

_____

Late maturing: _____

_____

Cultural Influences: Adolescent Initiation Ceremonies

1. What is the purpose of an *adolescent initiation ceremony*? (p. 526)

    _____

    _____

    _____

2. Describe three features common to adolescent initiation ceremonies. (pp. 526–527)

    A. _____

    _____

    _____

    B. _____

    _____

    _____

    C. _____

    _____

    _____

3. In the simplest societies, adolescent initiation ceremonies are more common for (boys / girls). Why is this the case? (p. 527)

    _____

    _____

    _____

Health Issues

Nutritional Needs

1. Of all age groups, the eating habits of adolescents are the (best / poorest). What factors contribute to this trend? (p. 531)

    _____

    _____

2. What is the most common nutritional problem of adolescence? (p. 531)

    _____

Serious Eating Disturbances

1. What is the strongest predictor of the onset of an eating disorder in adolescence? (p. 532)

    _____

2. Describe the physical and behavioral symptoms of *anorexia nervosa*. (p. 532)

_____

_____

_____

3. Explain how forces within the person, family, and larger culture contribute to anorexia nervosa. (p. 532)

Person: _____

_____

Family: _____

_____

Culture: _____

_____

4. Describe three approaches to treating anorexia nervosa, and note which is the most successful. (p. 533)

A. _____

B. _____

C. _____

5. True or False: Over 90 percent of anorexics make a full recovery. (p. 533)

6. Describe characteristics of *bulimia nervosa*. (p. 533)

_____

_____

_____

7. Bulimia is (more / less) common than anorexia. (p. 533)

8. Identify similarities and differences between persons with anorexia and bulimia. (p. 533)

Similarities: _____

_____

Differences: _____

_____

Injuries

1. The total rate of unintentional injuries (increases / decreases) during adolescence. Explain why this is the case. (p. 533)

_____

_____

_____

2. Outside of automobile accidents, the majority of adolescent deaths are caused by
_____. (p. 533)

3. How do coaches often contribute to sports injuries in adolescents? (p. 534)

_____

_____

_____

Sexual Activity

1. True or False: Exposure to sex, education about it, and efforts to limit the sexual curiosity of children and adolescents are very similar in nations around the world. (p. 534)

2. Contrast the messages that adolescents receive from parents and the media regarding sexual activity, and note the impact of such contradictory messages on adolescents' understanding of sex. (p. 535)

   Parents: _____

   _____

   Media: _____

   _____

   Impact: _____

   _____

3. The sexual attitudes and behavior of American adolescents have become (more / less) liberal over the past 30 years. (p. 535)

4. (Males / Females) tend to have their first sexual experience earlier than members of the opposite sex. (p. 535)

5. Cite personal, familial, peer, and educational variables linked to early and frequent teenage sexual activity. (pp. 535–536)

   Personal: _____

   Family: _____

   Peer: _____

   Educational: _____

6. Early sexual activity is (more / less) common among low-SES adolescents. Why is this the case? (pp. 536–537)

   _____

   _____

7. Discuss cognitive and social factors that may contribute to adolescents' reluctance to use contraception. (p. 538)

   Cognitive: _____

   _____

   _____

   Social: _____

   _____

   _____

8. Cite characteristics of adolescents who are more likely to use contraception. (p. 538)

_____

_____

9. Describe evidence suggesting that both genetic and prenatal biological influences contribute to homosexuality. (pp. 538–540)

Genetic: _____

_____

Prenatal biological influences: _____

_____

Sexually Transmitted Disease

1. True or False: Adolescents have the highest incidence of sexually transmitted disease (STD) of any age group. (p. 540)

2. True or False: Nearly all cases of AIDS that appear in young adulthood originate in adolescence. (p. 540)

3. True or False: Over 90 percent of high school students are aware of the basic facts about AIDS. (p. 540)

4. Discuss four ways of preventing STDs. (p. 542)

A. _____

_____

B. _____

_____

C. _____

_____

D. _____

_____

Adolescent Pregnancy and Parenthood

1. List three factors that heighten the incidence of adolescent pregnancy. (pp. 542–543)

A. _____

B. _____

C. _____

2. Summarize personal characteristics and life conditions that contribute to adolescent childbearing. (p. 543)

Personal characteristics: _____

_____

Life conditions: _____

_____

3. Discuss the consequences of adolescent parenthood in relation to the following areas: (p. 543)

Educational attainment: _____

_____

Marital patterns: _____

_____

Economic circumstances: _____

_____

4. True or False: Adolescent mothers are as knowledgeable about child development as are adult mothers, and they are just as effective at interacting with their children. (pp. 543–544)

5. Cite three factors that protect teenage mothers and their children from long-term difficulties. (p. 544)

A. _____

B. _____

C. _____

6. List three components of effective sex education programs. (p. 544)

A. _____

B. _____

C. _____

7. True or False: In European countries where contraception is readily available to teenagers, sexual activity is *not* more common than in the United States but pregnancy, childbirth, and abortion rates are much lower. (p. 544)

8. In addition to sex education and access to contraceptives, what other strategies are essential for preventing adolescent pregnancy and parenthood? (p. 544)

_____

_____

9. List characteristics of school programs that increase adolescent mothers' educational success and prevent additional childbearing. (p. 545)

_____

_____

_____

10. Older adolescent mothers display (more / less) effective parenting when they establish their own residence with the assistance of relatives. (p. 545)

11. True or False: Fewer than one-fourth of adolescent fathers maintain regular contact into the child's school-age years. (p. 545)

Substance Use and Abuse

1. Discuss the impact of culture on adolescent substance use. (p. 545)

_____

_____

_____

2. Distinguish the characteristics of adolescents who experiment with drugs from those of adolescents who are drug abusers. (p. 545)

_____

_____

_____

_____

3. Cite three life-long consequences of adolescent substance abuse. (p. 546)

   A. _____

   B. _____

   C. _____

4. List three components of school and community programs that reduce drug experimentation. (p. 547)

   A. _____

   _____

   B. _____

   _____

   C. _____

   _____

5. Discuss prevention and treatment strategies for drug abuse. (p. 547)

   Prevention: _____

   _____

   _____

   Treatment: _____

   _____

   _____

Social Issues: Health:
Parents and Teenagers (Don't) Talk About Sex

1. What percentage of parents report talking with their children about sex and contraception? (p. 536)

   _____

2. Explain why many parents avoid discussing sexual issues with their teenage children. (p. 536)

   _____

   _____

   _____

3. Why are adolescents reluctant to discuss sex with their parents? (p. 536)

_____

_____

_____

4. Describe qualities of successful parent–child communication about sex. (p. 536)

_____

_____

_____

Biology and Environment: Homosexuality: Coming Out to Oneself and Others

1. Describe the three-phase sequence that homosexual adolescents and adults move through in coming out to themselves and others. (p. 539)

   A. _____

   _____

   _____

   B. _____

   _____

   _____

   C. _____

   _____

   _____

2. For homosexual individuals, a first sense of their sexual orientation typically appears between the ages of _____ and _____. In what context does this typically occur? (p. 539)

   _____

3. True or False: Most adolescents resolve their feelings of confusion and discomfort at being attracted to same-sex individuals by crystallizing a gay, lesbian, or bisexual identity quickly—with a flash of insight into their sense of being different. (p. 539)

4. True or False: Most parents respond to their adolescent child's disclosure of homosexuality with severe rejection. (p. 539)

5. Explain how coming out has the potential to foster development in homosexual adolescents. (p. 539)

   _____

   _____

   _____

   _____

ASK YOURSELF . . .

For *Ask Yourself* questions for this chapter, please log on the Companion Website at *www.ablongman.com/berk*.

SUGGESTED STUDENT READINGS

Bruch, H. (2001). *The golden cage: The enigma of anorexia nervosa.* Cambridge, MA: Harvard University Press. Appropriate for students, parents, mental health professionals, and others interested in eating disorders, this book describes characteristics of anorexia nervosa, including danger signs, personal accounts, and factors that contribute to and sustain the disorder.

Carskadon, M. A. (2003). *Adolescent sleep patterns: Biological, social, and psychological influences.* New York: Cambridge University Press. A collection of chapters focusing on adolescent wake and sleep patterns, including the role of sleep deprivation in risky driving behavior, the effects of school and work on sleep habits, severe disturbances in adolescent sleep cycles, and benefits of later school start time.

Hayward, C. (Ed.). (2003). *Gender differences at puberty.* New York: Cambridge University Press. An ecological examination of the effects of puberty, this book focuses on the impact of puberty on physical, social, and psychological development. Other topics include: changes in body image, aggression, sexual abuse, and opposite sex relationships.

Merrick, E. (2001). *Reconceiving black adolescent child bearing.* New York: Barunch College. Based on the personal accounts of six African-American teenage girls, this book explores the effects of childbearing and adolescent development among lower-income minority youths.

PUZZLE 14.1 TERM REVIEW

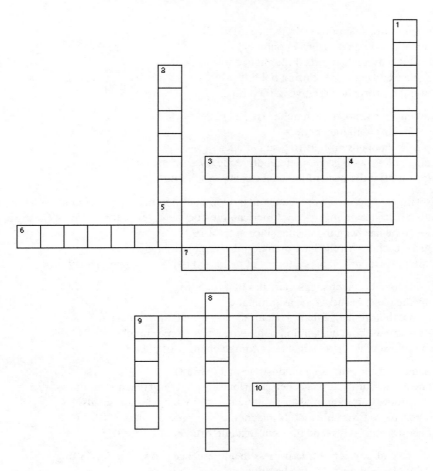

Across

3. _____ sexual characteristics are features visible on the outside of the body that do not involve the reproductive organs.
5. Adolescent _____ ceremony: rite of passage announcing to the community that a young person is making the transition into adolescence or adulthood
6. _____ nervosa: eating disorder in which individuals engage in strict dieting and excessive exercise accompanied by binge eating, often followed by deliberate vomiting or purging with laxatives
7. First menstruation
9. First ejaculation of seminal fluid
10. Body _____: conception of and attitude toward one's physical appearance

Down

1. Biological changes at adolescence leading to an adult-size body and sexual maturity
2. _____ nervosa: eating disorder in which individuals starve themselves due to a compulsive fear of becoming fat and a distorted body image
4. Transition between childhood and emerging adulthood
8. _____ sexual characteristics are those that directly involve the reproductive organs.
9. Growth _____: rapid gains in height and weight during adolescence

PRACTICE TEST #1

1. Research on body proportions demonstrates that (p. 519)
   a. the cephalocaudal trend reverses during puberty.
   b. boys are taller and heavier than girls throughout adolescence.
   c. the proximodistal trend continues during puberty.
   d. adolescents' shoulders broaden relative to their hips.

2. Which of the following is true about menarche? (p. 521)
   a. Female puberty begins with menarche.
   b. Menarche typically happens around 10 years of age.
   c. Breast and pubic hair growth is completed before the onset of menarche.
   d. Menarche happens after the peak of the adolescent growth spurt.

3. Which of the following is supported by research on individual differences in pubertal growth? (p. 523)
   a. Breast and pubic hair growth in African-American girls begins a year earlier than in Caucasian-American girls.
   b. The age of menarche has been increasing since at least 1900.
   c. Overweight girls reach menarche later than normal weight girls.
   d. Girls who attain pubertal milestones later are at increased risk for teen pregnancy.

4. Research on reactions to pubertal changes indicates that (p. 526)
   a. most girls view the onset of menarche as traumatic.
   b. most boys say that their first ejaculation occurred earlier than they expected.
   c. most boys do not know about ejaculation before the onset of spermarche.
   d. girls get much more social support than boys for the changes of puberty.

5. Studies of pubertal change and emotion demonstrate that (p. 528)
   a. higher hormone levels during adolescence contribute strongly to greater moodiness.
   b. mood swings are more common in older adolescents than younger adolescents.
   c. adolescents report more favorable moods than adults.
   d. low points of adolescents' days tend to occur in adult-structured settings.

6. The literature on the role of physical attractiveness in adolescence shows that (p. 530)
   a. the majority of adolescent girls want to be thinner.
   b. early maturing girls tend to have a positive body image.
   c. late maturing boys are more satisfied with their body image than on-time and early maturing boys.
   d. early maturing boys tend to be at less risk than late maturing boys for delinquency.

7. The most common nutritional problem of adolescence is (p. 531)
   a. obesity.
   b. iron deficiency.
   c. bulimia.
   d. anorexia.

8. Obese children (p. 531)
   a. tend to be attracted to the latest fad diets.
   b. usually have an extremely distorted body image.
   c. often reach menarche later than same-age peers.
   d. rarely outgrow their weight problem as teenagers.

9. _____ is the strongest predictor of the onset of an eating disorder in adolescence. (p. 532)
   a. Low self-worth
   b. Obesity
   c. Frequent, severe dieting
   d. Skipping breakfast

10. Adolescent girls with anorexia nervosa usually (p. 532)
    a. come from low-income homes.
    b. perform poorly in school.
    c. are emotionally inhibited.
    d. rely on intimate ties outside of the family.

11. Which of the following is supported by research on eating disorders during adolescence? (p. 532)
    a. Boys make up about 10 percent of anorexic cases.
    b. Late maturing girls are at greater risk than early maturing girls for anorexia.
    c. Both anorexics and bulimics are aware of their abnormal eating habits.
    d. Anorexia is usually easier to treat than bulimia.

12. In North America, _____ account(s) for 40 percent of deaths between 15 and 19 years of age. (p. 533)
    a. steroid drug use
    b. automobile accidents
    c. alcohol abuse
    d. firearms

13. In countries with strict gun regulations, including the prohibition of handguns, the firearm death rate among 15- to 19-year-olds is _____ times lower than in the United States. (p. 534)
    a. 2
    b. 5
    c. 8
    d. 16

14. Which of the following is supported by research on sexual behaviors among North American adolescents? (p. 535)
    a. Females tend to have their first intercourse earlier than males.
    b. Rates of teenage sexual activity in the United States and Canada are substantially higher than those in Western European countries.
    c. Since 1990, rates of extramarital sex among adolescents have declined.
    d. More than half of girls have had sexual intercourse by the age of 17.

15. Research on contraceptive use among North American adolescents demonstrates that (p. 538)
    a. more than half of sexually active adolescents do not use birth control.
    b. advances in perspective taking during adolescence contribute to an increase in the use of contraceptives.
    c. most who fail to use contraception do so because they cannot afford to pay for birth control devices.
    d. teenagers who report good relationships with their parents are more likely than others to use birth control.

16. Which of the following is supported by research on sexual orientation? (p. 540)
    a. Homosexual men tend to have a higher-than-average number of older brothers.
    b. Male homosexuality tends to be more common on the paternal than maternal side of families.
    c. More men than women are bisexual.
    d. Childhood gender nonconformity (e.g., boys' preference for "feminine" play) is not linked to homosexuality.

17. Studies on sexually transmitted diseases (STDs) demonstrate that (p. 540)
    a. adolescents have the highest rate of STDs of any age group.
    b. males are at greater risk than women for contracting HIV.
    c. most adolescents believe that oral contraceptives provide some protection against STDs.
    d. the incidence of HIV in adolescence is low relative to other age groups.

18. Research on teenage pregnancy in the United States shows that (p. 542)
    a. less than 10 percent of pregnancies to teenagers end in abortion.
    b. most pregnant teenage girls marry before giving birth.
    c. the number of teenage births is rapidly increasing.
    d. 20 percent of teenage girls who have sexual intercourse become pregnant annually.

19. Studies of adolescent pregnancy prevention suggest that (p. 544)
    a. distributing condoms in schools would increase rates of adolescent sexual activity.
    b. sex education courses are often given too early.
    c. distributing condoms in schools would decrease rates of adolescent childbirth and abortion.
    d. sex education in schools increases rates of early sex.

20. In the United States, at the end of high school, about (p. 545)
    a. 5 percent have engaged in heavy drinking during the past two weeks.
    b. 21 percent have tried at least one highly addictive and toxic substance, such as PCP, cocaine, or heroin.
    c. 80 percent have experimented with illegal drugs.
    d. 6 percent smoke cigarettes regularly.

PRACTICE TEST #2

1. The beginning of adolescence is marked by (p. 516)
   a. the thirteenth birthday.
   b. puberty.
   c. going to high school.
   d. the ability to independently take care of one's own physical well-being, including nutrition, safety, and hygiene.

2. When Margaret Mead returned from a trip to the Pacific Islands of Samoa, she stated that adolescence there (p. 516)
   a. is nonexistent as a developmental time period.
   b. lasts until a girl is pregnant or a boy becomes a father.
   c. is a period of stress and turbulence.
   d. is a very pleasant time.

3. Researchers refer to middle adolescence as a time when (p. 517)
   a. one's focus moves from self-centeredness to social awareness.
   b. adolescents begin to desire separateness from their parents.
   c. adolescents begin to consider vocational choices.
   d. pubertal changes are nearly complete.

4. The pituitary gland stimulates glands to release hormones that (p. 517)
   a. cause the secretion of growth hormone from the thyroid gland.
   b. decrease the production of thyroxine.
   c. cause body tissues to mature.
   d. stop the release of growth hormones as one approaches adolescence.

5. Adolescents are often disproportionately long-legged for a time because (p. 519)
   a. the cephalocaudal trend has reversed.
   b. chromosomal disorders are so common.
   c. they lack adequate nutrition.
   d. the proximodistal trend has increased since middle childhood.

6. When they reach menarche, girls typically (p. 526)
   a. report feeling "ashamed."
   b. say they were not informed before it occurred.
   c. tell a friend.
   d. report wanting to keep it a secret.

7. Half of all boys experience temporary breast enlargement during puberty because (p. 518)
   a. the testes secrete small amounts of estrogen.
   b. androgens cause breast enlargement.
   c. thyroxine stimulates breast enlargement when it is released too early.
   d. of a common developmental disorder due to a lack of testosterone.

8. Parent–adolescent conflict reaches its peak (p. 529)
   a. in early adolescence.
   b. in mid-adolescence.
   c. in late adolescence.
   d. just before the adolescent leaves home for college or independent living.

9. Which of the following adolescents will report the least positive body image? (p. 529)
   a. Zinta, an early-maturing girl
   b. Theo, an early-maturing boy
   c. Janelle, a girl who is maturing on time
   d. Fiona, a late-maturing girl

10. Adolescent girls may need _____ to make up for the loss of blood due to menstruation. (p. 531)
    a. folic acid
    b. calcium supplements
    c. extra iron
    d. more carbohydrates

11. Conception of and attitude toward one's physical appearance is known as (p. 530)
    a. body image.
    b. self-concept.
    c. self-esteem.
    d. self-respect.

12. Which of the following is true regarding anorexia nervosa? (p. 532)
    a. African-American girls are at greater risk than Asian-American girls because they tend to have larger builds.
    b. About half of all boys with anorexia are homosexual or bisexual.
    c. Anorexia occurs more often among economically advantaged girls than among economically disadvantaged girls.
    d. Less than 2 percent of people with anorexia actually die from it.

13. Which of the following factors is linked with increased contraceptive use among sexually active adolescents? (p. 534)
    a. Having a good relationship with parents and being able to talk openly with them about sex and contraception.
    b. Participation in sex education courses.
    c. Imitation of the sexually-responsible role-models seen in many prime-time TV shows.
    d. Sexual contact with multiple partners.

14. Twin studies of homosexuality have revealed that (p. 538)
    a. it is mostly related to environmental influences.
    b. male homosexuality is more commonly found on the paternal side of families.
    c. identical twins are no more likely to share a homosexual orientation than fraternal twins.
    d. it might be X-linked.

15. Which of the following accurately characterizes the three-phase sequence of gay and lesbian adolescents who are coming out to themselves and others? (p. 539)
    a. feeling different, confusion, acceptance
    b. confusion, feeling accepted, announcement
    c. feeling different, acceptance, integration
    d. feeling rejected, confusion, acceptance

16. In the United States, the adolescent pregnancy rate is (p. 542)
    a. much lower than that of other industrialized countries due to widely available access to birth control.
    b slightly lower than that of other industrialized countries.
    c the same as the rate in most other industrialized countries.
    d higher than that of most other industrialized countries.

17. According to your text, of all adolescent drug habits _____ has received the least attention but is one of the deadliest substances in the long run. (p. 546)
    a. cigarette smoking
    b. marijuana smoking
    c. caffeine use
    d. alcohol use

18. Research reveals that adolescents who experiment minimally with alcohol, tobacco, and marijuana (p. 545)
    a. are psychologically healthy.
    b. become addicts in adulthood.
    c. are less sociable than adolescents who do not experiment.
    d. are in the minority.

19. ___ percent of high school seniors drink alcohol daily, and ___ percent take illegal drugs daily. (p. 545)
    a. Twenty; 18
    b. Twelve; 15
    c. Eight; 12
    d. Three; 6

20. During the last decade, violence-related behaviors among high school students have (p. 546)
    a. remained steady.
    b. decreased.
    c. increased slightly
    d. increased greatly.

CHAPTER 15
COGNITIVE DEVELOPMENT IN ADOLESCENCE

BRIEF CHAPTER SUMMARY

During Piaget's formal operational stage, adolescents' abstract reasoning abilities become well developed. However, cross-cultural research challenges Piaget's view of formal operations as a universal change in cognition that results from adolescents' independent efforts to make sense of their world. Instead, it may be a culturally transmitted way of reasoning specific to literate societies and fostered by school experiences. According to the information-processing perspective, abstract, scientific reasoning is fostered by greater information-processing capacity, years of schooling, and increasingly sophisticated metacognition. Scientific reasoning develops gradually out of many specific experiences. The dramatic cognitive changes of adolescence are reflected in many aspects of everyday behavior, including argumentativeness, self-consciousness and self-focusing, idealism and criticism, and difficulties with planning and decision making.

By adolescence, boys are ahead of girls in mathematical performance, a difference related to biology, experience, social attitudes, and self-esteem. However, these sex differences appear only on some types of test items, such as complex word problems. Language continues to develop in subtle ways. For example, vocabulary expands, the grammatical complexity of speech increases, and communicative competence improves. School transitions create new adjustment problems for adolescents. Timing of school transitions, child-rearing practices, parent involvement in school, the peer culture, and characteristics of the learning environment affect school achievement during the teenage years. Although graduation rates have improved over the last half century, dropping out of school remains high in the United States and is related to a variety of family background and school variables that undermine life success.

During late adolescence, young people face a major life decision: the choice of an occupation. Factors that influence adolescents' vocational decisions include personality, family background, teachers, and gender stereotypes in the larger social environment, and access to vocational information. Compared to young people in European nations, American adolescents who terminate their education with a high school diploma have a more difficult time making the transition from school to a challenging, well-paid career.

LEARNING OBJECTIVES

After reading this chapter, you should be able to:

15.1   Describe the major characteristics of formal operational thought. (pp. 552–553)

15.2   Discuss recent research on formal operational thought and its implications for the accuracy of Piaget's formal operational stage. (pp. 553–555)

15.3   Explain how information-processing theorists account for cognitive change during adolescence. (pp. 555–556)

15.4   Summarize the development of scientific reasoning during adolescence. (pp. 556–557)

15.5   Describe cognitive and behavioral consequences of adolescents' newfound capacity for abstract reasoning. (pp. 558–561)

15.6   Describe sex differences in mental abilities during adolescence, along with factors that influence such differences. (pp. 561–564)

15.7   Describe changes in vocabulary, grammar, and pragmatics during adolescence. (pp. 564–565)

15.8   Discuss the impact of school transitions on adolescent adjustment, and cite ways to ease the strain of these changes. (pp. 565–567)

15.9   Discuss family, peer, and school influences on academic achievement during adolescence. (pp. 567–572)

15.10   Describe personal, family, and school factors related to dropping out, and cite ways to prevent early school leaving. (pp. 572–575)

15.11   Summarize the phases of vocational development and discuss factors that influence vocational choice. (pp. 576–579)

15.12   Describe the impact of part-time work on adolescents' adjustment, and discuss the problems faced by American non-college bound youths in making the transition from school to work, along with ways to help them. (pp. 579–581)

STUDY QUESTIONS

Piaget's Theory: The Formal Operational Stage

1.   Summarize the basic difference between concrete and formal operational reasoning. (p. 552)

_____

_____

_____

2.   Describe two features of formal operational reasoning, *hypothetico-deductive reasoning* and *propositional thought.* (pp. 552–553)

Hypothetico-deductive reasoning: _____

_____

_____

Propositional thought: _____

_____

_____

Follow-Up Research on Formal Operational Thought

1.   Cite examples illustrating that school-age children show signs of hypothetico-deductive reasoning and propositional thought but are not yet as competent at it as adolescents. (pp. 553–554)

Hypothetico-deductive reasoning: _____

_____

_____

Propositional thought: _____

_____

_____

2. Describe two reasons why many college students and adults are not fully formal operational. (p. 554)

A. _____

_____

B. _____

_____

3. True or False: Despite few opportunities to solve hypothetical problems, most people in tribal and village societies still master formal operational tasks. (p. 555)

An Information-Processing View of Adolescent Cognitive Development

1. Based on information-processing theory, cite five mechanisms of cognitive change in adolescence, and note which of these is central to the development of abstract thought. (pp. 555–556)

A. _____

B. _____

C. _____

D. _____

E. _____

Scientific Reasoning: Coordinating Theory with Evidence

1. Cite major changes in scientific reasoning from childhood into adolescence and adulthood. (pp. 556–557)

_____

_____

_____

2. Identify two factors that support adolescents' skill at coordinating theory with evidence. (p. 557)

A. _____

B. _____

3. Briefly explain how advances in metacognitive understanding promote adolescents' cognitive development. (p. 557)

_____

_____

_____

4. True or False: Like Piaget, information-processing theorists maintain that scientific reasoning develops from an abrupt, stagewise change. (p. 557)

Consequences of Abstract Thought

Argumentativeness

1. Explain how the development of abstract thought influences adolescents' argumentativeness. (pp. 558–559)

_____

_____

_____

Self-Consciousness and Self-Focusing

1. Describe two distorted images of the relation between self and others that appear at adolescence. (p. 559)

   Imaginary audience: _____

   _____

   _____

   Personal fable: _____

   _____

   _____

2. The imaginary audience and personal fable (do / do not) result from egocentrism, as Piaget suggested. Elaborate on your response. (pp. 559–560)

   _____

   _____

Idealism and Criticism

1. Explain how the emergence of formal operations leads to idealism and criticism in adolescence. (p. 560)

   _____

   _____

   _____

2. How are idealism and criticism advantageous to teenagers? (p. 560)

   _____

   _____

Planning and Decision Making

1. Briefly summarize changes in _cognitive self-regulation_ and _comprehension monitoring_ during adolescence. (p. 560)

   Cognitive self-regulation: _____

   _____

   Comprehension monitoring: _____

   _____

2. True or False: Like adults, adolescents use a rational process for planning and decision making in everyday life. (p. 560)

3. Describe two reasons why teenagers have difficulty with decision-making. (p. 561)

A. _____

_____

B. _____

_____

Sex Differences in Mental Abilities

1. Explain differences between boys and girls in specific mental abilities, particularly language and mathematics. (pp. 561–562)

_____

_____

_____

_____

2. Summarize how heredity and social pressures contribute to the gender gap in mathematics. (p. 562)

Heredity: _____

_____

Social pressures: _____

_____

3. True or False: Sex differences in cognitive abilities of all kinds have increased steadily over the past several decades. (p. 562)

4. Cite three strategies used to promote girls' interest in and confidence at math and science. (p. 562)

A. _____

B. _____

C. _____

Biology and Environment: Sex Differences in Spatial Abilities

1. Describe two spatial tasks on which individuals evidence a notable sex difference in performance. (p. 563)

A. _____

_____

B. _____

_____

2. True or False: Sex differences in spatial abilities persist throughout the lifespan. (p. 563)

3. Summarize biological and environmental factors that may contribute to sex differences in spatial abilities. (p. 563)

Biological: _____

_____

_____

Environmental: _____

_____

_____

Language Development

Vocabulary and Grammar

1. Describe three changes in adolescents' vocabularies. (p. 564)

   A. _____

   _____

   B. _____

   _____

   C. _____

   _____

2. Discuss two gains in grammatical development during the teenage years. (p. 564)

   A. _____

   _____

   B. _____

   _____

Pragmatics

1. Summarize gains in adolescents' communication skills. (pp. 564–565)

   _____

   _____

   _____

2. Explain the social function of teenage slang. (p. 565)

   _____

   _____

Learning in School

School Transitions

1. List several reasons why adolescents' grades decline at the transition to secondary school. (p. 565)

   A. _____

   B. _____

   C. _____

2. Contrast adolescents' adjustment to school transitions in districts with a 6-3-3 grade organization versus those with an 8-4 grade organization. (pp. 565–566)

6-3-3: _____

_____

_____

8-4: _____

_____

_____

3. The (earlier / later) the school transition occurs, the more dramatic and long-lasting its impact on adolescents' psychological well-being. (p. 566)

4. List three ways that parents, teachers, and peers can ease the strain of school transitions. (pp. 566–567)

A. _____

B. _____

C. _____

Academic Achievement

1. How do authoritative, authoritarian, permissive, and uninvolved parenting styles contribute to adolescents' academic achievement? Which is the most effective and why? (p. 568)

Authoritative: _____

Authoritarian: _____

Permissive: _____

Uninvolved: _____

Most effective: _____

2. How do parent-school partnerships foster academic achievement? (p. 568)

_____

_____

3. List four ways schools can strengthen parent-school partnerships. (pp. 568–569)

A. _____

B. _____

C. _____

D. _____

4. Summarize peer influences on adolescent academic achievement, noting how both family and the overall climate of the peer culture affect these influences. (p. 569)

_____

_____

5. Describe classroom learning experiences that foster academic achievement. (p. 570)

_____

_____

_____

6. True or False: A student from a disadvantaged family is just as likely to be placed in an academically-oriented, college-bound track as a student from a middle-SES background. What affect does this have on student achievement? (pp. 570, 572)

_____

_____

_____

7. Explain how the system of educational placement in the United States differs from that in Japan, China, and many Western European nations, and note the impact of these differences on student outcomes. (p. 572)

_____

_____

_____

_____

_____

Dropping Out

1. Cite two consequences of dropping out of high school. (pp. 572–573)

    A. _____

    B. _____

2. Summarize personal, familial, and school characteristics related to dropping out. (pp. 573–574, table 15.1 on p. 573)

    Personal: _____

    _____

    _____

    Familial: _____

    _____

    School: _____

    _____

3. Discuss four strategies for the prevention of early school leaving. (p. 574)

A. _____

_____

B. _____

_____

C. _____

_____

D. _____

_____

4. Over the past half-century, the percentage of American and Canadian adolescents completing high school has (increased / decreased) steadily. (pp. 574–575)

Social Issues: Education—High-Stakes Testing

1. Explain how the U.S. No Child Left Behind Act broadens high-stakes testing. (p. 571)

_____

_____

_____

2. Summarize potential benefits of high-stakes testing. (p. 571)

_____

_____

_____

3. Evidence indicates that high-stakes testing (undermines / upgrades) the quality of education. (p. 571)

4. Describe two concerns about high-stakes testing. (p. 571)

A. _____

_____

B. _____

_____

5. True or False: High-stakes testing has led to an increased emphasis on teaching for deeper understanding. (p. 571)

Social Issues: Education— Extracurricular Activities: Contexts for Positive Youth Development

1. What types of extracurricular activities promote diverse academic and social skills and have a lasting positive impact on adjustment? (p. 575)

_____

_____

2. Cite immediate and long-term benefits of involvement in extracurricular activities. (p. 575)

Immediate: _____

_____

Long-term: _____

_____

3. True or False: Adolescents who spend many afternoons and evenings engaged in unstructured activities show similar adjustment outcomes relative to adolescents who engage in structured, goal-oriented activities. (p. 575)

4. Who is especially likely to benefit from extracurricular activities, and what accounts for this effect? (p. 575)

_____

_____

Vocational Development

Selecting a Vocation

1. Describe the three phases of vocational development, noting the developmental period at which each occurs. (p. 576)

Fantasy period: _____

_____

Tentative period: _____

_____

Realistic period: _____

_____

Factors Influencing Vocational Choice

1. Match each of the following personality types that affect vocational development with the appropriate description. (p. 577)

____ Likes well-structured tasks and values social status; tends to choose business occupations

____ Prefers real-world problems and work with objects; tends toward mechanical occupations

____ Adventurous, persuasive, and a strong leader; drawn toward sales and supervisory positions

____ Enjoys working with ideas; likely to select scientific occupations

____ Has high need for emotional and individual expression; drawn toward fields such as writing, music, and the visual arts

____ Likes interacting with people; gravitates toward human service occupations

1. Investigative
2. Social
3. Realistic
4. Artistic
5. Conventional
6. Enterprising

2. The relationship between personality and vocational choice is (weak / moderate / strong). (p. 577)

3. Identify three reasons why young people's vocational aspirations correlate strongly with the jobs of their parents. (pp. 577–578)

    A. _____

    B. _____

    C. _____

4. Teachers (do / do not) play a powerful role in young adults' career decisions. (p. 578)

5. True or False: Over the past 30 years, young women's career preferences have remained strongly gender stereotyped, whereas young men have shown increasing interest in careers largely held by women. (p. 578)

6. Women's progress in entering and excelling at male-dominated professions has been (slow / rapid). (p. 578)

7. True or False: Sex differences in vocational achievement can be directly attributed to differences in ability. Elaborate on your response. (p. 578)

    _____

    _____

    _____

8. Cite two ways in which girls can be encouraged to maintain high career aspirations. (pp. 578–579)

    A. _____

    _____

    B. _____

    _____

9. What type of student is at-risk for becoming a "dreaming drifter," and how can schools better help these students to select an occupational goal that interests them and that fits with their personal attributes? (p. 579)

    _____

    _____

    _____

    _____

    _____

Making the Transition from School to Work

1. Non-college-bound high school graduates have (more / fewer) work opportunities than they did several decades ago. (p. 579)

2. Summarize the challenges faced by non-college-bound young adults in trying to gain employment, and describe the type of jobs they are likely to find. (p. 580)

    Challenges: _____

    _____

    Type of jobs: _____

    _____

3. Describe the nature of most jobs held by adolescents, and discuss the impact of heavy job commitment on adolescents' attitudes and behaviors. (p. 580)

_____

_____

_____

4. True or False: Like some European nations, the United States has a widespread training system designed to prepare youth for skilled business and industrial occupations and manual trades. (p. 580)

5. Summarize the features of Germany's work–study apprenticeship system, and explain how it creates a smooth transition from school to work. (p. 580)

_____

_____

_____

_____

6. Identify three major challenges to the implementation a national apprenticeship program in the United States. (p. 580)

A. _____

B. _____

C. _____

ASK YOURSELF . . .

For *Ask Yourself* questions for this chapter, please log on the Companion Website at *www.ablongman.com/berk*.

SUGGESTED STUDENT READINGS

Mortimer, J. T. (2003). *Working and growing up in America.* Cambridge, MA: Harvard University Press. Based on results from the Youth Development Study, which examined the effects of adolescent employment on development, this book highlights the impact of work experiences on cognitive and social development. The author presents factors contributing to both positive and negative outcomes associated with adolescent employment.

Ogbu, J. U. (2003). *Black American students in an affluent suburb: A study of academic disengagement.* Mahwah, NJ: Erlbaum. Examines factors that contribute to academic disengagement in black students of all socioeconomic backgrounds, including the impact of school race relations, discipline, culture, language, and peer relations.

West, A., & Pennell, H. (2003). *Underachievement in schools.* New York: Routledge. Addresses the many factors that contribute to underachievement in schools, including barriers experienced by educators and policymakers. The authors also provide practical advice for raising educational standards while promoting the achievement of all students.

PUZZLE 15.1 TERM REVIEW

Across

3. _____-deductive reasoning begins with a theory of all possible factors that could affect an outcome and inferences of specific hypotheses, which are then tested in a systematic fashion.

4. _____ necessity: specifies that the accuracy of conclusions drawn from premises rests on the rules of logic, not on real-world confirmation

5. Adolescents' belief that they are the focus of everyone's attention and concern is referred to as the _____ audience.

8. _____ monitoring: sensitivity to how well one understands a spoken or written message

9. Reasoning that views all knowledge as embedded in a framework of thought and that accepts the existence of multiple truths

10. _____ operational stage: Piaget's final stage, in which adolescents develop the capacity for abstract, scientific thinking

Down

1. The personal _____ refers to adolescents' belief that they are special and unique.

2. _____ thought: evaluating the logic of verbal statements without referring to real-world circumstances

6. Period of vocational development in which children explore career options through make-believe play

7. Period of vocational development in which adolescents weigh vocational options against their interests, abilities, and values

9. Period of vocational development in which adolescents focus on a general career category and eventually settle on a single occupation

PRACTICE TEST #1

1. In the formal operational stage, children first become capable of (p. 552)
   a. animistic thinking.
   b. transitive inference.
   c. analogical problem solving.
   d. hypothetico-deductive reasoning.

2. In one study, an experimenter hid a poker chip in her hand and asked participants to evaluate the truthfulness of the following statement: "The chip in my hand is green and it is not green." A young person in the formal operational stage would MOST agree that this statement is (p. 553)
   a. always false, regardless of the color of the poker chip.
   b. false if the poker chip is red.
   c. always true, regardless of the color of the poker chip.
   d. true if the poker chip is green.

3. Research demonstrates that (p. 555)
   a. over three-quarters of North American college students pass Piaget's formal operational problems.
   b. college course content does not seem to promote formal operational thinking.
   c. in many tribal and village societies, formal operational tasks are not mastered at all.
   d. formal operational reasoning usually emerges in all contexts at once.

4. Advances in _____ are central to the development of abstract thought. (p. 557)
   a. metacognition
   b. cognitive self-regulation
   c. attention
   d. strategy use

5. Compared to adults, adolescents tend to (p. 557)
   a. master information processing skills in sequential order.
   b. deliberately isolate variables when solving problems.
   c. show a self-serving bias in their reasoning skills.
   d. actively seek disconfirming evidence on hypothetical reasoning tasks.

6. The emergence of the personal fable during adolescence is partly an outgrowth of gains in _____. (p. 559)
   a. perspective taking
   b. self-regulation
   c. processing capacity
   d. social problem solving

7. Research on decision making demonstrates that teenagers are (p. 560)
   a. less likely than adults to assess the likelihood of various possible outcomes.
   b. more likely than adults to identify the pros and cons of each alternative.
   c. more likely than adults to learn from mistakes and make better future decisions.
   d. less likely than adults to act on impulse.

8. Studies on sex differences in mental abilities show that (p. 561)
   a. boys attain higher scores than girls in general intelligence.
   b. boys attain higher scores than girls in writing achievement.
   c. girls attain higher scores than boys in mathematical ability.
   d. girls attain higher scores than boys in reading achievement.

9. Sex differences in mathematical ability (p. 562)
   a. are first apparent during the middle school years.
   b. are largest among academically talented students.
   c. are larger in countries where women are in the labor force.
   d. have increased over the past several decades.

10. Adolescents improved capacity for _____ permits them to master irony and sarcasm. (p. 564)
   a. cognitive self-regulation
   b. sustained attention
   c. comprehension monitoring
   d. abstract thinking

11. Research on school transitions shows that (p. 565)
   a. students rate their secondary school learning experiences more favorably than their elementary school learning experiences.
   b. students feel more academically competent in high school than in junior high school.
   c. the later a school transition occurs, the less negative its impact on the child.
   d. children's grades decline with each school change.

12. Studies on helping adolescents adjust to school transitions suggest that (p. 566)
   a. school districts should consider changing 6-3-3 schools to 8-4 schools.
   b. homerooms hinder adolescents' growing desire for autonomy.
   c. during the first year following a school transition, students should be assigned to classes with changing groups of new peers.
   d. schools should stress competition and differential treatment by ability.

13. Of all the parenting approaches, _____ parenting predicts the poorest grades among adolescents. (p. 568)
   a. authoritative
   b. permissive
   c. authoritarian
   d. uninvolved

14. Highly-controlling, but noncoercive, parenting (p. 568)
   a. is linked to better grades among African-American teenagers.
   b. is associated with lower grades among American adolescents.
   c. is linked to lower grades among Chinese immigrant youths.
   d. is associated with higher grades among adolescents living in rural areas.

15. Parental involvement in school predicts academic success (p. 568)
   a. among both black and white adolescents.
   b. only among adolescents in middle- to high-SES families.
   c. only among white teenagers.
   d. only among adolescents living in rural areas.

16. Research on peer influences during adolescence indicates that (p. 569)
   a. most adolescents place peer acceptance above responding to parental expectations.
   b. teenagers whose parents value achievement generally choose friends who share those values.
   c. even high-achieving minority youths tend to associate with peers that engage in problem behaviors, like drug use and truancy.
   d. peers tend to have only minimal influence on teenagers' academic performance.

17. _____ tend(s) to occur in classrooms that emphasize competition and public comparison of students. (p. 570)
   a. Better attendance
   b. Declines in motivation
   c. Increases in academic achievement
   d. Higher educational expectations

18. Which of the following is supported by research on tracking in high school? (p. 572)
    a. It is relatively easy for high ability students to break out of low tracks.
    b. Low-SES minority students are equally distributed among college and non-college tracks.
    c. Tracking prevents many low-achieving students from dropping out of school.
    d. The performance level of high ability students in low tracks tends to drop to that of their trackmates.

19. What percentage of American and Canadian youth leaves high school without a diploma? (p. 572)
    a. 2
    b. 5
    c. 11
    d. 18

20. According to Holland's research on vocational choice, _____ people are drawn to sales and supervisory positions and politics. (p. 577)
    a. investigative
    b. social
    c. conventional
    d. enterprising

PRACTICE TEST #2

1. Piaget used the pendulum problem to test for (p. 552)
   a. propositional thought.
   b. logical necessities.
   c. hypothetico-deductive reasoning.
   d. metacognitive knowledge.

2. Formal operational thought (p. 553)
   a. is shown in specific situations and on specific tasks.
   b. is quickly generalized to a wide variety of situations and tasks.
   c. makes it easy to analyze the themes of a Shakespearean play.
   d. is not affected by experience with a task.

3. Which individual would not master formal operational tasks at all? (p. 555)
   a. George, an American high school student
   b. Gus, a college sophomore majoring in English
   c. Ghenniaa, the chief of a tribal society in Tonga
   d. Grady, the custodian at George's high school

4. Many researchers believe that _____ (is / are) at the heart of advanced cognitive development. (p. 557)
   a. postformal reasoning abilities
   b. neurochemicals
   c. genetic influences
   d. sophisticated metacognitive understanding

5. Research on the development of scientific reasoning shows that (p. 557)
   a. reasoning skill is unaffected by formal schooling.
   b. formal operational abilities develop in a similar, stepwise fashion on a variety of tasks.
   c. individuals are not capable of demonstrating metacognitive understanding until early adulthood.
   d. adolescents and adults show few individual differences in scientific reasoning skills.

6. The ability to think about theories, deliberately isolate variables, and actively seek disconfirming evidence (p. 557)
   a. begins to appear in middle childhood.
   b. is fully present by the end of the school years.
   c. is rarely present before adolescence.
   d. does not occur until adulthood.

7. Teenagers' argumentativeness and self-focus is a consequence of (p. 558)
   a. self-consciousness.
   b. abstract thought.
   c. adolescent egocentrism.
   d. anxiety.

8. When Rudy's father wouldn't let him borrow the car, Rudy said, "Dad, you don't know what it's like to be 16!" This distortion is known as (p. 559)
   a. the imaginary audience.
   b. the adolescent superiority complex.
   c. cognitive alienation.
   d. the personal fable.

328

9. With regard to mathematics, (p. 562)
   a. both girls and boys see it as a "male domain."
   b. researchers do not believe math skills are related to genetics.
   c. fewer and fewer girls are enrolling in advanced high school math courses.
   d. girls more often blame math errors on lack of studying.

10. School changes such as the transitions from elementary to junior high school and from junior high to high school (p. 566)
   a. do not affect students' grade point averages.
   b. affect adolescents more negatively, the later the change occurs.
   c. are related to strong increases in self-esteem for all children, regardless of the timing of school changes.
   d. temporarily depress adolescents' psychological well-being.

11. Which parenting style is linked to adolescent achievement? (p. 568)
   a. progressive
   b. authoritarian
   c. authoritative
   d. permissive

12. _____ in eighth grade strongly predicted students' grade point averages in tenth grade. (p. 568)
   a. Popularity with peers
   b. Physical maturity
   c. Parent involvement
   d. Relationships with teachers

13. When African-American high school sophomores were interviewed, what did the high achievers have in common? (p. 569)
   a. two-parent homes
   b. belief in the struggle against oppression
   c. at least one African-American teacher who encouraged them to succeed
   d. higher self-esteem

14. Research on ability grouping shows that (p. 570)
   a. students in low-ability groups evidence gains in academic achievement since instruction is adapted to meet their needs.
   b. mixed-ability classes are preferable, at least into the early years of secondary school.
   c. good students from low-SES families are just as likely to be placed in academically-oriented, college-bound tracks as are students of equal ability from middle-SES homes.
   d. mixed-ability groups stifle high-achieving students and provide few, if any, intellectual or social benefits to low-achieving students.

15. High school drop-out rates are highest among _____ adolescents. (p. 572)
   a. African-American
   b. White
   c. Asian-American
   d. Hispanic

16. Students at risk for dropping out benefit from (p. 574)
   a. remedial instruction in small classes.
   b. greater emotional distance from teachers.
   c. less focus on vocations and more emphasis on basic academics.
   d. larger classes where they feel less "on the spot."

17. Early and middle adolescence is characterized by which phase of vocational development? (p. 576)
    a. fantasy period
    b. tentative period
    c. realistic period
    d. crystallization period

18. Nissa wants to be a physicist or an engineer. According to Holland, she is a(n) _____ person. (p. 577)
    a. realistic
    b. conventional
    c. investigative
    d. enterprising

19. The best predictor of occupational status is (p. 577)
    a. years of education.
    b. parents' income.
    c. high school GPA.
    d. career aspirations.

20. The term "drifting dreamers" is used to refer to adolescents who (p. 579)
    a. are at risk for dropping out of high school.
    b. opt to enter the workforce after high school rather than pursuing a college education.
    c. remain stuck in the fantasy phase of vocational development.
    d. are highly ambitious with regard to vocational development but who lack knowledge of their preferred vocation and the educational requirements of their chosen field.

CHAPTER 16
EMOTIONAL AND SOCIAL DEVELOPMENT
IN ADOLESCENCE

BRIEF CHAPTER SUMMARY

Erikson's stage of identity versus identity confusion recognizes the formation of a coherent set of values and life plans as the major personality achievement of adolescence. An organized self-concept and a more differentiated sense of self-esteem prepare the young person for constructing an identity. Adolescents vary in their degree of progress toward developing a mature identity. Identity achievement and moratorium are adaptive statuses associated with positive personality characteristics, parents who offer a "secure base" from which teenagers can confidently move out into the wider world, and schools and communities offering rich and varied opportunities for exploration. Teenagers who remain in identity foreclosure or identity confusion tend to have adjustment difficulties.

Piaget's theory of moral development served as the inspiration for Kohlberg's expanded cognitive-developmental perspective. According to Kohlberg, from late childhood into adulthood, morality changes from concrete, externally controlled reasoning to more abstract, principled justifications for moral choices. Although Kohlberg's theory emphasizes a "masculine" morality of justice rather than a "feminine" morality of care, it does not underestimate the moral maturity of females. A broad range of experiences, including personality, family, school, peer, and cultural factors, fosters moral development. As individuals advance through Kohlberg's stages, moral reasoning becomes better related to behavior.

Biological, social, and cognitive forces combine to make early adolescence a period of gender intensification. Over the adolescent years, relationships with parents and siblings change as teenagers strive to establish a healthy balance between family connection and separation. As adolescents spend more time with peers, intimacy and loyalty become central features of friendship. Adolescent peer groups are organized into tightly knit groups called cliques. Sometimes several cliques with similar values form a crowd, which grants the adolescent an identity within the larger social structure of the school. Although dating relationships increase in intimacy with age, they lag behind same-sex friendships. Peer pressure rises in adolescence, but most teenagers do not blindly conform to the dictates of agemates.

Depression is the most common psychological problem of the teenage years, resulting from a diverse combination of biological and environmental factors. When it is severe, it often leads to suicidal thoughts. The suicide rate increases dramatically at adolescence. Although many teenagers become involved in some delinquent activity, only a few are serious and repeat offenders. Personal, family, school, peer, and neighborhood factors are related to delinquency.

LEARNING OBJECTIVES

After reading this chapter, you should be able to:

16.1 Discuss Erikson's theory of identity development. (pp. 586–587)

16.2 Describe changes in self-concept and self-esteem during adolescence. (pp. 587–589)

16.3 Describe the four identity statuses, noting how each is related to psychological adjustment, and describe the factors that influence identity development. (pp. 589–592)

16.4 Describe Piaget's theory of moral development and Kohlberg's extension of it, noting research that evaluates the accuracy of each. (pp. 594–598)

16.5 Discuss sex differences in moral reasoning, with particular attention to Gilligan's argument. (p. 598–599)

16.6 Describe the factors that influence moral reasoning, and discuss the relationship between moral reasoning and behavior. (pp. 599–603)

16.7 Explain why early adolescence is a period of gender intensification, and cite factors that promote the development of an androgynous gender identity. (pp. 603–604)

16.8 Discuss familial influences on adolescent development, including the impact of the parent–child relationship, family circumstances, and sibling interaction. (pp. 604–607)

16.9. Describe the characteristics of adolescent friendships and peer groups, and discuss the contribution of each to emotional and social development. (pp. 607–611)

16.10 Describe adolescent dating relationships. (pp. 611–612)

16.11 Discuss the influence of peer pressure during adolescence, noting how parental behavior is related to adolescent conformity. (pp. 612–613)

16.12 Discuss factors related to adolescent depression and suicide, along with approaches for prevention and treatment. (pp. 613–618)

16.13 Discuss factors related to delinquency, and cite strategies for prevention and treatment. (pp. 618–621)

STUDY QUESTIONS

Erikson's Theory: Identity versus Identity Confusion

1. Explain what is involved in constructing an identity. (p. 586)

_____

_____

2. Discuss Erikson's notion of an *identity crisis*. (p. 586)

_____

_____

3. Current theorists (do / do not) agree with Erikson that the process of identity development constitutes a "crisis." (p. 586)

4. Describe the negative outcome of Erikson's psychological conflict of adolescence—*identity confusion*. (p. 587)

_____

_____

_____

Self-Understanding

Changes in Self-Concept

1. True or False: Young adolescents often provide contradictory self-descriptions, such as describing themselves as both shy and outgoing. (p. 587)

2. Compared to school-age children, teenagers place (more / less) emphasis on social virtues, such as being friendly, considerate, kind, and cooperative. Why is this the case? (p. 587)

_____

_____

Changes in Self-Esteem

1. Cite three new dimensions of self-esteem that emerge during adolescence. (p. 588)

   A. _____   B. _____

   C. _____

2. True or False: Except for temporary declines associated with school transitions, self-esteem rises in most adolescents. (p. 588)

Influences on Self-Esteem

1. Explain how both parents and the larger social environment influence adolescents' self-esteem. (pp. 588–589)

   Parents: _____

   _____

   Social environment: _____

   _____

Paths to Identity

1. Match each of the following identity statuses with the appropriate description. (p. 589)

   ____ Committed to values and goals without taking time to explore alternatives
   ____ Have not yet made definite commitments and are still exploring alternatives
   ____ Committed to self-chosen values and goals after having already explored alternatives
   ____ Lack clear direction; are not committed to values and goals and are not actively seeking them

   1. Identity achievement
   2. Moratorium
   3. Identity foreclosure
   4. Identity diffusion

2. Most adolescents start out at "lower" statuses, such as _____ and _____, but by late adolescence, they have moved toward "higher" statuses, including _____ and _____. (p. 590)

3. True or False: Most adolescent girls follow a different path to identity formation than do boys: They postpone the task of establishing an identity, focusing instead on intimacy development. (p. 590)

Identity Status and Psychological Well-Being

1. True or False: Research supports the conclusion that identity achievement and moratorium are healthy routes to a mature self-definition, whereas identity foreclosure and identity diffusion are maladaptive. (p. 590)

2. Summarize personality characteristics associated with each identity status. (pp. 590–591)

   Identity achievement and moratorium: _____

   _____

   _____

   Identity foreclosure: _____

   _____

   _____

Identity diffusion: _____

_____

_____

Influences on Identity Development

1. Match the following identity statuses with the appropriate description of associated personality, familial, school, community, and larger cultural factors. Descriptions may apply to more than one identity status. (pp. 591–592)

____ Assume that absolute truth is always attainable

____ Lack confidence in the prospect of ever knowing anything with certainty

____ Appreciate that they can use rational criteria to choose among alternatives

____ Feel attached to parents but are also free to voice their own opinions

____ Have close bonds with parents but lack healthy separation

____ Report the lowest levels of warm, open communication at home

____ Fostered by classrooms that promote high-level thinking, as well as extracurricular and community activities that permit teens to take on responsible roles

1. Identity achievement
2. Moratorium
3. Identity foreclosure
4. Identity diffusion

2. Discuss four ways in which adults can support healthy identity development in adolescents. (pp. 591–592)

A. _____

_____

B. _____

_____

C. _____

_____

D. _____

_____

Cultural Influences:
Identity Development Among Ethnic Minority Adolescents

1. What is an *ethnic identity*? (p. 593)

_____

_____

2. Explain why ethnic minority adolescents often experience unique problems in developing a sense of identity. (p. 593)

_____

_____

3. True or False: Many minority high school students are diffused or foreclosed on ethnic identity issues. (p. 593)

4. List three ways in which minority adolescents can be helped to resolve identity conflicts constructively. (p. 593)

   A. _____

   B. _____

   C. _____

5. What is a *bicultural identity*, and how does it benefit minority adolescents? (p. 593)

   _____

   _____

   _____

Moral Development

Piaget's Theory of Moral Development

1. Describe the main characteristics of Piaget's heteronomous and autonomous stages of moral development, noting the age at which children display each type of moral understanding. (p. 594)

   Heteronomous: _____

   _____

   _____

   Age: _____

   Autonomous: _____

   _____

   _____

   Age: _____

2. Piaget (underestimated / overestimated) young children's ability to make moral judgments. (p. 595)

3. True or False: Piaget's theory accurately describes the general direction of change in moral judgment. (p. 595)

Kohlberg's Extension of Piaget's Theory

1. Explain Kohlberg's approach to the study of moral development. (p. 595)

   _____

   _____

2. True or False: Kohlberg emphasized that it is the *way an individual reasons* about a dilemma, not the *content of the response,* which determines moral maturity. (p. 595)

3. List two factors that Kohlberg believed to promote moral understanding. (p. 595)

   A. _____

   B. _____

4. Explain the basic characteristics of moral reasoning at each of Kohlberg's three levels: (pp. 595–598)

Preconventional: _____

_____

Conventional: _____

_____

Postconventional: _____

_____

5. Match each of the following moral orientations with the appropriate description. (pp. 596–597, chart on p. 596)

_____ Laws must be obeyed under all circumstances; rules must be
enforced in the same even-handed manner for everyone, and
each member of society has a personal duty to uphold them
_____ Right action is defined by self-chosen ethical principles of
conscience that are valid for all humanity, regardless of law
and social agreement
_____ Ignore people's intentions and focus on fear of authority
and avoidance of punishment as reasons for behaving morally
_____ Desire to obey rules because they promote social harmony
_____ Regard laws and rules as flexible and emphasize fair procedures
for interpreting and changing the law in order to protect individual
rights and the interests of the majority
_____ View right action as flowing from self-interest; reciprocity is
understood as equal exchange of favors

1. Punishment and obedience orientation
2. Instrumental purpose orientation
3. "Good boy–good girl" orientation
4. Social-order-maintaining orientation
5. Social contract orientation
6. Universal ethical principle orientation

6. True or False: Longitudinal research suggests that individuals do not move through the stages of moral development in the order in which Kohlberg suggested. (p. 598)

7. True or False: The development of moral understanding is very slow and gradual. (p. 598)

8. Moral reasoning for real-life problems tends to fall at a (lower / higher) stage than does reasoning related to hypothetical dilemmas. Explain why this is the case. (p. 598)

_____

_____

9. True or False: Kohlberg's stages develop in a neat, stepwise fashion. (p. 598)

Are There Sex Differences in Moral Reasoning?

1. Carol Gilligan believes that feminine morality emphasizes an *ethic of care* that is devalued in Kohlberg's model. Explain what she meant by this. (p. 598)

_____

_____

_____

2. True or False: Research supports Gilligan's claim that Kohlberg's approach underestimates females' moral maturity. (p. 598)

3. Summarize research findings on sex differences in moral development. (p. 599)

_____

_____

_____

Influences on Moral Reasoning

1. Explain how having a flexible, open-minded approach to new information and experiences fosters gains in moral reasoning. (p. 599)

_____

_____

_____

2. Describe child-rearing practices that promote gains in moral development. (p. 599)

_____

_____

_____

3. True or False: Years of schooling is one of the most powerful predictors of moral maturity. (p. 599)

4. Cite characteristics of peer interaction that promote moral understanding and movement to higher moral stages. (p. 600)

_____

_____

_____

5. True or False: Cross-cultural research shows that individuals in industrialized nations move through Kohlberg's stages more quickly and advance to higher levels of moral reasoning than do individuals in village societies. Based on your response, provide some possible explanations. (p. 600)

_____

_____

_____

Moral Reasoning and Behavior

1. There is a (weak / moderate / strong) relationship between moral thought and action. Elaborate on your response by citing research findings on the relationship between moral reasoning and behavior. (p. 601)

_____

_____

_____

Religious Involvement and Moral Development

1. During adolescence, formal religious involvement (increases / declines). (p. 601)

2. Summarize the benefits derived by adolescents who remain involved in a religious community. (p. 601)

_____

_____

_____

Social Issues: Education— Development of Civic Responsibility

1. What is *civic responsibility*? List its three components. (p. 602)

   A. _____

   B. _____

   C. _____

2. Summarize family, school, and community influences that contribute to adolescents' civic responsibility. (p. 602)

   Family: _____

   _____

   School: _____

   _____

   Community: _____

   _____

3. Cite two aspects of involvement in extracurricular activities and youth organizations that account for their lasting impact. (p. 602)

   A. _____

   B. _____

Gender Typing

1. What is *gender intensification*? (p. 603)

   _____

   _____

2. Although it occurs in both sexes, gender intensification is stronger for (boys / girls). (p . 603)

3. Discuss biological, social, and cognitive factors associated with gender intensification. (pp. 603–604)

   Biological: _____

   _____

   _____

   Social: _____

   _____

   _____

Cognitive: _____

_____

_____

4. (Androgynous / Gender-typed) adolescents tend to be psychologically healthier. (p. 604)

The Family

1. During adolescence, _____—establishing oneself as a separate, self-governing individual— becomes a salient task. (p. 604)

Parent-Child Relationships

1. Describe parenting practices that foster adolescent autonomy. (pp. 604–605)

_____

_____

_____

2. Explain why maintenance of an authoritative parenting style involves special challenges and adjustments during the adolescent years. (p. 605)

_____

_____

_____

3. Discuss the life transition that parents may be experiencing as their adolescent children are undergoing their own life transitions, and note how this impacts the parent–child relationship. (pp. 605–606)

_____

_____

_____

_____

4. True or False: The quality of the parent–child relationship is the most consistent predictor of mental health throughout adolescence. (p. 606)

5. Explain how mild parent–child conflict is beneficial during adolescence. (p. 606)

_____

_____

_____

Family Circumstances

1. True or False: Maternal employment reduces the amount of time that parents spend with their teenagers and is harmful to adolescent development. (p. 606)

Siblings

1. During adolescence, teenagers invest (more / less) time and energy in siblings. Why is this the case? (p. 607)

_____

_____

2. Sibling relationships become (more / less) intense during adolescence, in both positive and negative feelings. (p. 607)

Peer Relations

Friendships

1. Cite the two characteristics of friendship emphasized by teenagers. (p. 608)

A. _____   B. _____

2. List three changes that result from adolescents' revised view of friendship. (p. 608)

A. _____

B. _____

C. _____

3. Briefly discuss how friendships change during the transition to middle or junior high school. (p. 609)

_____

_____

_____

4. Summarize sex differences in the nature of adolescents' close friendships. (p. 609)

_____

_____

_____

5. True or False: Androgynous boys are just as likely as girls to form intimate same-sex ties, whereas boys who identify strongly with the traditional masculine role are less likely to do so. (p. 609)

6. Cite four reasons why gratifying childhood and adolescent friendships are related to psychological health and competence during early adulthood. (pp. 609–610)

A. _____

_____

B. _____

_____

C. _____

_____

D. _____

_____

Cliques and Crowds

1. Differentiate between cliques and crowds, noting the characteristics of each. (p. 610)

   Cliques: _____

   _____

   Crowds: _____

   _____

2. Provide some examples of typical high school crowds. (p. 610)

   _____

   _____

3. True or False: Peer group values are often an extension of values learned in the home. (p. 610)

4. Describe the function of mixed-sex cliques in early adolescence. (p. 611)

   _____

   _____

   _____

5. True or False: Crowds increase in importance from early to late adolescence. (p. 611)

Dating

1. Describe younger and older adolescents' different reasons for dating. (p. 611)

   Younger: _____

   _____

   Older: _____

   _____

2. True or False: Early dating is positively associated with social maturity. Briefly expand on your response. (pp. 611–612)

   _____

   _____

3. Describe the unique challenges faced by homosexual adolescents in initiating and maintaining romances. (p. 612)

   _____

   _____

   _____

4. Cite some of the possible benefits of adolescent dating. (p. 612)

   _____

   _____

Peer Pressure and Conformity

1. True or False: Conformity to peer pressure is greater during adolescence than during childhood or young adulthood. (p. 612)

2. Describe the differing spheres of influence of parents and peers during the adolescent years. (p. 613)

Parents: _____

_____

Peers: _____

_____

3. Summarize the link between parenting behavior and adolescents' conformity to peer pressure. (p. 613)

_____

_____

_____

Problems of Development

Depression

1. About _____ to _____ percent of American teenagers have experienced one or more depressive episodes, and _____ to _____ percent are chronically depressed. (p. 614)

2. Summarize consequences of adolescent depression. (p. 614)

_____

_____

3. Explain why adolescents' depressive symptoms tend to be overlooked by parents and teachers. (p. 614)

_____

_____

4. Kinship studies of identical and fraternal twins reveal that heredity (does / does not) play an important role in depression. (p. 614)

5. Explain how experience combines with biology to activate depression in youths. (p. 614)

_____

_____

_____

6. Biological changes associated with puberty (can / cannot) account for sex differences in depression. Elaborate on your response. (p. 615)

_____

_____

_____

7. Describe how stressful life events and gender-typed coping styles account for girls' higher rates of depression. (p. 615)

_____

_____

_____

Suicide

1. True or False: Suicide is currently the leading cause of death among young people in the United States and Canada. (p. 616)

2. True or False: Adolescent suicide rates are roughly equivalent in all industrialized countries. (p. 616)

3. Discuss sex differences in suicidal behavior, noting whether boys or girls are more likely to kill themselves. (p. 616)

_____

_____

_____

4. True or False: Gay, lesbian, and bisexual youth are three times more likely to attempt suicide than are other adolescents. (p. 616)

5. Describe two types of young people who tend to commit suicide. (p. 616)

A. _____

_____

B. _____

_____

6. Cite cognitive changes that contribute to the rise in suicide among adolescents. (pp. 616–617)

_____

_____

7. List five warning signs of suicide. (p. 617)

A. _____

B. _____

C. _____

D. _____

E. _____

8. Discuss four ways of responding to an adolescent who might be suicidal. (p. 617—chart)

A. _____

_____

B. _____

_____

C. _____

_____

D. _____

_____

9. What types of treatments are available for depressed and suicidal adolescents? (pp. 617–618)

_____

_____

_____

10. True or False: Teenage suicides often take place in clusters. Elaborate on your response. (p. 618)

_____

_____

Delinquency

1. Explain why delinquency rises during early adolescence, remains high in middle adolescence, and then declines into young adulthood? (p. 618)

_____

_____

2. Describe personal, familial, peer, school, and neighborhood factors associated with delinquency. (p. 620)

Personal: _____

_____

Familial: _____

_____

Peer: _____

_____

School: _____

_____

Neighborhood: _____

_____

3. Describe characteristics of the most effective treatment programs for adolescent delinquency. (p. 620–621)

_____

_____

_____

At The Threshold

1. List five factors that foster resilience in adolescence. (pp. 621–622)

A. _____

B. _____

C. _____

D. _____

E. _____

Biology and Environment: Two Routes to Adolescent Delinquency

1. Identify two paths to adolescent delinquency. (p. 619)

   A. _____

   B. _____

2. Longitudinal research reveals that the (early / late) onset type is far more likely to lead to a life course pattern of aggression and criminality. (p. 619)

3. True or False: Adolescent-onset delinquent youth show significantly higher levels of serious offenses, involvement with deviant peers, substance abuse, unsafe sex, dangerous driving, and time spent in correctional facilities than do childhood-onset delinquent youth. (p. 619)

4. Describe characteristics that distinguish early-onset from late-onset delinquent youth. (p. 619)

   Early-onset: _____

   _____

   _____

   Late-onset: _____

   _____

   _____

ASK YOURSELF . . .

For *Ask Yourself* questions for this chapter, please log on the Companion Website at *www.ablongman.com/berk.*

SUGGESTED STUDENT READINGS

Gibbs, J. C. (2003). *Moral development and reality: Beyond the theories of Kohlberg and Hoffman.* Thousand Oaks, CA: Sage. Examines moral development and social behavior in children and adolescents, including practical, research-based recommendations for promoting moral development in the classroom.

Marcovitz, H. (2004). *Teens and family issues.* Folcroft, PA: Mason Crest Publishers. Based on results from the Gallup Youth Study, which surveys teenagers' perspectives on family, peers, school, social issues, and other relevant topics, this book examines the importance of family relationships for health development.

Quinsey, V. L., Lalumiere, M., & Skilling, T. A. (2003). *Juvenile delinquency: Understanding the origins of individual differences.* Washington, DC: American Psychological Association. An ecological approach to understanding juvenile aggression and delinquency, this book explores the origins of antisocial behavior, sex differences in juvenile delinquency, and interventions used to treat violent offenders.

PUZZLE 16.1 TERM REVIEW

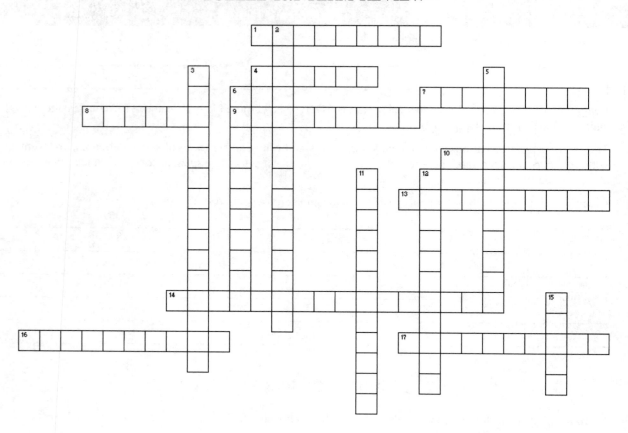

Across

1. Identity_____: identity status of individuals who have no commitments to values and goals and are not actively trying to reach them
4. _____ identity: aspect of the self that includes sense of ethnic group membership and attitudes associated with that membership
7. Sense of self as a separate, self-governing individual
8. Small group of 5 to 7 members who are good friends
9. Identity versus identity _____: Erikson's psychological conflict of adolescence
10. A well-organized conception of the self made up of values, beliefs, and goals to which the individual is solidly committed
13. Identity status of individuals who are exploring alternatives in an effort to find values and goals to guide their life
14. Kohlberg's highest level of moral development; morality is defined in terms of abstract principles and values that apply to all situations and societies
16. Identity constructed by adolescents who explore and adopt values from both their subculture and the dominant culture
17. _____ morality: Piaget's second stage of moral development; children view rules as flexible, socially-agreed-upon principles that can be revised

Down

2. Gender _____: increased gender stereotyping of attitudes and behavior
3. Kohlberg's first level of moral development; moral understanding is based on rewards, punishments, and the power of authority figures
5. Kohlberg's second level of moral development; moral understanding is based on conforming to social rules to ensure positive relationships and social order
6. Identity _____ : identity status of individuals who have explored and committed themselves to self-chosen values and goals
11. _____ morality: Piaget's first stage of moral development; children view rules as permanent, unchangeable features of the external world
12. Identity _____: identity status of individuals who have accepted ready-made values and goals that authority figures have chosen for them
15. A large, loosely organized group consisting of several cliques; membership is based on reputation and stereotype

PRACTICE TEST #1

1. Erikson's theory recognizes _____ as the major personality achievement of adolescence. (p. 586)
   a. initiative
   b. identity
   c. intimacy
   d. industry

2. Compared with school-age children, adolescents tend to place emphasis on _____ in their self-descriptions. (p. 587)
   a. social virtues
   b. personality traits
   c. talents
   d. physical characteristics

3. Which of the following is a new dimension of self-esteem that is added during the teenage years? (p. 588)
   a. academic competence
   b. close friendship
   c. physical/athletic competence
   d. physical appearance

4. Which of the following is supported by research on self-esteem during adolescence? (p. 588)
   a. Boys score lower than girls in overall self-worth.
   b. Authoritarian parenting is associated with favorable self-esteem.
   c. Asians score higher than Caucasians on self-esteem.
   d. Caucasian-Americans' self-esteem is less positive than that of African-Americans.

5. Jason has decided to go to law school simply because his father and his grandfather are lawyers. Jason did not explore alternatives. According to Marcia, Jason's identity status is (p. 589)
   a. identity diffusion.
   b. moratorium.
   c. identity achievement.
   d. identity foreclosure.

6. Which of the following is supported by research on identity? (p. 590)
   a. Adolescents who go to college settle on a self-definition earlier than those who go to work after high school.
   b. Teenagers who find it difficult to realize their occupational goals because they lack training are at risk for long-term moratorium.
   c. Identity achievement and moratorium are psychologically healthy routes to a mature self-definition.
   d. Persistently foreclosed teenagers are the least mature in identity development.

7. Adolescents who have close bonds with parents, but lack opportunities for healthy separation, tend to be in a state of (p. 591)
   a. identity achievement.
   b. moratorium.
   c. foreclosure.
   d. diffusion.

8. Children in Piaget's heteronomous morality stage (p. 594)
   a. want to maintain the affection and approval of others by being a "good person."
   b. view rules as unchangeable and requiring strict obedience.
   c. base their moral understanding on rewards, punishments, and the power of authority figures.
   d. view right action as what satisfies their needs or otherwise results in a personal advantage.

9. Kohlberg emphasized that it is the _____ and *not* the _____ that determines moral maturity when presented with the Heinz dilemma. (p. 595)
   a. way an individual reasons about the dilemma; content of the response
   b. content of the response; way an individual reasons about the dilemma
   c. final outcome for Heinz; way in which that outcome was achieved
   d. emotional reaction to the dilemma; justification of the response

10. In response to the Heinz dilemma, Gillian says, "You shouldn't steal the drug because everybody will think you're a criminal and you won't be able to face anyone again." Gillian is most likely in which of the following stages? (pp. 596–597)
   a. social-contract orientation
   b. "good boy–good girl" orientation
   c. instrumental purpose orientation
   d. social-order-maintaining orientation

11. In Kohlberg's theory, at the _____, individuals define morality in terms of abstract principles and values that apply to all situations and societies. (p. 597)
   a. postconventional level
   b. social-order-maintaining orientation
   c. conventional level
   d. instrumental purpose orientation

12. Research on Kohlberg's stages indicates that (p. 598)
   a. responses to Kohlberg's hypothetical dilemmas typically fall at a lower stage compared to moral reasoning in everyday situations.
   b. individuals use the same level of moral reasoning across tasks and situations.
   c. progress through Kohlberg's stages is not consistently related to age.
   d. the development of moral reasoning is very slow and gradual.

13. Research on Gilligan's claims regarding sex differences in moral reasoning has demonstrated that (p. 599)
   a. adolescent and adult females display reasoning at the same stage as their male counterparts, and sometimes higher.
   b. males show more advanced moral reasoning in care-based understanding in real-life situations, but purposely hide this trait in hypothetical situations for fear of appearing "too feminine."
   c. themes of justice are more likely to appear in males' responses, whereas themes of caring are more likely to appear in females' explanations.
   d. females fall behind males in moral development on everyday moral problems but not on hypothetical dilemmas.

14. Flexible and open-minded individuals have greater gains in moral development because they (p. 599)
   a. have more opportunities for social participation, which in turn enhances exposure to others' perspectives and allows them to derive insights from that exposure.
   b. are less likely to be interested in others' moral ideas and justifications.
   c. have difficulty adapting to new experiences and so spend great amounts of time thinking about their own actions as well as actions of those around them.
   d. are more likely to put their own thoughts and preferences aside and adopt the perspectives of the predominant peer culture.

15. Longitudinal research demonstrates that moral reasoning advances in late adolescence and emerging adulthood only (p. 599)
   a. among postconventional thinkers.
   b. as long as a person remains in college.
   c. among identity-achieved individuals.
   d. among females.

16. Cross-cultural research on Kohlberg's theory demonstrates that (p. 600)
    a. individuals in village societies rarely move beyond stage 1.
    b. moral reasoning is advanced in collectivist cultures relative to individualistic cultures.
    c. Kohlberg's levels represent a universal progression of moral reasoning.
    d. young people in industrialized nations move though Kohlberg's stages more quickly than those in village societies.

17. During early adolescence, (p. 603)
    a. the onset of dating leads to a decrease in gender intensification.
    b. teenagers who explore non-gender-typed activities are less identity achieved than their peers.
    c. girls become increasingly likely to experiment with "other gender" activities and behavior.
    d. teenagers move toward a more traditional gender identity.

18. Throughout adolescence, _____ is the single most constant predictor of mental health. (p. 606)
    a. identity status
    b. the quality of parent–child relationships
    c. academic performance
    d. the quality of friendships

19. When asked about the meaning of friendship, teenagers stress which of the following characteristics? (p. 608)
    a. intimacy and loyalty
    b. common interests and trust
    c. proximity and common interests
    d. popularity and athletic ability

20. As teenagers move through adolescence, (p. 610)
    a. the importance of mixed-sex cliques declines.
    b. deviant crowds gain members.
    c. crowd membership becomes increasingly important.
    d. "brains" and "normal" crowds lose members.

PRACTICE TEST #2

1. Erikson's psychosocial conflict of adolescence is (p. 586)
    a. initiative versus shame and doubt.
    b. identity versus identity confusion.
    c. intimacy versus isolation.
    d. exploration versus stagnation.

2. According to Erikson, resolution of the adolescent psychological conflict requires (p. 586)
    a. successful outcomes at earlier stages.
    b. an above-average IQ.
    c. a variety of romantic partners.
    d. permissive parenting.

3. When asked about their outlook on life, teenagers from industrialized countries were (p. 588)
    a. hopeless.
    b. worried.
    c. optimistic.
    d. indifferent.

4. Which of the following statements is true? (p. 589)
    a. Caucasian adolescents have higher self-esteem than African-American adolescents do.
    b. African-American girls are more satisfied with their physical appearance than are Caucasian girls.
    c. Caucasian girls are more satisfied with their peer relationships than are African-American girls.
    d. Teenagers who go to schools with many others of their own SES or ethnic group do not differ in self-esteem from those who are minorities in their schools.

5. The impetus behind commitments such as vocational choices and religious ideals (p. 589)
    a. is the search for self.
    b. is peer pressure.
    c. is parental values.
    d. is biological maturation.

6. What identity status is associated with inflexibility and intolerance? (p. 590)
    a. diffusion
    b. foreclosure
    c. achievement
    d. moratorium

7. Research on identity construction indicates that (p. 591)
    a. girls often postpone the task of identity development to focus instead on intimacy development.
    b. adolescents who go to work after high school settle on an identity status earlier than do college-bound youths.
    c. adolescents typically retain the same identity status across adolescence and adulthood.
    d. most adolescents experience a serious identity crisis.

8. Desiree is in Piaget's stage of heteronomous morality. Approximately what age is she? (p. 594)
    a. 2 to 5
    b. 5 to 10
    c. 10 to 15
    d. 15 to 20

9. Kohlberg's stage of punishment and obedience corresponds to Selman's (p. 596)
   a. social informational stage.
   b. self-reflective stage.
   c. third-party stage.
   d. societal stage.

10. _____ asserted that the morality of girls and women is based on "an ethic of care." (p. 598)
   a. Gilligan
   b. Harter
   c. Kohlberg
   d. Marcia

11. Gender intensification is strongest (p. 603)
   a. for boys in late adolescence.
   b. for girls in late adolescence.
   c. for boys in early adolescence.
   d. for girls in early adolescence.

12. Immigrant parents (p. 606)
   a. usually allow their adolescents to have more freedom than non-immigrants.
   b. have adolescents who prefer more restrictive parenting practices than non-immigrants.
   c. react more strongly to adolescent disagreement than non-immigrants.
   d. do not believe children should have independence until they leave home.

13. Compared with teens in other nations, American adolescents spend _____ time on schoolwork, and _____ time with other adolescents outside of school. (p. 607)
   a. more; more
   b. less; more
   c. more; less
   d. less; less

14. Tightly structured groups of adolescent peers are called (p. 610)
   a. cliques.
   b. clusters.
   c. crowd.
   d. clans.

15. Who is most likely to give in to peer pressure? (p. 613)
   a. elementary school children
   b. early adolescents
   c. middle adolescents
   d. late adolescents

16. _____ is the most common psychological problem of adolescence. (p. 614)
   a. Anxiety
   b. Delinquency
   c. Depression
   d. Social phobia

17. In adolescence, depression (p. 614)
   a. occurs at the same rate as it did in middle childhood.
   b. peaks around the time of puberty.
   c. occurs equally as often in girls as in boys.
   d. does not seem to affect identity development.

18. Adolescent attempts at suicide (p. 616)
    a. occur equally often in girls and boys.
    b. occur more often in boys.
    c. occur more often in girls.
    d. are decreasing among girls and boys.

19. Gay, lesbian, and bisexual youths (p. 616)
    a. do not commit suicide.
    b. have an extremely low suicide rate.
    c. have the same suicide rate as heterosexual youths.
    d. have a higher suicide rate than heterosexual youths.

20. Delinquency (p. 618)
    a. rises during early adolescence, remains high during middle adolescence, and decreases into young adulthood.
    b. rises during early adolescence, then decreases to a low level for middle and late adolescence.
    c. begins to rise during middle adolescence, and stays high until adulthood.
    d. is low until late adolescence, when it rises and stays high during early adulthood.

CHAPTER 17
EMERGING ADULTHOOD

BRIEF CHAPTER SUMMARY

Emerging adulthood is a recent period in development that is marked by great challenge and uncertainty. Young people between the ages of 18 and 25 who live in industrialized nations are making decisions regarding education, romantic commitments, and careers later than young people of past generations. Released from the oversight of parents but not yet immersed in adult roles, emerging adults are free to explore many different life paths. Changes in reasoning capacity permit emerging adults to revise their political and religious perspectives.

Cultural changes have contributed to the appearance of this new period in development. The economies of industrialized nations have become more technical and information based—requiring higher levels of education for well-paid careers. Prosperous nations continue to experience gains in life expectancy and less reliance on young people's labor. Such changes delay the need for financial independence and career commitment among emerging adults, allowing more time for exploring options. These benefits, however, are not always available to those living in impoverished areas.

To transition to adulthood successfully, emerging adults must acquire new knowledge and skills. Researchers who study postformal thought have shown that college students make substantial strides in cognition Younger and older students vary in their employment of relativistic thinking, with older students more aware of multiple truths. Exposure to multiple viewpoints encourages young people to look at themselves. As self-understanding increases, emerging adults experience advances in identity in the areas of love, work, and worldviews.

Taking a more active role in their own development and participating in vigorous explorations, emerging adults face increased risks. Feelings of loneliness peak during the late teens and early twenties as young people begin to live on their own and move more frequently. Certain personal attributes and social supports increase resilience and foster successful passage through this period.

LEARNING OBJECTIVES

After reading this chapter, you should be able to:

17.1   Describe emerging adulthood and explain the emergence of this new period of development. (pp. 630–631)

17.2   Describe the cultural changes that contributed to emerging adulthood and explain whether the benefits of this period are available to everyone. (pp. 631–632)

17.3   Compare emerging adulthood with adolescence and state what cognitive, emotional, and social changes emerging adults experience. (pp. 632–637)

17.4   Discuss the risks faced by emerging adults and what factors foster resilience and successful passage into adulthood. (pp. 637–638)

STUDY QUESTIONS

1. Describe the new phase of development known as *emerging adulthood*. (p. 630)

_____

_____

_____

A Period of Unprecedented Exploration

1. True or False: About 85 percent of American and Canadian young people who enroll in higher education earn their bachelor's degree by age 25. (p. 630)

2. The average age of first marriage is (increasing / declining) in industrialized nations. (p. 630)

3. Explain how extended education and delayed career entry and marriage create residential instability for emerging adults. (p. 630)

_____

_____

_____

Cultural Change and Emerging Adulthood

1. Describe two cultural factors that have contributed to the development of emerging adulthood as a new period of development. (p. 631)

    A. _____

    _____

    B. _____

    _____

2. True or False: Emerging adulthood is largely limited to developed nations. (p. 631)

3. Emerging adulthood (is / is not) common in low-SES and ethnic minority youths. Elaborate on your response. (p. 632)

_____

_____

_____

4. Explain how globalization is expected to impact emerging adulthood. (p. 632)

_____

_____

Cognitive Changes

1. Research has shown that college students (do / do not) make substantial gains in cognition. (p. 632)

2. Summarize changes in thought that occur across the college years. Be sure to discuss *relativistic thinking* in your response. (pp. 632–633)

   _____

   _____

   _____

   _____

3. True or False: Residence hall living is one of the most consistent predictors of cognitive development during the college years. (p. 633)

Emotional and Social Changes

1. Explain how dating relationships change from adolescence into emerging adulthood. (p. 633)

   _____

   _____

2. Describe how partner similarity and communication affect the likelihood of forming an intimate romantic bond during emerging adulthood. (pp. 633–634)

   Partner similarity: _____

   _____

   _____

   Communication: _____

   _____

   _____

3. True or False: Emerging adults' attachment relationships to their parents have little influence on their romantic partnerships. (p. 634)

4. Explain why cohabitation is much more likely to lead to the break up of a romantic relationship in North American couples than in their Western European counterparts. (p. 634)

   _____

   _____

   _____

5. Summarize how work-related goals and pursuits differ for young men and women. (pp. 634–635)

   _____

   _____

   _____

6. Describe four experiences common to women who continue to achieve at a high level during the college years. (p. 635)

A. _____

_____

B. _____

_____

C. _____

_____

D. _____

_____

7. True or False: Young adults report that constructing a worldview, or set of beliefs and values to live by, is more important than finishing their education and settling into a career or marriage. (p. 635)

8. True or False: The overwhelming majority of emerging adults develop worldviews that focus on concern for the self. (p. 635)

9. Compared to older people, emerging adults are (more / less) likely to be involved in organizations devoted to specific issues of concern to them. (p. 635)

10. Compared to previous generations, far (more / fewer) American, Canadian, and Western European young people vote and engage in political party activities. (p. 636)

11. Summarize the development of religious beliefs during emerging adulthood, including the relationship between parenting practices and religious development. (p. 636)

_____

_____

_____

_____

Risk and Resilience in Emerging Adulthood

1. True or False: Feelings of loneliness peak during the late teens and early twenties. Elaborate on your response. (p. 637)

_____

_____

_____

2. Summarize cognitive, emotional, and social assets and social supports that support development during emerging adulthood. (pp. 637–638)

Cognitive assets: _____

_____

_____

Emotional assets: _____

_____

_____

Social assets: _____

_____

_____

Social supports: _____

_____

_____

ASK YOURSELF . . .

For *Ask Yourself* questions for this chapter, please log on the Companion Website at *www.ablongman.com/berk*.

SUGGESTED STUDENT READINGS

Arnett, J. J., & Galambos, N. L. (2003). *Exploring cultural conceptions of the transition to adulthood: New directions for child and adolescent development #100*. San Francisco: Jossey-Bass. A cross-cultural examination of the transition to adulthood, including leaving the family home, continuing education, marriage, and parenthood.

Eccles, J. S., & Gootman, J. (Eds.). (2002). *Community programs to promote youth development*. Washington, DC: National Academy Press. Using up-to-date research on community programs for adolescents and young adults, this book addresses the ability of these programs to meet the developmental needs of young people. The authors also provide recommendations for improving community-based programs, including directions for future research.

Goldscheider, F., & Goldscheider, C. (1999). *The changing transition to adulthood: Leaving and returning home*. Thousand Oaks, CA: Sage. Reflecting on major events in the 20th century, this book examines the multitude of reasons that adolescents and young adults ultimately leave and return to the family home. The authors also address the impact of external factors, including ethnicity, gender, religion, and socioeconomic status.

PUZZLE 17.1 TERM REVIEW

Across

2. _____ thought: development beyond Piaget's formal operational stage
3. _____ adulthood: new period of development extending from the late teens to the mid-twenties

Down

1. _____ thinking: viewing knowledge as embedded in a framework of thought

PRACTICE TEST #1

1. The term emerging adulthood refers to a time period (p. 630)
    a. during the twenties.
    b. extending from the mid-thirties to the fifties.
    c. during the thirties.
    d. extending from the late teens to the mid-twenties.

2. During the emerging adulthood period (p. 629)
    a. young adults are free to experiment more than they did during adolescence because of a lack of social expectations.
    b. over 80 percent of young people enroll in college.
    c. young adults gain greater residential stability than they had in earlier years.
    d. young people are less likely to explore political and religious alternatives than they were in adolesence.

3. Research on the period of emerging adulthood has revealed that (p. 630)
    a. only about half of American young people earn a bachelor's degree by age 25.
    b. young people are getting married earlier than in past generations.
    c. the majority of young people graduate with the major declared their first year in college.
    d. less than half of young people cohabitate with a romantic partner before marriage.

4. In 2002 in the United States, the average age of first marriage was _____ for women and _____ for men. (p. 630)
    a. 25; 27
    b. 19; 23
    c. 23; 19
    d. 27; 29

5. Which of the following is true about North American 18- to 25-year-olds? (p. 630)
    a. Over 50 percent will move in with a romantic partner.
    b. More than half move in and out of fraternity and sorority houses during college.
    c. More than half will return to their parents' home for at least a brief period after first leaving.
    d. Over 50 percent become parents for the first time.

6. Which of the following is supported by research on emerging adulthood? (p. 631)
    a. In developing countries, the majority of young people do not experience emerging adulthood.
    b. Gains in life expectancy during the past century have contributed to a decline in the period of emerging adulthood.
    c. The period of emerging adulthood is extended for low-SES and ethnic minority young people.
    d. Most theorists predict that emerging adulthood will become less common as globalization accelerates.

7. _____ is one of the most consistent predictors of cognitive development among college students. (p. 633)
    a. Living at home
    b. Exposure to logical, internally consistent beliefs
    c. Living on campus
    d. Exposure to singular and truthful viewpoints

8. Which of the following is supported by research on romantic relationships during emerging adulthood? (p. 633)
    a. Most romantic relationships during emerging adulthood are more short-lived.
    b. Romantic relationships involve a deeper sense of emotional intimacy during emerging adulthood than during adolescence.
    c. Most romantic partners meet in nonconventional ways, such as at bars or through personal ads.
    d. During emerging adulthood, the more different partners are, the more likely they are to stay together.

9. Most mentors during emerging adulthood are (p. 634)
   a. parents.
   b. nonparental relatives.
   c. professors.
   d. work supervisors.

10. Which of the following is supported by research on work during emerging adulthood? (p. 635)
    a. Identity achievement in the vocational realm is more challenging for men than women.
    b. Mathematically talented women are more likely to choose careers in engineering, math, or physical science rather than in medicine or other health professions.
    c. Women with male mentors tend to be more successful in their careers than those with female mentors.
    d. Female high school valedictorians are more likely than men to show a drop in estimates of intelligence during the college years.

11. Which of the following is supported by research on civic and political commitments during emerging adulthood? (pp. 635–636)
    a. Emerging adults are less likely than older adults to be involved in organizations devoted to improving communities.
    b. Compared with previous generations, more North American emerging adults vote.
    c. More than 80% of college freshman have done volunteer work.
    d. The majority of emerging adults have participated in political demonstrations.

12. Emerging adults (p. 636)
    a. often struggle to reconcile religious or spiritual beliefs with scientific principles.
    b. attend religious services at higher rates than at any other time throughout the lifespan.
    c. are rarely involved in religious activities.
    d. who were raised in authoritative homes are less likely to hold religious beliefs that were similar to their parents'.

13. Research on religion during emerging adulthood has found that (p. 636)
    a. emerging adults who feel securely attached to their parents are more likely than others to hold religious beliefs similar to their parents.
    b. attendance at religious services increases to its highest level throughout the lifespan.
    c. more than half of North American emerging adults practice formal religious activities.
    d. emerging adults with authoritarian parents are more likely than others to integrate their parents' religious perspectives into their own beliefs.

14. Research has found that 18- to 24-year-olds spend more time _____ than any age group younger than 40. (p. 637)
    a. by themselves
    b. working
    c. participating in religious activities
    d. engaging in political party activities

15. Research on resilience during emerging adulthood demonstrates that (p. 637)
    a. supportive community environments are less crucial for successful passage through this period than they were at earlier ages.
    b. a strong mentor can overcome the impact of a poor parental relationship during this period.
    c. even multiple, negative life events rarely undermine development during this period.
    d. emerging adults are less resilient than children and adolescents.

PRACTICE TEST #2

1. Most North American people report feeling truly adult only after reaching (pp. 629–630)
   a. the late teens.
   b. the early twenties.
   c. the late twenties and early thirties.
   d. the late thirties and the early forties.

2. The literature on emerging adulthood has found that (p. 631)
   a. little individual differences exist in the timing of attainment of adult milestones, such as independent living, launching of career, marriage, and parenthood.
   b. emerging adults experiment more with various activities and roles than they did during adolescence.
   c. little individual differences exist in the order of attainment of adult milestones, such as independent living, launching of career, marriage, and parenthood.
   d. emerging adulthood facilitates identity development.

3. Today, _____ percent of American and _____ percent of Canadian high school graduates pursue college. (p. 631)
   a. 50; 75
   b. 70; 90
   c. 70; 75
   d. 85; 95

4. Which factor contributes to the great numbers of young adults who delay career commitments during their early twenties? (p. 631)
   a. Computer technology has decreased the amount of information that today's workers must know.
   b. Lifespan longevity decreases the pressing need for young people's labor.
   c. Fewer individuals are choosing to attend graduate school.
   d. Fewer students, proportionally, are attending college than a generation before.

5. Research on romantic relationships during emerging adulthood has demonstrated that (p. 634)
   a. couples who stay together despite difficult moments are less likely to express happiness over time.
   b. in North America, cohabitation before marriage is associated with increased conflict resolution skills.
   c. North American cohabiters tend to be less androgynous than couples who do not live together.
   d. early memories of attachment can affect the quality of love relationships.

6. Which of the following is accurate? (p. 635)
   a. Most young women prefer to focus on family or career, but not both.
   b. Identity achievement in the vocational realm is more challenging for women than for men.
   c. Mathematically talented women tend to continue in programs for the gifted throughout high school and choose more demanding careers.
   d. Women's high self-confidence about succeeding in male-dominated fields expands their occupational choices.

7. Jade, a computer graphics designer and self-described introvert, enjoys reading and painting in her spare time. Which of the following people would be a good long-term partner for her? (p. 633)
   a. Terry, who is extremely outgoing and loves to do things with a large group of friends
   b. Tom, an engineer who enjoys outdoor activities
   c. Ted, whom she met at a singles club
   d. Tony, an artist she met at work

8. The role of a _____ includes acting as a teacher who enhances a young person's occupational skills, or serves as a guide who acquaints a person with the values and customs of a working setting. (pp. 634–635)
   a. mentor
   b. teacher
   c. tutor
   d. parent

9. The exploration of alternative roles, values, and behaviors in college leads to substantial gains in _____, development beyond Piaget's formal operational stage. (p. 632)
   a. postformal thought
   b. postoperational thought
   c. globalization
   d. preoperational thought

10. Advances in identity occur in which three areas? (p. 633)
    a. love, work, world views
    b. college, employment, parenthood
    c. romantic relationships, careers, attainment of wealth
    d. job security, relationship security, financial security

11. Andrew is an emerging adult. He is likely to say that _____ is essential for him to attain adult status. (p. 635)
    a. getting married
    b. settling into a career
    c. constructing a worldview
    d. finishing his education

12. According to your text, what types of assets promote development through resilience so that young people can make a smooth transition to adulthood? (p. 638)
    a. authoritarian parenting, a strong peer support group, completion of college
    b. academic success, discovery of a life partner early in adulthood, early parenthood
    c. interpersonal skills, extrapersonal skills, cognitive maturity
    d. cognitive assets, emotional and social assets, social supports

13. Joy is an emerging adult. In which of the following activities is she more likely to be involved? (p. 636)
    a. volunteering time with organizations that protect the environment
    b. avoiding community service in favor of personal self-improvement activities
    c. running for a political office
    d. campaigning for political candidates

14. Because globalization will foster economic progress and heighten awareness of events, lifestyles, and practices in faraway places, theorists predict that (p. 632)
    a. emerging adulthood will become increasingly common.
    b. college attendance rates will decrease in favor of internships and apprenticeships similar to those in European countries.
    c. the developmental phase known as emerging adulthood will disappear.
    d. it will be harder for young people to form global identities.

15. The rate of _____ is at its highest level through the lifespan between the ages of 19 and 22. (p. 637)
    a. binge drinking
    b. church attendance
    c. voting
    d. cohabitation

PUZZLE 1.1

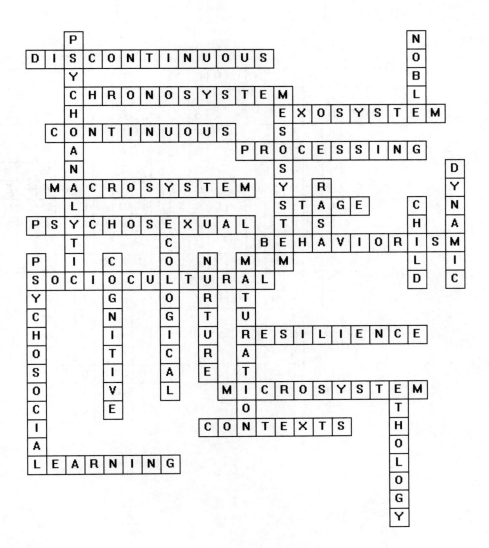

PUZZLE 1.2

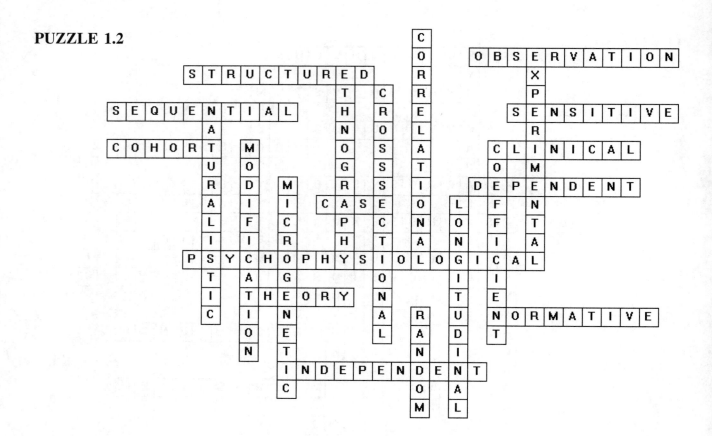

PUZZLE 2.1

PUZZLE 2.2

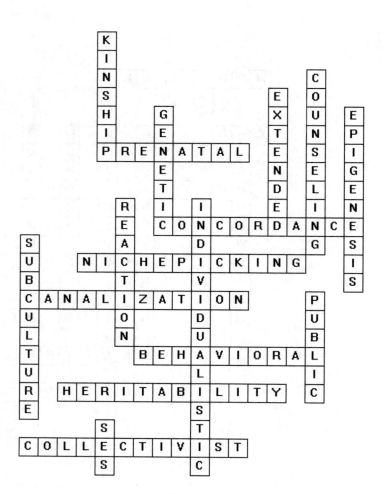

PUZZLE 3.1

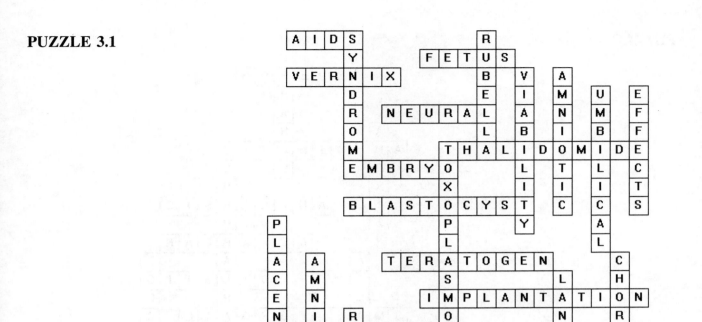

A-5

PUZZLE 4.1

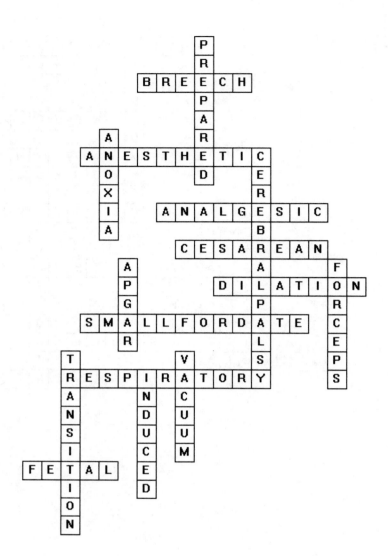

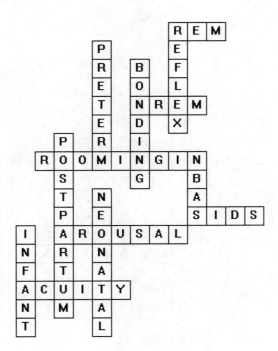

PUZZLE 5.1

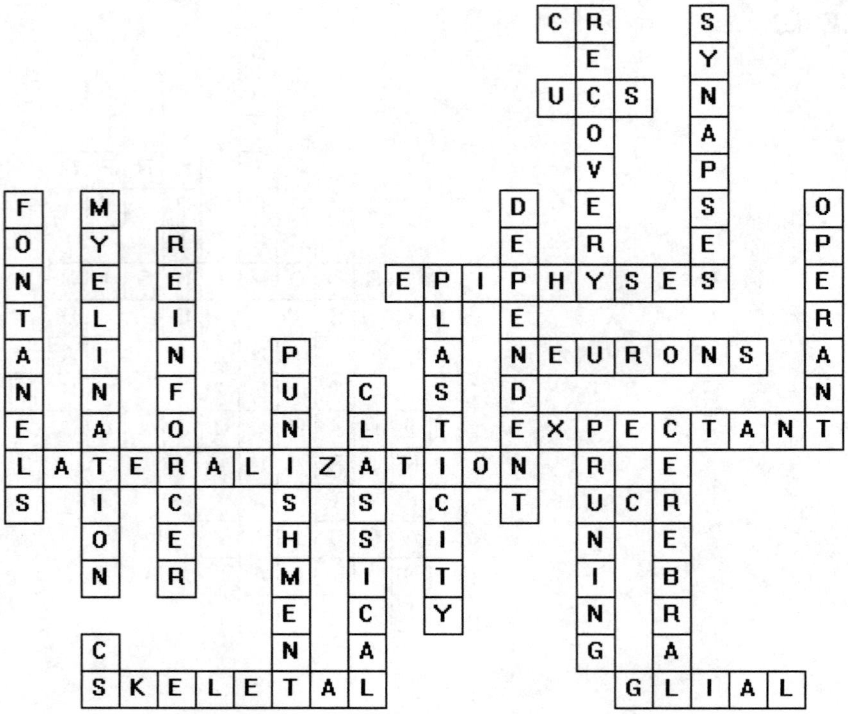
CR
RECOVERY
UCS
SYNAPSES
EPIPHYSES
FONTANELS
MYELINATION
REINFORCER
DEPENDENT
OPERANT
PLASTICITY
NEURONS
PUNISHMENT
CLASSICAL
EXPECTANT
LATERALIZATION
PRUNING
CEREBRA
UCR
CS
SKELETAL
GLIAL

PUZZLE 5.2

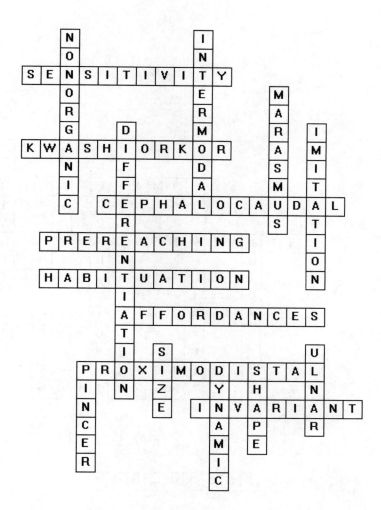

PUZZLE 6.1

PUZZLE 7.2

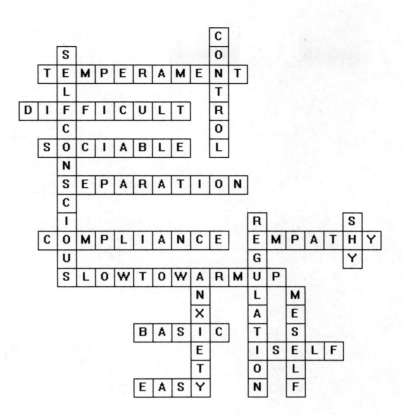

PUZZLE 8.1

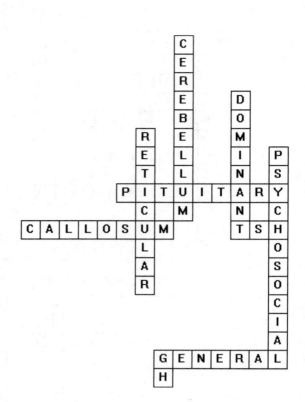

PUZZLE 9.1

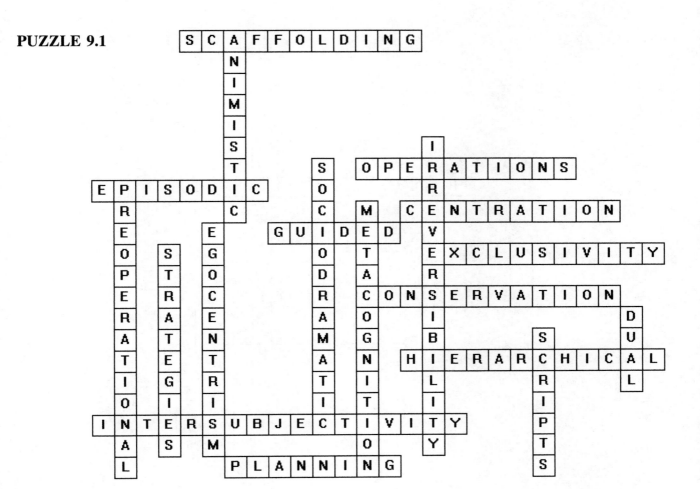

PUZZLE 9.2

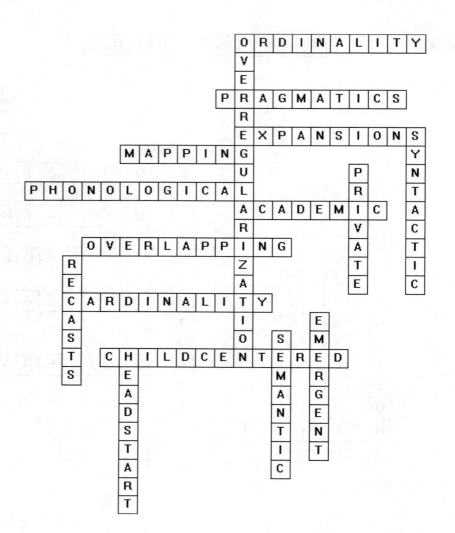

PUZZLE 10.1

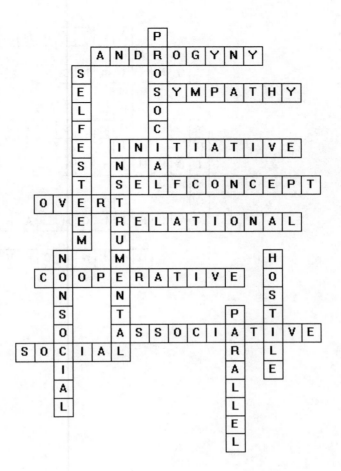

PUZZLE 10.2

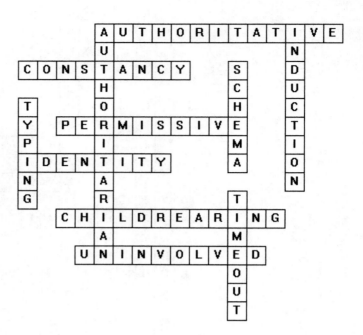

PUZZLE 11.1

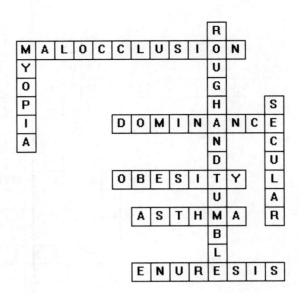

PUZZLE 12.1

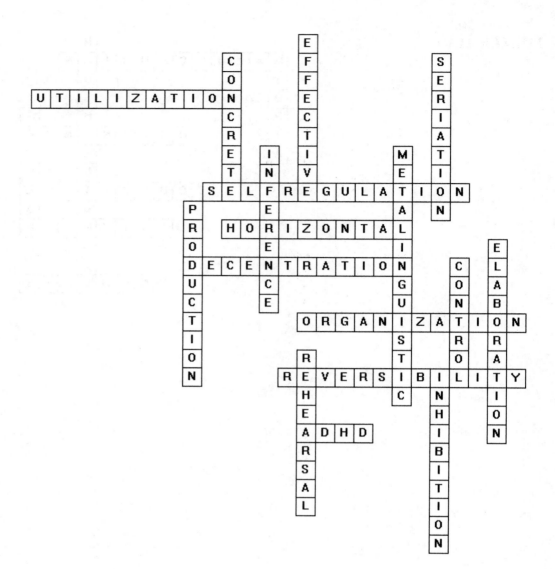

PUZZLE 12.2

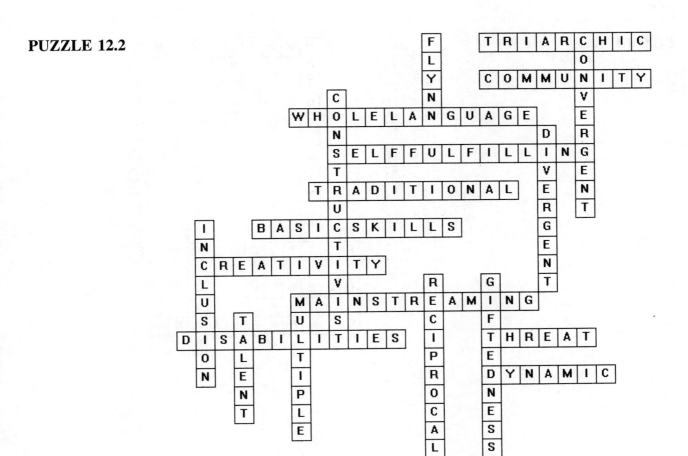

PUZZLE 13.1

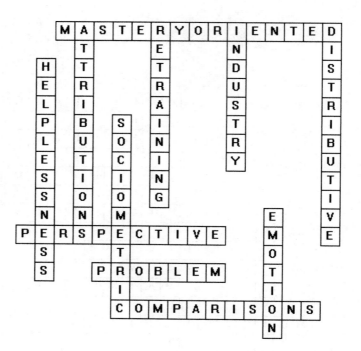

PUZZLE 13.2

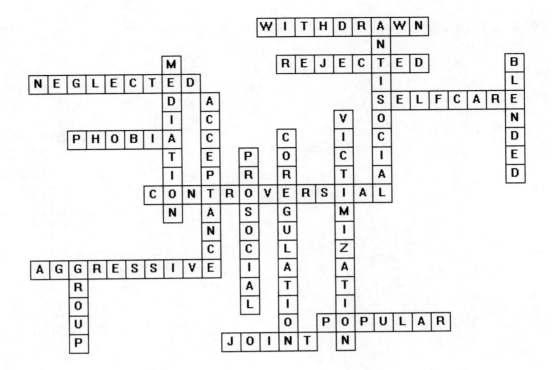

PUZZLE 14.1

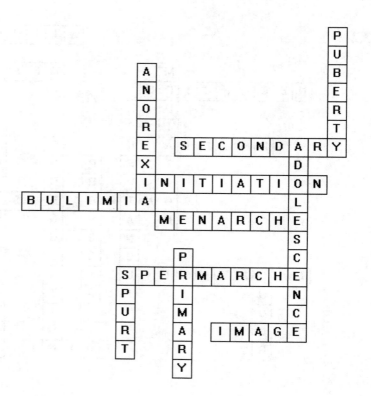

PUZZLE 15.1

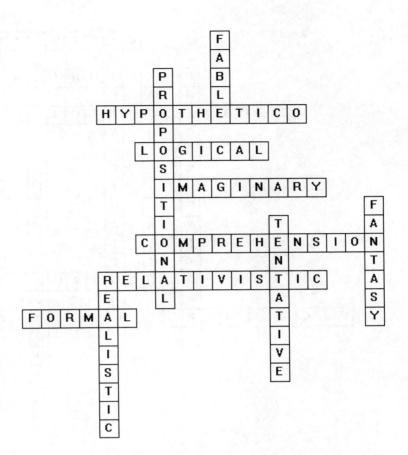

PUZZLE 16.1

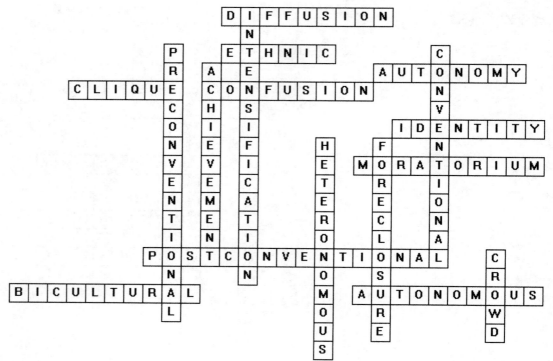

PUZZLE 17.1

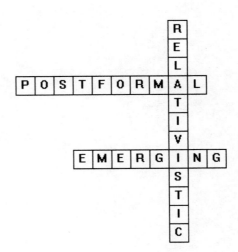

PRACTICE TEST ANSWERS

CHAPTER 1

Practice Test #1

1.	d	11.	b
2.	b	12.	a
3.	a	13.	b
4.	d	14.	c
5.	d	15.	b
6.	d	16.	d
7.	c	17.	a
8.	d	18.	d
9.	b	19.	b
10.	a	20.	c

Practice Test #2

1.	a	11.	d
2.	b	12.	c
3.	d	13.	c
4.	d	14.	a
5.	a	15.	d
6.	d	16.	a
7.	d	17.	d
8.	b	18.	d
9.	a	19.	a
10.	b	20.	d

CHAPTER 2

Practice Test #1

1.	a	11.	b
2.	b	12.	d
3.	a	13.	c
4.	b	14.	d
5.	d	15.	d
6.	b	16.	b
7.	c	17.	d
8.	a	18.	d
9.	d	19.	a
10.	c	20.	a

Practice Test #2

1.	a	11.	c
2.	d	12.	d
3.	c	13.	d
4.	c	14.	a
5.	a	15.	c
6.	b	16.	b
7.	a	17.	d
8.	b	18.	b
9.	c	19.	d
10.	d	20.	d

CHAPTER 3

Practice Test #1

1.	a	11.	b
2.	d	12.	b
3.	d	13.	d
4.	b	14.	a
5.	a	15.	a
6.	b	16.	d
7.	d	17.	d
8.	c	18.	b
9.	d	19.	c
10.	c	20.	b

Practice Test #2

1.	c	11.	a
2.	d	12.	c
3.	d	13.	a
4.	d	14.	c
5.	a	15.	a
6.	d	16.	d
7.	b	17.	a
8.	b	18.	a
9.	b	19.	d
10.	c	20.	d

CHAPTER 4

Practice Test #1

1.	b	11.	b
2.	d	12.	d
3.	a	13.	d
4.	a	14.	a
5.	a	15.	a
6.	b	16.	c
7.	c	17.	b
8.	b	18.	a
9.	a	19.	c
10.	a	20.	a

Practice Test #2

1.	c	11.	b
2.	a	12.	c
3.	b	13.	d
4.	a	14.	d
5.	d	15.	d
6.	a	16.	b
7.	c	17.	a
8.	a	18.	b
9.	c	19.	c
10.	d	20.	d

CHAPTER 5

Practice Test #1

1.	c	11.	b
2.	d	12.	a
3.	d	13.	a
4.	b	14.	a
5.	d	15.	b
6.	c	16.	d
7.	a	17.	c
8.	d	18.	a
9.	c	19.	a
10.	a	20.	d

Practice Test #2

1.	a	11.	c
2.	b	12.	a
3.	a	13.	c
4.	c	14.	a
5.	c	15.	a
6.	d	16.	a
7.	d	17.	a
8.	d	18.	c
9.	a	19.	a
10.	c	20.	b

CHAPTER 6

Practice Test #1

1.	c	11.	a
2.	b	12.	c
3.	d	13.	a
4.	a	14.	d
5.	a	15.	d
6.	a	16.	a
7.	d	17.	c
8.	a	18.	d
9.	d	19.	a
10.	a	20.	a

Practice Test #2

1.	c	11.	a
2.	c	12.	a
3.	d	13.	a
4.	b	14.	c
5.	a	15.	d
6.	b	16.	a
7.	a	17.	d
8.	c	18.	a
9.	a	19.	b
10.	b	20.	a

CHAPTER 7

Practice Test #1

1.	b	11.	a
2.	d	12.	c
3.	d	13.	b
4.	c	14.	c
5.	b	15.	a
6.	a	16.	a
7.	d	17.	b
8.	a	18.	a
9.	c	19.	a
10.	b	20.	d

Practice Test #2

1.	d	11.	d
2.	a	12.	d
3.	a	13.	c
4.	d	14.	d
5.	b	15.	b
6.	a	16.	d
7.	a	17.	c
8.	a	18.	a
9.	a	19.	a
10.	a	20.	c

CHAPTER 8

Practice Test #1

1.	b	11.	b
2.	a	12.	d
3.	d	13.	a
4.	b	14.	c
5.	d	15.	a
6.	c	16.	c
7.	a	17.	c
8.	d	18.	d
9.	c	19.	d
10.	d	20.	a

Practice Test #2

1.	b	11.	d
2.	a	12.	a
3.	b	13.	c
4.	c	14.	c
5.	c	15.	d
6.	c	16.	a
7.	a	17.	d
8.	d	18.	b
9.	d	19.	a
10.	b	20.	b

CHAPTER 9

Practice Test #1

1.	d	11.	c
2.	d	12.	c
3.	c	13.	a
4.	c	14.	d
5.	a	15.	a
6.	a	16.	a
7.	b	17.	b
8.	d	18.	c
9.	c	19.	b
10.	d	20.	a

Practice Test #2

1.	a	11.	c
2.	c	12.	b
3.	b	13.	a
4.	c	14.	a
5.	a	15.	c
6.	d	16.	d
7.	b	17.	d
8.	b	18.	a
9.	c	19.	b
10.	d	20.	c

CHAPTER 10

Practice Test #1

1.	b	11.	d
2.	a	12.	d
3.	c	13.	b
4.	d	14.	b
5.	d	15.	a
6.	a	16.	a
7.	d	17.	d
8.	a	18.	c
9.	c	19.	a
10.	b	20.	c

Practice Test #2

1.	c	11.	b
2.	b	12.	c
3.	d	13.	a
4.	a	14.	c
5.	c	15.	c
6.	a	16.	a
7.	d	17.	d
8.	b	18.	c
9.	a	19.	d
10.	b	20.	b

CHAPTER 11

Practice Test #1

1.	a	11.	a
2.	b	12.	d
3.	d	13.	d
4.	a	14.	d
5.	c	15.	a
6.	d	16.	b
7.	d	17.	c
8.	a	18.	b
9.	b	19.	d
10.	b	20.	c

Practice Test #2

1.	c	11.	c
2.	a	12.	c
3.	b	13.	c
4.	a	14.	b
5.	d	15.	c
6.	d	16.	a
7.	d	17.	d
8.	c	18.	c
9.	d	19.	d
10.	b	20.	a

CHAPTER 12

Practice Test #1

1. c	11. b
2. c	12. c
3. a	13. a
4. d	14. a
5. b	15. d
6. d	16. c
7. b	17. b
8. d	18. a
9. a	19. d
10. d	20. c

Practice Test #2

1. a	11. a
2. a	12. c
3. d	13. c
4. b	14. a
5. d	15. d
6. c	16. a
7. b	17. a
8. a	18. b
9. b	19. d
10. d	20. c

CHAPTER 13

Practice Test #1

1.	a	11.	d
2.	b	12.	d
3.	c	13.	b
4.	b	14.	b
5.	c	15.	b
6.	a	16.	d
7.	d	17.	c
8.	a	18.	c
9.	c	19.	d
10.	c	20.	a

Practice Test #2

1.	c	11.	b
2.	a	12.	d
3.	c	13.	c
4.	b	14.	b
5.	d	15.	d
6.	d	16.	a
7.	c	17.	a
8.	c	18.	c
9.	b	19.	c
10.	a	20.	d

CHAPTER 14

Practice Test #1

1.	a	11.	a
2.	d	12.	b
3.	a	13.	d
4.	b	14.	c
5.	d	15.	d
6.	c	16.	a
7.	b	17.	a
8.	d	18.	d
9.	c	19.	c
10.	c	20.	b

Practice Test #2

1.	b	11.	a
2.	d	12.	b
3.	d	13.	a
4.	c	14.	d
5.	a	15.	a
6.	c	16.	d
7.	a	17.	a
8.	b	18.	a
9.	a	19.	d
10.	c	20.	b

CHAPTER 15

Practice Test #1

1.	d	11.	d
2.	a	12.	a
3.	c	13.	d
4.	a	14.	a
5.	c	15.	a
6.	a	16.	b
7.	a	17.	b
8.	d	18.	d
9.	b	19.	c
10.	d	20.	d

Practice Test #2

1.	c	11.	c
2.	a	12.	c
3.	a	13.	b
4.	d	14.	b
5.	b	15.	d
6.	c	16.	a
7.	b	17.	b
8.	d	18.	c
9.	a	19.	a
10.	d	20.	a

CHAPTER 16

Practice Test #1

1.	b	11.	a
2.	a	12.	d
3.	b	13.	a
4.	d	14.	a
5.	d	15.	b
6.	a	16.	d
7.	c	17.	d
8.	b	18.	b
9.	a	19.	a
10.	b	20.	a

Practice Test #2

1.	b	11.	d
2.	a	12.	c
3.	c	13.	b
4.	b	14.	a
5.	a	15.	b
6.	b	16.	c
7.	b	17.	b
8.	b	18.	c
9.	a	19.	d
10.	a	20.	a

CHAPTER 17

Practice Test #1

1.	d	9.	c
2.	a	10.	d
3.	a	11.	c
4.	a	12.	c
5.	c	13.	a
6.	a	14.	a
7.	c	15.	a
8.	b		

Practice Test #2

1.	c	9.	a
2.	b	10.	a
3.	c	11.	c
4.	b	12.	d
5.	d	13.	a
6.	b	14.	a
7.	d	15.	a
8.	a		

NOTES

NOTES

NOTES

NOTES

NOTES

NOTES

NOTES

NOTES

NOTES

NOTES

NOTES

NOTES

NOTES

NOTES

NOTES

NOTES

NOTES

NOTES

NOTES

NOTES

NOTES

NOTES

NOTES

NOTES

NOTES

NOTES

NOTES

NOTES

NOTES

NOTES